FREE Study Skills DVD Offer

Dear Customer,

Thank you for your purchase from Mometrix! We consider it an honor and a privilege that you have purchased our product and we want to ensure your satisfaction.

As a way of showing our appreciation and to help us better serve you, we have developed a Study Skills DVD that we would like to give you for <u>FREE</u>. This DVD covers our *best practices* for getting ready for your exam, from how to use our study materials to how to best prepare for the day of the test.

All that we ask is that you email us with feedback that would describe your experience so far with our product. Good, bad, or indifferent, we want to know what you think!

To get your FREE Study Skills DVD, email <u>freedvd@mometrix.com</u> with *FREE STUDY SKILLS DVD* in the subject line and the following information in the body of the email:

- The name of the product you purchased.
- Your product rating on a scale of 1-5, with 5 being the highest rating.
- Your feedback. It can be long, short, or anything in between. We just want to know your impressions and experience so far with our product. (Good feedback might include how our study material met your needs and ways we might be able to make it even better. You could highlight features that you found helpful or features that you think we should add.)
- Your full name and shipping address where you would like us to send your free DVD.

If you have any questions or concerns, please don't hesitate to contact me directly.

Thanks again!

Sincerely,

Jay Willis
Vice President
<u>jay.willis@mometrix.com</u>
1-800-673-8175

Series 7 Exam SECRETS

Study Guide
Your Key to Exam Success

Written and edited by the Mometrix Financial Industry Certification Test Team

Printed in the United States of America

This paper meets the requirements of ANSI/NISO Z39.48-1992 (Permanence of Paper).

Mometrix offers volume discount pricing to institutions. For more information or a price quote, please contact our sales department at sales@mometrix.com or 888-248-1219.

Paperback
ISBN 13: 978-1-61072-866-9
ISBN 10: 1-61072-866-1

Ebook
ISBN 13: 978-1-62120-691-0
ISBN 10: 1-62120-691-2

Hardback
ISBN 13: 978-1-5167-0566-5
ISBN 10: 1-5167-0566-1

DEAR FUTURE EXAM SUCCESS STORY

First of all, **THANK YOU** for purchasing Mometrix study materials!

Second, congratulations! You are one of the few determined test-takers who are committed to doing whatever it takes to excel on your exam. **You have come to the right place.** We developed these study materials with one goal in mind: to deliver you the information you need in a format that's concise and easy to use.

In addition to optimizing your guide for the content of the test, we've outlined our recommended steps for breaking down the preparation process into small, attainable goals so you can make sure you stay on track.

We've also analyzed the entire test-taking process, identifying the most common pitfalls and showing how you can overcome them and be ready for any curveball the test throws you.

Standardized testing is one of the biggest obstacles on your road to success, which only increases the importance of doing well in the high-pressure, high-stakes environment of test day. Your results on this test could have a significant impact on your future, and this guide provides the information and practical advice to help you achieve your full potential on test day.

Your success is our success

We would love to hear from you! If you would like to share the story of your exam success or if you have any questions or comments in regard to our products, please contact us at **800-673-8175** or **support@mometrix.com**.

Thanks again for your business and we wish you continued success!

Sincerely,
The Mometrix Test Preparation Team

> **Need more help? Check out our flashcards at:**
> **http://MometrixFlashcards.com/Series**

TABLE OF CONTENTS

Introduction

Thank you for purchasing this resource! You have made the choice to prepare yourself for a test that could have a huge impact on your future, and this guide is designed to help you be fully ready for test day. Obviously, it's important to have a solid understanding of the test material, but you also need to be prepared for the unique environment and stressors of the test, so that you can perform to the best of your abilities.

For this purpose, the first section that appears in this guide is the **Secret Keys**. We've devoted countless hours to meticulously researching what works and what doesn't, and we've boiled down our findings to the five most impactful steps you can take to improve your performance on the test. We start at the beginning with study planning and move through the preparation process, all the way to the testing strategies that will help you get the most out of what you know when you're finally sitting in front of the test.

We recommend that you start preparing for your test as far in advance as possible. However, if you've bought this guide as a last-minute study resource and only have a few days before your test, we recommend that you skip over the first two Secret Keys since they address a long-term study plan.

If you struggle with **test anxiety**, we strongly encourage you to check out our recommendations for how you can overcome it. Test anxiety is a formidable foe, but it can be beaten, and we want to make sure you have the tools you need to defeat it.

Secret Key #1 – Plan Big, Study Small

There's a lot riding on your performance. If you want to ace this test, you're going to need to keep your skills sharp and the material fresh in your mind. You need a plan that lets you review everything you need to know while still fitting in your schedule. We'll break this strategy down into three categories.

Information Organization

Start with the information you already have: the official test outline. From this, you can make a complete list of all the concepts you need to cover before the test. Organize these concepts into groups that can be studied together, and create a list of any related vocabulary you need to learn so you can brush up on any difficult terms. You'll want to keep this vocabulary list handy once you actually start studying since you may need to add to it along the way.

Time Management

Once you have your set of study concepts, decide how to spread them out over the time you have left before the test. Break your study plan into small, clear goals so you have a manageable task for each day and know exactly what you're doing. Then just focus on one small step at a time. When you manage your time this way, you don't need to spend hours at a time studying. Studying a small block of content for a short period each day helps you retain information better and avoid stressing over how much you have left to do. You can relax knowing that you have a plan to cover everything in time. In order for this strategy to be effective though, you have to start studying early and stick to your schedule. Avoid the exhaustion and futility that comes from last-minute cramming!

Study Environment

The environment you study in has a big impact on your learning. Studying in a coffee shop, while probably more enjoyable, is not likely to be as fruitful as studying in a quiet room. It's important to keep distractions to a minimum. You're only planning to study for a short block of time, so make the most of it. Don't pause to check your phone or get up to find a snack. It's also important to **avoid multitasking**. Research has consistently shown that multitasking will make your studying dramatically less effective. Your study area should also be comfortable and well-lit so you don't have the distraction of straining your eyes or sitting on an uncomfortable chair.

The time of day you study is also important. You want to be rested and alert. Don't wait until just before bedtime. Study when you'll be most likely to comprehend and remember. Even better, if you know what time of day your test will be, set that time aside for study. That way your brain will be used to working on that subject at that specific time and you'll have a better chance of recalling information.

Finally, it can be helpful to team up with others who are studying for the same test. Your actual studying should be done in as isolated an environment as possible, but the work of organizing the information and setting up the study plan can be divided up. In between study sessions, you can discuss with your teammates the concepts that you're all studying and quiz each other on the details. Just be sure that your teammates are as serious about the test as you are. If you find that your study time is being replaced with social time, you might need to find a new team.

2

Secret Key #2 – Make Your Studying Count

You're devoting a lot of time and effort to preparing for this test, so you want to be absolutely certain it will pay off. This means doing more than just reading the content and hoping you can remember it on test day. It's important to make every minute of study count. There are two main areas you can focus on to make your studying count:

Retention

It doesn't matter how much time you study if you can't remember the material. You need to make sure you are retaining the concepts. To check your retention of the information you're learning, try recalling it at later times with minimal prompting. Try carrying around flashcards and glance at one or two from time to time or ask a friend who's also studying for the test to quiz you.

To enhance your retention, look for ways to put the information into practice so that you can apply it rather than simply recalling it. If you're using the information in practical ways, it will be much easier to remember. Similarly, it helps to solidify a concept in your mind if you're not only reading it to yourself but also explaining it to someone else. Ask a friend to let you teach them about a concept you're a little shaky on (or speak aloud to an imaginary audience if necessary). As you try to summarize, define, give examples, and answer your friend's questions, you'll understand the concepts better and they will stay with you longer. Finally, step back for a big picture view and ask yourself how each piece of information fits with the whole subject. When you link the different concepts together and see them working together as a whole, it's easier to remember the individual components.

Finally, practice showing your work on any multi-step problems, even if you're just studying. Writing out each step you take to solve a problem will help solidify the process in your mind, and you'll be more likely to remember it during the test.

Modality

Modality simply refers to the means or method by which you study. Choosing a study modality that fits your own individual learning style is crucial. No two people learn best in exactly the same way, so it's important to know your strengths and use them to your advantage.

For example, if you learn best by visualization, focus on visualizing a concept in your mind and draw an image or a diagram. Try color-coding your notes, illustrating them, or creating symbols that will trigger your mind to recall a learned concept. If you learn best by hearing or discussing information, find a study partner who learns the same way or read aloud to yourself. Think about how to put the information in your own words. Imagine that you are giving a lecture on the topic and record yourself so you can listen to it later.

For any learning style, flashcards can be helpful. Organize the information so you can take advantage of spare moments to review. Underline key words or phrases. Use different colors for different categories. Mnemonic devices (such as creating a short list in which every item starts with the same letter) can also help with retention. Find what works best for you and use it to store the information in your mind most effectively and easily.

3

Secret Key #3 – Practice the Right Way

Your success on test day depends not only on how many hours you put into preparing, but also on whether you prepared the right way. It's good to check along the way to see if your studying is paying off. One of the most effective ways to do this is by taking practice tests to evaluate your progress. Practice tests are useful because they show exactly where you need to improve. Every time you take a practice test, pay special attention to these three groups of questions:

- The questions you got wrong
- The questions you had to guess on, even if you guessed right
- The questions you found difficult or slow to work through

This will show you exactly what your weak areas are, and where you need to devote more study time. Ask yourself why each of these questions gave you trouble. Was it because you didn't understand the material? Was it because you didn't remember the vocabulary? Do you need more repetitions on this type of question to build speed and confidence? Dig into those questions and figure out how you can strengthen your weak areas as you go back to review the material.

Additionally, many practice tests have a section explaining the answer choices. It can be tempting to read the explanation and think that you now have a good understanding of the concept. However, an explanation likely only covers part of the question's broader context. Even if the explanation makes sense, **go back and investigate** every concept related to the question until you're positive you have a thorough understanding.

As you go along, keep in mind that the practice test is just that: practice. Memorizing these questions and answers will not be very helpful on the actual test because it is unlikely to have any of the same exact questions. If you only know the right answers to the sample questions, you won't be prepared for the real thing. **Study the concepts** until you understand them fully, and then you'll be able to answer any question that shows up on the test.

It's important to wait on the practice tests until you're ready. If you take a test on your first day of study, you may be overwhelmed by the amount of material covered and how much you need to learn. Work up to it gradually.

On test day, you'll need to be prepared for answering questions, managing your time, and using the test-taking strategies you've learned. It's a lot to balance, like a mental marathon that will have a big impact on your future. Like training for a marathon, you'll need to start slowly and work your way up. When test day arrives, you'll be ready.

Start with the strategies you've read in the first two Secret Keys—plan your course and study in the way that works best for you. If you have time, consider using multiple study resources to get different approaches to the same concepts. It can be helpful to see difficult concepts from more than one angle. Then find a good source for practice tests. Many times, the test website will suggest potential study resources or provide sample tests.

4

Practice Test Strategy

If you're able to find at least three practice tests, we recommend this strategy:

UNTIMED AND OPEN-BOOK PRACTICE

Take the first test with no time constraints and with your notes and study guide handy. Take your time and focus on applying the strategies you've learned.

TIMED AND OPEN-BOOK PRACTICE

Take the second practice test open-book as well, but set a timer and practice pacing yourself to finish in time.

TIMED AND CLOSED-BOOK PRACTICE

Take any other practice tests as if it were test day. Set a timer and put away your study materials. Sit at a table or desk in a quiet room, imagine yourself at the testing center, and answer questions as quickly and accurately as possible.

Keep repeating timed and closed-book tests on a regular basis until you run out of practice tests or it's time for the actual test. Your mind will be ready for the schedule and stress of test day, and you'll be able to focus on recalling the material you've learned.

Secret Key #4 – Pace Yourself

Once you're fully prepared for the material on the test, your biggest challenge on test day will be managing your time. Just knowing that the clock is ticking can make you panic even if you have plenty of time left. Work on pacing yourself so you can build confidence against the time constraints of the exam. Pacing is a difficult skill to master, especially in a high-pressure environment, so **practice is vital**.

Set time expectations for your pace based on how much time is available. For example, if a section has 60 questions and the time limit is 30 minutes, you know you have to average 30 seconds or less per question in order to answer them all. Although 30 seconds is the hard limit, set 25 seconds per question as your goal, so you reserve extra time to spend on harder questions. When you budget extra time for the harder questions, you no longer have any reason to stress when those questions take longer to answer.

Don't let this time expectation distract you from working through the test at a calm, steady pace, but keep it in mind so you don't spend too much time on any one question. Recognize that taking extra time on one question you don't understand may keep you from answering two that you do understand later in the test. If your time limit for a question is up and you're still not sure of the answer, mark it and move on, and come back to it later if the time and the test format allow. If the testing format doesn't allow you to return to earlier questions, just make an educated guess; then put it out of your mind and move on.

On the easier questions, be careful not to rush. It may seem wise to hurry through them so you have more time for the challenging ones, but it's not worth missing one if you know the concept and just didn't take the time to read the question fully. Work efficiently but make sure you understand the question and have looked at all of the answer choices, since more than one may seem right at first.

Even if you're paying attention to the time, you may find yourself a little behind at some point. You should speed up to get back on track, but do so wisely. Don't panic; just take a few seconds less on each question until you're caught up. Don't guess without thinking, but do look through the answer choices and eliminate any you know are wrong. If you can get down to two choices, it is often worthwhile to guess from those. Once you've chosen an answer, move on and don't dwell on any that you skipped or had to hurry through. If a question was taking too long, chances are it was one of the harder ones, so you weren't as likely to get it right anyway.

On the other hand, if you find yourself getting ahead of schedule, it may be beneficial to slow down a little. The more quickly you work, the more likely you are to make a careless mistake that will affect your score. You've budgeted time for each question, so don't be afraid to spend that time. Practice an efficient but careful pace to get the most out of the time you have.

Secret Key #5 – Have a Plan for Guessing

When you're taking the test, you may find yourself stuck on a question. Some of the answer choices seem better than others, but you don't see the one answer choice that is obviously correct. What do you do?

The scenario described above is very common, yet most test takers have not effectively prepared for it. Developing and practicing a plan for guessing may be one of the single most effective uses of your time as you get ready for the exam.

In developing your plan for guessing, there are three questions to address:

- When should you start the guessing process?
- How should you narrow down the choices?
- Which answer should you choose?

When to Start the Guessing Process

Unless your plan for guessing is to select C every time (which, despite its merits, is not what we recommend), you need to leave yourself enough time to apply your answer elimination strategies. Since you have a limited amount of time for each question, that means that if you're going to give yourself the best shot at guessing correctly, you have to decide quickly whether or not you will guess.

Of course, the best-case scenario is that you don't have to guess at all, so first, see if you can answer the question based on your knowledge of the subject and basic reasoning skills. Focus on the key words in the question and try to jog your memory of related topics. Give yourself a chance to bring the knowledge to mind, but once you realize that you don't have (or you can't access) the knowledge you need to answer the question, it's time to start the guessing process.

It's almost always better to start the guessing process too early than too late. It only takes a few seconds to remember something and answer the question from knowledge. Carefully eliminating wrong answer choices takes longer. Plus, going through the process of eliminating answer choices can actually help jog your memory.

Summary: Start the guessing process as soon as you decide that you can't answer the question based on your knowledge.

How to Narrow Down the Choices

The next chapter in this book (**Test-Taking Strategies**) includes a wide range of strategies for how to approach questions and how to look for answer choices to eliminate. You will definitely want to read those carefully, practice them, and figure out which ones work best for you. Here though, we're going to address a mindset rather than a particular strategy.

Your chances of guessing an answer correctly depend on how many options you are choosing from.

How many choices you have	How likely you are to guess correctly
5	20%
4	25%
3	33%
2	50%
1	100%

You can see from this chart just how valuable it is to be able to eliminate incorrect answers and make an educated guess, but there are two things that many test takers do that cause them to miss out on the benefits of guessing:

- Accidentally eliminating the correct answer
- Selecting an answer based on an impression

We'll look at the first one here, and the second one in the next section.

To avoid accidentally eliminating the correct answer, we recommend a thought exercise called **the $5 challenge**. In this challenge, you only eliminate an answer choice from contention if you are willing to bet $5 on it being wrong. Why $5? Five dollars is a small but not insignificant amount of money. It's an amount you could afford to lose but wouldn't want to throw away. And while losing $5 once might not hurt too much, doing it twenty times will set you back $100. In the same way, each small decision you make—eliminating a choice here, guessing on a question there—won't by itself impact your score very much, but when you put them all together, they can make a big difference. By holding each answer choice elimination decision to a higher standard, you can reduce the risk of accidentally eliminating the correct answer.

The $5 challenge can also be applied in a positive sense: If you are willing to bet $5 that an answer choice *is* correct, go ahead and mark it as correct.

Summary: Only eliminate an answer choice if you are willing to bet $5 that it is wrong.

8

Which Answer to Choose

You're taking the test. You've run into a hard question and decided you'll have to guess. You've eliminated all the answer choices you're willing to bet $5 on. Now you have to pick an answer. Why do we even need to talk about this? Why can't you just pick whichever one you feel like when the time comes?

The answer to these questions is that if you don't come into the test with a plan, you'll rely on your impression to select an answer choice, and if you do that, you risk falling into a trap. The test writers know that everyone who takes their test will be guessing on some of the questions, so they intentionally write wrong answer choices to seem plausible. You still have to pick an answer though, and if the wrong answer choices are designed to look right, how can you ever be sure that you're not falling for their trap? The best solution we've found to this dilemma is to take the decision out of your hands entirely. Here is the process we recommend:

Once you've eliminated any choices that you are confident (willing to bet $5) are wrong, select the first remaining choice as your answer.

Whether you choose to select the first remaining choice, the second, or the last, the important thing is that you use some preselected standard. Using this approach guarantees that you will not be enticed into selecting an answer choice that looks right, because you are not basing your decision on how the answer choices look.

This is not meant to make you question your knowledge. Instead, it is to help you recognize the difference between your knowledge and your impressions. There's a huge difference between thinking an answer is right because of what you know, and thinking an answer is right because it looks or sounds like it should be right.

Summary: To ensure that your selection is appropriately random, make a predetermined selection from among all answer choices you have not eliminated.

Test-Taking Strategies

This section contains a list of test-taking strategies that you may find helpful as you work through the test. By taking what you know and applying logical thought, you can maximize your chances of answering any question correctly!

It is very important to realize that every question is different and every person is different: no single strategy will work on every question, and no single strategy will work for every person. That's why we've included all of them here, so you can try them out and determine which ones work best for different types of questions and which ones work best for you.

Question Strategies

READ CAREFULLY

Read the question and answer choices carefully. Don't miss the question because you misread the terms. You have plenty of time to read each question thoroughly and make sure you understand what is being asked. Yet a happy medium must be attained, so don't waste too much time. You must read carefully, but efficiently.

CONTEXTUAL CLUES

Look for contextual clues. If the question includes a word you are not familiar with, look at the immediate context for some indication of what the word might mean. Contextual clues can often give you all the information you need to decipher the meaning of an unfamiliar word. Even if you can't determine the meaning, you may be able to narrow down the possibilities enough to make a solid guess at the answer to the question.

PREFIXES

If you're having trouble with a word in the question or answer choices, try dissecting it. Take advantage of every clue that the word might include. Prefixes and suffixes can be a huge help. Usually they allow you to determine a basic meaning. Pre- means before, post- means after, pro - is positive, de- is negative. From prefixes and suffixes, you can get an idea of the general meaning of the word and try to put it into context.

HEDGE WORDS

Watch out for critical hedge words, such as *likely, may, can, sometimes, often, almost, mostly, usually, generally, rarely,* and *sometimes.* Question writers insert these hedge phrases to cover every possibility. Often an answer choice will be wrong simply because it leaves no room for exception. Be on guard for answer choices that have definitive words such as *exactly* and *always.*

SWITCHBACK WORDS

Stay alert for *switchbacks.* These are the words and phrases frequently used to alert you to shifts in thought. The most common switchback words are *but, although,* and *however.* Others include *nevertheless, on the other hand, even though, while, in spite of, despite, regardless of.* Switchback words are important to catch because they can change the direction of the question or an answer choice.

10

FACE VALUE

When in doubt, use common sense. Accept the situation in the problem at face value. Don't read too much into it. These problems will not require you to make wild assumptions. If you have to go beyond creativity and warp time or space in order to have an answer choice fit the question, then you should move on and consider the other answer choices. These are normal problems rooted in reality. The applicable relationship or explanation may not be readily apparent, but it is there for you to figure out. Use your common sense to interpret anything that isn't clear.

Answer Choice Strategies

ANSWER SELECTION

The most thorough way to pick an answer choice is to identify and eliminate wrong answers until only one is left, then confirm it is the correct answer. Sometimes an answer choice may immediately seem right, but be careful. The test writers will usually put more than one reasonable answer choice on each question, so take a second to read all of them and make sure that the other choices are not equally obvious. As long as you have time left, it is better to read every answer choice than to pick the first one that looks right without checking the others.

ANSWER CHOICE FAMILIES

An answer choice family consists of two (in rare cases, three) answer choices that are very similar in construction and cannot all be true at the same time. If you see two answer choices that are direct opposites or parallels, one of them is usually the correct answer. For instance, if one answer choice says that quantity x increases and another either says that quantity x decreases (opposite) or says that quantity y increases (parallel), then those answer choices would fall into the same family. An answer choice that doesn't match the construction of the answer choice family is more likely to be incorrect. Most questions will not have answer choice families, but when they do appear, you should be prepared to recognize them.

ELIMINATE ANSWERS

Eliminate answer choices as soon as you realize they are wrong, but make sure you consider all possibilities. If you are eliminating answer choices and realize that the last one you are left with is also wrong, don't panic. Start over and consider each choice again. There may be something you missed the first time that you will realize on the second pass.

AVOID FACT TRAPS

Don't be distracted by an answer choice that is factually true but doesn't answer the question. You are looking for the choice that answers the question. Stay focused on what the question is asking for so you don't accidentally pick an answer that is true but incorrect. Always go back to the question and make sure the answer choice you've selected actually answers the question and is not merely a true statement.

EXTREME STATEMENTS

In general, you should avoid answers that put forth extreme actions as standard practice or proclaim controversial ideas as established fact. An answer choice that states the "process should be used in certain situations, if..." is much more likely to be correct than one that states the "process should be discontinued completely." The first is a calm rational statement and doesn't even make a definitive, uncompromising stance, using a hedge word *if* to provide wiggle room, whereas the second choice is a radical idea and far more extreme.

11

BENCHMARK

As you read through the answer choices and you come across one that seems to answer the question well, mentally select that answer choice. This is not your final answer, but it's the one that will help you evaluate the other answer choices. The one that you selected is your benchmark or standard for judging each of the other answer choices. Every other answer choice must be compared to your benchmark. That choice is correct until proven otherwise by another answer choice beating it. If you find a better answer, then that one becomes your new benchmark. Once you've decided that no other choice answers the question as well as your benchmark, you have your final answer.

PREDICT THE ANSWER

Before you even start looking at the answer choices, it is often best to try to predict the answer. When you come up with the answer on your own, it is easier to avoid distractions and traps because you will know exactly what to look for. The right answer choice is unlikely to be word-for-word what you came up with, but it should be a close match. Even if you are confident that you have the right answer, you should still take the time to read each option before moving on.

General Strategies

TOUGH QUESTIONS

If you are stumped on a problem or it appears too hard or too difficult, don't waste time. Move on! Remember though, if you can quickly check for obviously incorrect answer choices, your chances of guessing correctly are greatly improved. Before you completely give up, at least try to knock out a couple of possible answers. Eliminate what you can and then guess at the remaining answer choices before moving on.

CHECK YOUR WORK

Since you will probably not know every term listed and the answer to every question, it is important that you get credit for the ones that you do know. Don't miss any questions through careless mistakes. If at all possible, try to take a second to look back over your answer selection and make sure you've selected the correct answer choice and haven't made a costly careless mistake (such as marking an answer choice that you didn't mean to mark). This quick double check should more than pay for itself in caught mistakes for the time it costs.

PACE YOURSELF

It's easy to be overwhelmed when you're looking at a page full of questions; your mind is confused and full of random thoughts, and the clock is ticking down faster than you would like. Calm down and maintain the pace that you have set for yourself. Especially as you get down to the last few minutes of the test, don't let the small numbers on the clock make you panic. As long as you are on track by monitoring your pace, you are guaranteed to have time for each question.

DON'T RUSH

It is very easy to make errors when you are in a hurry. Maintaining a fast pace in answering questions is pointless if it makes you miss questions that you would have gotten right otherwise. Test writers like to include distracting information and wrong answers that seem right. Taking a little extra time to avoid careless mistakes can make all the difference in your test score. Find a pace that allows you to be confident in the answers that you select.

Keep Moving

Panicking will not help you pass the test, so do your best to stay calm and keep moving. Taking deep breaths and going through the answer elimination steps you practiced can help to break through a stress barrier and keep your pace.

Final Notes

The combination of a solid foundation of content knowledge and the confidence that comes from practicing your plan for applying that knowledge is the key to maximizing your performance on test day. As your foundation of content knowledge is built up and strengthened, you'll find that the strategies included in this chapter become more and more effective in helping you quickly sift through the distractions and traps of the test to isolate the correct answer.

Now it's time to move on to the test content chapters of this book, but be sure to keep your goal in mind. As you read, think about how you will be able to apply this information on the test. If you've already seen sample questions for the test and you have an idea of the question format and style, try to come up with questions of your own that you can answer based on what you're reading. This will give you valuable practice applying your knowledge in the same ways you can expect to on test day.

Good luck and good studying!

14

Regulatory Requirements

SEC Act of 1934

The Securities Exchange Act of 1934 is the foundational law of American stock trading. After the 1929 stock market crash, many critics blamed the crash and subsequent depression on rampant speculation in an unregulated stock trading atmosphere, including selling short, buying on margin, and selling on margin. In response, the Congress passed the **SEC Act**, which established rules and regulations for stock trading in America, including the formation of the **Securities and Exchange Commission (SEC)** to enforce those laws.

In addition to creating the Securities and Exchange Commission, the SEC Act of 1934 requires that stock exchanges file their registration papers with the SEC and requires any companies that trade on the exchanges to file their registration papers. It also established capital requirements and set rigid limits on borrowing and lending for purposes of buying on margin. It set rules governing insider trading and created general rules for trading stocks and other securities, including how customer accounts are handled, and the "customer protection rule." In addition, it set standards for ownership and administration of exchanges and broker firms.

SROs

SROs are **self-regulatory organizations**. These types of organizations are not backed with government power, but nonetheless are granted limited power and authority to enforce regulations and standards within their industry and over the members belonging to the organization. Examples of SROS are the Financial Industry Regulatory Authority (FINRA), the Municipal Securities Rulemaking Board (MSRB), the New York Stock Exchange (NYSE), and the Chicago Board Options Exchange (CBOE).

State Requirements for Becoming a Licensed Stockbroker

After the Series 7 exam, there might be **additional licensing exams** which one would need to pass in order to ensure that a particular state grants him a stockbroker's license. Some states, for example, require that one pass the Series 63 and Series 65 exams, while others may simply require that one pass the Series 66 exam. States also have varying requirements for continuing education.

Registration, Continuing Education, and Termination of Registered Representatives (RR)

All candidates for brokerage must have a **sponsoring broker** before they register to take the Series 7 exam. Usually, this occurs by means of a firm that has hired the candidate. The sponsoring firm needs to file an application form and pay processing fees with the **Central Registration Depository (CRD)**. The applicant must submit his fingerprints through an approved facility (such as a local police station) and schedule his exam time. Among the continuing education requirements for RRs is to complete an exam covering various topics of regulation. This exam needs to be taken two years after one gains his license and then every three years after that. In addition to these exams, there is a "broker-age firm element," which is a requirement for broker dealers to ensure that their employed RRs are up-to-date on various topics related to their particular jobs. Regarding the termination of a registered representative from his firm, a broker dealer is required to issue a form explaining the reason for the RR's departure, including the relevant ethical and legal factors.

Form U4 and Form U5

The **Form U-4** is the form filed by a prospective RR's sponsoring firm, outlining the applicant's **employment history** over the previous ten years. This must be exhaustive, explaining all of the applicant's full-time employment, part-time employment, unemployment, full-time education, and other things. Any gaps longer than three months are not permissible. The U-4 also requires the applicant's residential history for the previous five years. The **Form U-5** is the form filed by a broker dealer upon a registered representative's **departure** from the firm. This form must explain any investigations, allegations, charges, litigation, regulatory actions, and customer complaints made against the RR. The U-5 must be filed within thirty days, and the RR must be given a copy of it.

Permitted and Restricted Activities for Non-Registered Individuals

According to "**NASD Notice to Members 00-50**," non-registered individuals are restricted in their ability to contact potential customers, being allowed to contact them for only three reasons: (1) to invite the customer to events, sponsored by a registered firm, at which registered individuals will make solicitations, (2) to ask whether the customer would desire to speak with a registered individual, and (3) to determine whether the customer desires literature from a registered firm. There are also restrictions on registered firms in their employment of non-registered individuals. They are not permitted to discuss investment products with customers or pre-qualify potential customers. Registered firms need to instruct such individuals on relevant regulations and penalties for noncompliance (including some amount of oversight to ensure compliance), and the firms need to perform background checks on them as well. Moreover, non-registered persons, since they are not in the direct service of soliciting customers for investments, should be paid according to a salary or an hourly wage, not by commissions.

Registration Requirements and Exemptions for Investment Advisers

Investment advisers must register either with the SEC or with the securities agency for the state where they principally conduct their business. Generally, the rule is that investment advisers who manage **over $100 million** in customer assets must register with the **SEC,** while those handling less must register with their **state securities agency**. Investment advisers registering with the SEC are required to file the Form ADV Part 1A through the **Investment Adviser Registration Depository (IARD) system**, in addition to the submission of other documents. There are some exemptions to the requirement for investment advisers to register with the SEC: (1) if all the adviser's clients reside in the same state as the adviser's principal location of business, (2) if the adviser provides no advice or reports concerning securities on a national securities exchange, (3) if the adviser does not provide advisory service to a registered investment company or a business development security, (4) if the adviser is servicing a charitable organization, or (5) if the adviser is providing advice for church employee pension plans.

Gifts and Gratuities and Non-Cash Compensation

According to **MSRB Rule G-20**, brokers are forbidden from giving **gifts and gratuities**, the sum of whose value exceeds $100, to other persons per year. The exceptions to this include employees and partners, so long as the payments are made as ordinary business compensation in municipal securities. On the other hand, the $100 limit does not prohibit various meals or tickets to events hosted by the broker (or similar items), nor does it prohibit events which the IRS permits to be deducted as business expenses, nor does it prohibit gifts of reminder advertising, so long as all these gifts are not excessive or suspicious. In connection with primary offerings of municipal securities, brokers may not accept or request **non-cash compensation**. However, there are various exceptions to this rule, including gifts below $100 (so long as they are not intended to secure a sale), occasional meals or tickets to events (again, if not intended to secure a sale), and other conditions.

REGULATIONS REGARDING POLITICAL CONTRIBUTIONS

The **Investment Advisers Act of 1940** prohibits investment advisers from providing their services to any government client for a period of two years following any political contribution they have made. And this rule applies not merely to those who make contributions to officials who are elected or to officials who later become elected, but to all officials who *may* become elected. Furthermore, advisers are forbidden from soliciting contributions for various officials or candidates if he is also pursuing or providing business with the government.

Communications

ODD

Options are riskier than other types of investments, so before engaging in their first options transaction, investors are required to receive an **Options Disclosure Document (ODD)** that articulates these increased risks and their tax implications. (For instance, if the investor is selling call options, he could have an unlimited maximum loss potential.) The investor must read and sign this document before his brokerage account is permitted to include options.

ADVERTISEMENTS
MUNICIPAL FUND SECURITIES

Municipal fund securities, in addition to not being materially false or misleading, must include certain disclosures. These disclosures can be divided into basic disclosures and additional disclosures for identified products. **Basic disclosures** include statements that an investor ought to consider his objectives, risks, charges, and expenses before investing, that he can gain additional information about municipal fund securities in the issuer's official statement, and that the official statement ought to be carefully perused before investing. **Additional disclosures** for identified products are complex and vary according to the products. An example is that if the advertised municipal security has the characteristics of a money market fund, the advertisement must include a statement noting that the security is not guaranteed by any government agency.

BASIC DISCLOSURE

According to the MSRB, **product advertisements** for municipal fund securities must include a basic disclosure which states (a) that investors should carefully consider the costs and risks of such securities, (b) that further information on municipal fund securities is available in the issuer's official statement, (c) that the broker is the underwriter of the securities for which the official statement (mentioned elsewhere in the advertisement) can be supplied, if he indeed is, and (d) that the official statement should be carefully read. **Municipal securities advertisements** are also required to offer a legend explaining the relevance of performance data, noting that future results cannot be guaranteed on the basis of past performance, that an investor may lose more than his original investment, and that even current performance may be worse than the (past) performance indicated in the advertisement. Additionally, such advertisements should note any sales loads or other nonrecurring fee, including whether such fees are reflected in the advertisement's performance data. Lastly, to whatever extent this is applicable to the performance data, the advertisement should include the total annual operating expense ratio of municipal securities (gross of fee waivers or expense reimbursements).

17

STANDARDS AND APPROVAL

The general standard for all municipal securities advertisements is that they may not be **materially false or misleading**. The prohibition of misleading information includes an appraisal of the clarity of the information, its emphases, its intended audience, and other relevant factors which go beyond the technical accuracy of the information. Advertisement for municipal securities must be approved in writing by a municipal securities principal or a general securities principal prior to the advertisement's first display. Records of this approval should be maintained by each broker dealer and municipal securities dealer involved.

PROFESSIONAL ADVERTISEMENTS, PRODUCT ADVERTISEMENTS, AND NEW ISSUE ADVERTISEMENTS

Professional advertisements are advertisements related to the skills, services, or facilities of some professional broker or dealer of municipal securities. The requirements for these advertisements are the same as the more general requirements for municipal securities advertisements; they must not be materially false or misleading. **Product advertisements** are advertisements related to specific municipal securities, issues of municipal securities, or features of municipal securities. These also must not be materially false or misleading. **New issue advertisements** are specific types of product advertisements dealing with the new issue of municipal securities. These advertisements have specific requirements related to accuracy at the time of sale (if showing initial reoffering prices or yields for securities, the date for such information must be provided) and accuracy at the time of publication (there must be a disclaimer noting that the advertised securities may no longer be available at the time of publication, or that they may be available only at a different price).

INVESTMENT COMPANY PRODUCTS

FINRA requires that advertisements for investment company products not be **misleading**, even in part. The term "misleading" is intentional, since it goes beyond mere falsity. Whether an advertisement is misleading is determined according to the context, intended audience, and clarity of the advertisement. Moreover, FINRA guidelines specifically analyze advertised claims **of tax-free or tax-exempt returns** (since there are questions of whether the taxes are actually deferred, in addition to whether the taxes in question are local, state, or federal), comparisons (which must be clear, fair, and balanced), and predictions or projections (which are allowed only if stated as theoretical extensions of mathematical principles).

VARIABLE CONTRACTS AND MUTUAL FUNDS

All advertisements for investing companies, including those advertisements for variable contracts and mutual funds, are required to be registered with the **Advertising Regulation Department** of FINRA within ten business days of the advertisement's first use or publication. This requirement for such advertisements also includes written or electronically distributed form letters which are to be delivered to twenty-five or more potential customers. A number of SEC regulations also exist for advertisements of variable contracts and mutual funds. These include *SEC Rule 482* (the "Omitting Prospectus Rule"), *SEC Rule 433* (which applies to free writing prospectuses), *SEC Rule 135a* (which permits a general discussion of product attributes without a specific identification of the product), and *SEC Rule 34b-1* (which requires performance data for mutual fund and variable annuity advertisements to comply with Rule 482).

GOVERNMENT SECURITIES, COLLATERALIZED MORTGAGE OBLIGATIONS, AND CERTIFICATES OF DEPOSIT

Advertisements for government securities are required to be filed with FINRA's Advertising Regulation Department within ten business days of the advertisements' first use. Advertisements for **collateralized mortgage obligations (CMOs)** must likewise be filed within ten days of their first use with the Advertising Regulation Department. Specifically, the advertisements must be filed for review, and they cannot be used until all the changes designated by the department have been made. Moreover, the **National Association of Securities Dealers (NASD)** is concerned with the possibility of CMO advertisements being materially misleading, inasmuch as they are advertised as alternatives to certificates of deposit (CDs), implicitly communicating that CMOs offer the same level of security and guarantee as CDs. Advertisements for certificates of deposit (CDs) generally have the same regulations governing them as for other types of advertisements.

RESEARCH REPORTS

Research reports are any documents which communicate information related to the characteristics, strengths, and weaknesses of some particular stock, financial instrument, industry, commodity, or geographic region. These reports are generally prepared by **investment research teams** (or individuals) in stock brokerages or investment banks, and they ordinarily include "actionable" recommendations, i.e., recommendations for investment. **Research reports** need not be done "in house," but can also be performed by a third party. Third parties in such situations are defined as persons or entities lacking any affiliation or contractual relationship with the entity being researched or any of the entity's affiliates who would have an interest in the report's contents, and making all decisions about the content of their report independently of the input of the entity being researched or its affiliates. A number of regulations govern the distribution of research reports by brokers, such as ones clarifying whether the distribution of a research report constitutes an offer to sell. These regulations also differ according to the differing content of the reports.

INFORMATION BARRIERS AND QUIET PERIODS

Information barriers are any restrictions on the flow of information or data which is not intended to be released to the public, but which nonetheless can be gained by employees of a company in the employees' ordinary course of work. This information is, of course, related to **investment decisions and recommendations**. The barriers tend to work to forbid the flow of such information between employees, as well as between employees and non-employees.

Quiet periods are the durations of time when an issuer of *initial public offerings (IPOs)* are forbidden by the SEC from publicly promoting themselves, including the publication of research reports.

COLD CALLING

Cold calling is an interaction with a potential customer, usually by telephone, for which the customer had no previous anticipation. ("Warm calling" occurs after a customer has expressed some interest in an investment product.) FINRA has various rules governing cold calling, including a prohibition of calls before **8 A.M. and after 9 P.M.** and a prohibition of cold-calling those who have placed themselves on the **do-not-call list** (either for specific firms or for the national list, kept by the Federal Trade Commission). While cold calling is forbidden in the above situations, that does not mean that all phone solicitations are so forbidden. The time-of-day restraint is not applicable, for example, to those with whom one has established a business relationship or to those who have invited or permitted one to call. Similarly, people listed do-not-call registries can still be called, without any rules being violated, if there is a personal relationship, established business relationship, or prior express written consent.

Evaluating the Customer's Investment Profile

ASSESSING A CUSTOMER'S INVESTMENT PROFILE
FINANCIAL FACTORS

Many investors are not sure how much risk they should be taking, and it is the broker's job to help them figure this out. **Primary financial factors** in making this determination include the client's household income, his net worth (his total assets—including deferred assets, like retirement plans, and marketable securities—minus his liabilities), including his liquid net worth (the component of his net worth which can easily be converted to cash), the money he has available for investment, and additional background items, such as:

- whether he is a homeowner
- whether he has employee stock options
- what insurance he has, including life and disability insurance
- what his credit score is
- what his tax bracket is

NONFINANCIAL FACTORS

Many investors are not sure how much risk they should be taking, and it is the broker's job to help them figure this out. Various **nonfinancial factors** in making this determination include:

- the investor's age (older couples should generally employ less risk, since they have less time to gain from investment)
- his marital status (couples who are recently married might desire something relating buying a house)
- his dependents (the more dependents, the less desired risk)
- his educational needs (including those of his children)
- his employment situation
- his previous investment experience

CUSTOMER-SPECIFIC FACTORS AFFECTING THE SELECTION OF SECURITIES

The customer-specific factors which affect the selection of his securities for investment purposes can be categorized into three sections: his **risk tolerance**, his **investment time horizon**, and his **investment objectives**. Risk tolerance and investment time horizon are dependent upon a number of financial and nonfinancial factors which a broker must grasp in assessing a customer's investment profile. The investment objectives of a customer include how much emphasis he puts on the following *goals*:

- capital preservation
- increased current income
- capital growth
- total return (i.e. growth with income)
- tax advantages of different investments
- diversification in one's portfolio
- liquidity

20

- acquiring trading profits
- balancing short-term and long-term risks

PORTFOLIO OR ACCOUNT DIVERSIFICATION AND PRINCIPLES OF ASSET ALLOCATION

Diversification for portfolios or accounts is the possession of several varied types of securities, usually so that different parts of one's portfolio offset risks in other parts. (And it can be contrasted with **concentration**, which involves an emphasis upon some specific type of asset.) Part of diversification involves **asset allocation**, where one takes an investor's portfolio and divides it into different categories, such as cash, stocks, and bonds. **Strategic asset allocation** seeks to structure a portfolio for long-term investment (e.g. having fewer stocks for older investors, all other things being equal), whereas **tactical asset allocation** seeks to structure a portfolio in response to particular market conditions (e.g. decreasing stocks in the short term if the market as a whole is expected to fare poorly). An important characteristic of a portfolio is its **volatility**, that is, its tendency to fluctuate in its returns or losses according to the market's own fluctuations. Generally, portfolios follow the principle that an increased chance of return comes with an increased risk. A broker should also help an investor construct his portfolio according to the various tax ramifications of the assets in question.

PORTFOLIO THEORY

Portfolio theory is a branch of **finance theory** which mathematically seeks to maximize the return and/or minimize risk for a given portfolio. A widely used model in portfolio theory is the **capital asset pricing model (CAPM)**, which functions according to the following formula:

$$E(R_i) = R_f + \beta_i(E(R_m) - R_f)$$

$E(R_i)$ = expected return on the capital asset

R_f = risk-free rate of return, such as interest from government bonds

β_i = beta, or the sensitivity of the asset to the market as a whole (where 1 means that stock prices change with the market, and >1 means that they change more than the market does)

$E(R_m)$ = expected return of the market

The concept of an asset's **beta coefficient** is an important feature of portfolio theory, as is an alpha coefficient in other models. An asset's **alpha coefficient** is a measure of an asset's return after its risk is accounted for, i.e. after the compensation for the risk is deducted.

DIVERSIFICATION OF MUNICIPAL INVESTMENTS

There are three main factors relevant to the diversification of municipal investments: geography, type, and rating:

- **Geographic diversification** involves municipal investments which are outside one's own state or other governmental jurisdiction. The reason for this kind of diversification is that it offsets the risk of certain events that would bear a cost on only one municipality, such as natural disasters or political changes. By diversifying geographically, one can offset these risks.
- **Type diversification** refers to the different types of municipal investments. Most municipal investments are bonds, but municipal bonds can be further subdivided into other categories, such as general obligation bonds and revenue obligation bonds.
- **Rating diversification** refers to the risk that the bond issuer will be unable to repay its bond debts. This simply involves the ordinary investment tradeoff of risk and reward.

Customer Accounts

Opening Customer Accounts

REQUIREMENTS AND APPROVALS FOR OPENING NEW ACCOUNTS

In order to open a **new account** for a customer, a broker will need to get the customer's full legal name and date of birth, address and phone number or phone numbers, Social Security number, occupation and employer, citizenship status, annual income, and net worth. In addition, the broker must get the customer's banking and investment references, identify what investment experience and objectives the customer has, and learn whether or not the customer is an employee of another brokerage firm. Finally, the broker must also get the names and occupations of all parties authorized to make trades in the account.

CASH, MARGIN, OPTION, RETIREMENT, AND DAY TRADING ACCOUNTS

Cash accounts are ordinary brokerage accounts where the customer deposits cash to purchase various securities. Regulation T requires that customers with **cash accounts** pay for their securities within two days of having bought them. **Margin accounts** are brokerage accounts where, instead of paying his own cash, the customer is lent cash from the broker, with various securities and cash being used as collateral. **Options accounts** are brokerage accounts where the customer can trade various options, which are generally riskier than ordinary stocks or bonds. **Retirement accounts** are brokerage accounts aimed for the purposes of providing retirement income. **Day trading accounts** are brokerage accounts opened specifically for the purposes of trading various financial instruments within the same day, depending upon speculation for one's profits.

PRIME BROKERAGE, DVP/RVP, ADVISORY OR FEE-BASED, AND DISCRETIONARY ACCOUNTS

Prime brokerage accounts are **brokerage accounts** where special customers receive a special set of services. These services can include cash management and securities lending, as well as mutual funds. **Delivery Versus Payment (DVP)** accounts involve a procedure where a security buyer's payment is due at the time of delivery. **Receive Versus Payment (RVP)** accounts involve a procedure where a security buyer's payment is due at the time of receipt. **Advisory accounts** are brokerage accounts where the customer works closely with a financial advisor but retains the final say over investment decisions. **Fee-based accounts** are brokerage accounts where a customer's financial advisor is compensated as a percentage of the client's assets rather than according to commissions. **Discretionary accounts** are accounts where brokers have the authority to engage in securities transactions apart from the client's consent. These accounts require the client and broker to sign a discretionary disclosure. (These are also called managed accounts.)

DIFFERENT TYPES OF ACCOUNT REGISTRATION

Brokers can register accounts for many kinds of different customers, including individuals and institutions. Some of these accounts can also be **joint accounts**, that is, accounts which are shared by two or more people. These are most likely created for people who have good grounds to trust one another, such as relatives or business partners. One kind of joint account is **Joint Tenants with Rights of Survivorship (JTWROS),** in which all the individuals for the account have equal authority over the account's assets, retaining control even if other joint tenants die. This kind of account differs from **Joint Tenants in Common (JTIC)**, where the different individuals do *not* retain any rights of survivorship over the account. In JTIC accounts, survivors do not necessarily acquire the control over assets which was previously held by a tenant who has died. Instead, each tenant gets to distribute the assets as he desires through a will.

Brokers can register accounts for a number of different businesses, not simply individuals. They can register accounts for **sole proprietorships** (individually-owned businesses), **partnerships** (businesses owned by two or more individuals who manage and operate it), and **corporations** (a business legally separate from its owners). Furthermore, brokers can open accounts for **unincorporated associations**, which are voluntary unions of individuals for some common purpose, generally non-profit ones. They can also open accounts for **marital property** (or community property), where property acquired by either spouse is owned by the author as well, and **trust accounts**, where a trustee manages an account for the sake of another.

Brokers can register **custodial accounts**, which are accounts managed by an adult for the sake of minor (under 18 or 21 years old, depending on the relevant state's legislation), and are therefore a type of trust account. These accounts can be either UGMA or UTMA accounts, depending on the legislation in the state governing such an account—the **Uniform Gifts to Minors Act** or the **Uniform Transfers to Minors Act**. UGMA accounts are extensions of UTMA accounts, since they allow the transferal of gifts (including art, real estate, royalties, and intangible assets) as well as securities and cash. **Numbered accounts** are accounts where the account holder's name is kept confidential, identified by a number or some code word.

Transfer on death (TOD) accounts provide the account holder with a means of easily passing on his assets to others without the various hassles and delays of probate. He simply specifies which assets go to which persons. **Estate accounts** are accounts held in the name of the estate of some deceased person, handled by his representative.

DIFFERENT TYPES OF ACCOUNT AUTHORIZATIONS

One means of account authorization is **power of attorney (POA)**, where the authority to represent someone in legal, private, or business matters is held by another person; these must be formalized in writing. Another means is by **corporate resolution**, where a corporation as a unit performs some action. This is usually accomplished with a legal document, voted upon by the corporation's board of directors. **Trading authorization** can serve as a lesser substitute for power of attorney. There are different degrees of trading authorization, where the client grants a level of power to a broker (or some other agent) for the trading of his securities. This is less than the authorization granted in power of attorney, since it applies only to trading (and only to the trading that the client specifies). **Discretionary accounts** are accounts where a broker is authorized to make securities transactions on the client's behalf without the client's consent. These require the signing of a discretionary disclosure for written confirmation.

ELEMENTS OF CUSTOMER SCREENING
CIP, KYC, AND ISSUES OF DOMESTIC OR FOREIGN RESIDENCY

The **Customer Identification Program (CIP)** was implemented in various companies as a result of the Patriot Act, requiring financial institutions to better assess persons who wish to engage in financial activity. Each institution must employ its own CIP as befits its size and ordinary operations. CIP programs seek to assess the riskiness of their customers and verify their identities. **Know Your Customer (KYC)** forms are documents specifically designed to acquire relevant information about customers, so that brokers or other agents can assess the client's willingness to assume risk, his knowledge of investments and finance, and his actual assets. Important information about the client includes his place of residence and citizenship. Brokers should seek to gain this kind of information from their clients, such as whether they qualify as bona fide foreign residents.

RELEVANCE OF CORPORATE INSIDERS, EMPLOYEES OF A BROKER-DEALER, AND EMPLOYEES OF AN SRO

Corporate insiders are individuals who are particularly privy to a corporation's "**inside**" information; this definition includes directors and officers for the company in addition to anyone owning over 10% of the voting shares, and really anyone who has access to **material but non-public knowledge**. These insiders have an extra set of restrictions for any securities transactions they wish to make, and brokers should consider them accordingly. Another consideration which brokers have to make is whether their clients are employees of a broker-dealer. Just as corporate insiders are subject to various trading restrictions based upon their inside knowledge, so also employees of broker-dealers (especially of competing broker-dealers) carry their own set of risks. Particularly, the broker's company must receive consent from the employee's own institution. Employees of self-regulatory organizations (SROs) likewise are subject to these restrictions. As with employees of other broker-dealers, brokers are required to obtain the consent of a client's institution if he is employed for an SRO.

REQUIRED DISCLOSURES RELATED TO MARGIN ACCOUNTS AND DAY TRADING ACCOUNTS

Margin trading can be profitable, but it includes risks of loss greater than with buying stocks with cash, and customers wishing to trade on margin must be informed of these risks. This notification must be provided by the broker before the client opens a margin account, and the client must be reminded of the risks every year, in writing. You must let customers know that because since they're using borrowed money, it is quite possible that they'll lose more money than they have in their account. You must also tell them that margin calls must be met immediately, that borrowing rules are subject to change at any time, and that if some of their stocks must be sold to meet a margin call, the brokerage house and not the customer chooses which stocks will be sold. Some brokerage firms actively encourage **day trading** and specialize in catering to day trading clients. These firms have a special obligation to educate their customers who are potential day traders in order to make sure they have some idea of what day trading entails and the risks involved. They must furnish to the customer a risk disclosure form which outlines all the risks involved in day trading, and they must specifically approve the account for day trading, or have the client sign a form affirming that they don't intend to use the account to day trade.

Maintaining Customer Accounts

Maintenance of Customer Account Records

Brokers have obligations not only to acquire customer information, but also to **maintain their customer account records**. This includes an appropriate assessment of the customer's changing assets and his investment objectives, as well as any updates for changes in address. Further, brokers must hold customer mail and send required notifications to their customers, such as the notifications required to inform customers of the risks of various accounts.

Physical Receipt, Delivery, and Safeguarding of Cash, Cash Equivalents, and Checks

Since the broker is acting for the sake of the client's assets, it is imperative that he appropriately receive and guard any **physical assets** owned by the client and given to the broker's care, such as cash, cash equivalents, and checks. Measures for the **physical safeguarding** of these assets generally include something as simple as a safe or a locked drawer, with access being provided only to authorized persons. Brokers should periodically modify safe codes and other means of access in order to stave off the risk of theft.

Receipt, Delivery, and Safeguarding of Securities

In order to receive securities, customers must have the **cash on hand**, or **line of credit**, or **stocks** to cover a transaction at the time of the transaction. It is the job of the registered representative to ensure this. If stocks are required, and the customer doesn't have them on hand, but says they're listed in a street name at another firm, the rep must call the other firm and confirm this before making the trade. The broker is generally required to safeguard the client's securities, that is, to hold the securities on the client's behalf. Since some securities come with physical certificates, it can also be the broker's job to ensure that these physical assets are appropriately safeguarded.

Instances When Account Activity Can Be Restricted or Refused

Account activity can be restricted in different ways for different accounts. A **mutual fund, or open-end investment company**, must state in its prospectus whether it intends to engage in the following practices and how big a part these activities will play in their investment portfolio: buying stocks and bonds on margin, short selling, taking part in joint investment accounts, or distributing its own securities without an underwriter. If these activities aren't listed in the prospectus, in detail, the investment company is forbidden from participating in them. Since **money market funds** are not insured by the FDIC, the SEC requires that the front cover of a money market prospectus plainly state that federal government does not guarantee the money, and that there is no guarantee that the fund will be able to maintain a net asset value of one dollar. Another restriction on money market funds is that they must stay mainly invested in short-term securities—the average maturity in their portfolio cannot exceed 90 days, and no security in the portfolio can have a maturity of more than 13 months. Additionally, customers with **cash brokerage accounts** are not permitted to sell securities before they have fully paid for the shares. Doing so subjects one's account to trading restrictions for ninety days.

Closing an Account

If someone wishes to **close his brokerage account**, whether due to dissatisfaction with his broker, or due to a need for the funds for some other purpose, he can contact his broker with his account information and let him know. He should let his broker know if he wants any of his investment holdings to be sold or transferred to a different broker. If the account is not closed within three business days of the request, he should notify his broker. Regulations require that the closing of a brokerage account not be delayed except for just cause. After the account closure, he should check his account for any remaining funds or securities that should not have been left there.

TRANSFERRING ACCOUNTS BETWEEN BROKER-DEALERS

A customer wishing to transfer his account between broker-dealers needs to complete an **account transfer form** with the new broker-dealer, stating whatever securities he held with the old broker-dealer. At this point, the new broker-dealer can send transfer instructions to the old broker-dealer. After the new broker-dealer sends these instructions to the old one, the old broker-dealer has three business days to confirm or else make an exception for some information in the request (e.g. an invalid account number of Social Security number). Once the account is validated, the old-broker dealer then has three more business days to execute the account transfer. A common means of account transfers is through the **Automated Customer Account Transfer Service (ACATS)**. Using this service requires membership in the **National Securities Clearing Corporation (NSCC)**.

ACCOUNT REGISTRATION CHANGES

Accounts can be registered under different categories, such as individual, joint, and custodial. If a customer desires to **change the registration** for his account, different firms will ordinarily have some process and form for the customer to fill out, requiring the signatures of all the owners involved. These processes are different if certain owners are dropping from the account. Doing so may require the notarized signatures of the other owners of the account. If the primary account holder is dropping from the account, then a new account may need to be opened.

INTERNAL TRANSFERS

Internal transfers are **transfers** which customers make with funds between or among their own accounts (or accounts with which they are closely associated). **Transfer on death (TOD)** permits securities to pass from an account owner directly to some assigned TOD beneficiary upon the owner's death. The benefit of this is that such a transfer eliminates the need to go through probate. In this type of transfer, however, the beneficiaries need to ensure that the transferred funds and assets are re-registered in their own names. **Divorce transfers** can vary according to the terms specified by the parties to be divorced. It is not uncommon for brokerage accounts to be split 50-50.

ANTI-MONEY LAUNDERING COMPLIANCE

Money laundering is the deliberate concealment of the source of illegally-obtained funds, and due to its deception and harm, a number of regulations and procedures exist for anti-money laundering compliance:

- **Suspicious activity reports (SARs)** are made by financial institutions to the U.S. Treasury Department (specifically, the Financial Crimes Enforcement Network, or FinCEN), detailing information about suspicious individuals or transactions.
- The **Bank Secrecy Act (BSA),** passed in 1970, established responsibilities for financial institutions to federal government agencies, requiring the institutions to maintain records for cash purchases of negotiable instruments, to file any such purchases totaling over $10,000, and to report any suspicious activity.
- **Currency transaction reports (CTRs)** must be filed by financial institutions to the federal government for any currency transaction exceeding $10,000. Before 1986, out of regard for financial privacy, these were not required.

- The **Office of Foreign Asset Control (OFAC)** is a section of the U.S. Treasury Department tasked with the objective of national security other foreign policy goals through economic and trade sanctions, as well as the tracking of terrorist activity. Their relevance to anti-money laundering compliance is to discover any financial activity involving the financing of terrorism.
- The OFAC has compiled a list of **Specially Designated Nationals (SDNs)**, that is, people or groups of people with whom U.S. citizens and institutions are prohibited from doing business.

DELIVERY OF ANNUAL REPORTS AND NOTICES OF CORPORATE ACTIONS

A broker is responsible for informing his customer of various actions taken by corporations in which the customer has some share or interest. This includes notifying the customer about **annual reports** for the corporation (as well as interim reports, if necessary) and notices of various **corporate actions**. If a corporation has split its stock, tendered new stock, established some kind of shareholder voting by proxy, announced plans to repurchase stock, or done some other action which is worthy of the customer's attention, the broker should seek to notify him.

RETAINING BOOKS AND RECORDS

One of the duties of a broker for his customers is to retain various **books and records**. According to **MSRB Rule G-8**, these include records of original entry, account records, securities records, and subsidiary records, such as records for municipal securities in transfer, municipal securities to be validated, municipal securities borrowed or loaned, and municipal securities transactions not completed on the settlement date. The broker should also maintain records for put options and repurchase agreements, records for agency transactions, records for transactions as principal, records concerning primary offerings, and other records. Essentially, the broker should maintain a paper trail for all of his customer's substantial activity.

PRIVACY REGULATIONS

A number of **privacy regulations** govern broker-dealers. Financial institutions are prohibited from disclosing nonpublic personal information about any customers to third parties not affiliated with the customer (except in certain circumstances where the institution informs the customer and he does not opt out), and they are required to provide customers with a notice of the institution's privacy policies and practices. Institutions must also develop processes and standards for the protection of their customers' information. The bulk of these regulations are contained in **Regulation S-P**, issued by the SEC to protect customers from the risk of identity theft or fraud and from unauthorized access to their private information.

Margin Accounts

REQUIREMENTS AND CHARACTERISTICS

Margin accounts are brokerage accounts in which the customer purchases securities using cash he borrowed from the broker. Since purchasing securities on credit is a riskier venture for the broker than a customer who purchases them with his own cash, it is necessary for the broker to approve any clients wishing to do so. Moreover, customers will generally be required to offer securities and cash as **collateral**. Brokerage firms will also have restrictions on what kind of accounts can be margin accounts, as well as what kind of securities can be purchased in margin accounts. Margin accounts require a certain portion of the account to be owned by the client, not the broker. If the value of certain stocks drops, then the client might be required to place more cash in the account or to sell off some of the securities. At one time, prior to the stock market crash of 1929, investors could buy stocks with only ten percent down. After the crash and after much blame for the crash was placed on speculators, the rule was changed in order to reduce the leverage and risk in margin trading. Currently, investors must put at least fifty percent of the stock price down in cash. To open an account, they must be approved based on their credit history. For their first purchase on margin, they must use at least $2,000.

REQUIRED DISCLOSURES

Due to the **increased risks** of margin accounts, brokerage firms must disclose some of the risks to customers. For instance, customers should know that they can lose more funds than they deposit, that they might be forced to sell assets in their accounts (or that the brokerage firm might itself sell such assets), and that the brokerage firm's maintenance margin requirement might increase. Since the broker is lending money to the client, it is imperative that the broker or firm disclose the rate of interest the client will be charged for the borrowed money. Likewise, since the client will have to collateralize some assets in order to hold the account, the broker should disclose information to the client regarding such hypothecation.

PRODUCT OR STRATEGY SPECIFIC REQUIREMENTS

Since margin accounts use a broker's money, there can be additional requirements and restrictions placed upon it for different investment products or strategies. Some securities, since they are declared **very low-risk** (e.g. U.S. Treasury bonds) do not fall subject to these restrictions, since the restrictions are meant to regulate the increased riskiness of margin accounts. However, the restrictions do apply to such investments as mutual funds. Per **Regulation T**, the shares of mutual funds (open-end investment companies) may not be purchased on margin. This is due to the fact that they're part of a continuous public offering. Once bought and held for thirty days, however, they may be used as collateral for a margin purchase of other securities.

LONG AND SHORT MARGIN ACCOUNTS

In a margin account, a client can take two different courses of action: either he can borrow money with which he will buy securities, or he can borrow securities directly. The first type of margin account is a long margin account, and the second is a short margin account. In a **long margin account**, the customer uses money lent to him by the broker, in addition to some of his money, to purchase a security (or set of securities), hoping to make a profit on the security, pay back the broker, and pocket the extra cash. Long margin accounts are therefore fitting for bull markets, since the customer's profit depends on the increased value of the security. In a **short margin account**, the customer will generally sell the security (or set of securities) he has just borrowed from the broker, hope for the price to decrease, purchase the security at a lower price, and return the security to the broker while pocketing the extra cash. Short margin accounts are therefore fitting for bear markets, since the customer's profit depends on the decreased value of the security.

INITIAL MARGIN REQUIREMENT

When a customer wishes to set up a margin account with his broker, he cannot simply request that the entire account be given as a loan. Instead, there is some specific portion of the account which he must contribute himself, and it is this equity which is the **initial margin requirement**. These requirements are not merely stipulated by brokerage firms, either, but are subject to government regulation. The initial margin requirement, as determined by Regulation T of the Financial Reserve Board is 50%. Different brokerage firms are free to establish their own initial margin requirement levels in excess of this percentage.

MARGIN REQUIREMENTS FOR SHORT SALE ACCOUNTS

Since short sales involve the selling of stocks which an investor does not own (so that he can buy them back cheaper and return the stocks to their owner, pocketing the difference), there are stricter **margin requirements**. Whereas ordinary margin accounts have margin requirements of 50% (and long positions also have 50% requirements), short sale accounts, according to Regulation T requirements, have margin requirements of 150%. If an investor engages in a short sale for $5,000, then the margin requirement for his short sale account is $7,500.

EXCESS EQUITY, BALANCE, AND BUYING POWER FOR SMAS

Special memorandum accounts (SMAs) are like lines of credit, where an investor is permitted to take out more on margin if he has more equity in his margin account. The balance of an SMA depends upon the initial margin requirement, stipulated by Regulation T as 50% minimum, and higher for different financial institutions. Thus, if a customer deposits more of his money into the account, or if the value of the stock he has purchased on margin in his margin account increases, then the line of credit in his SMA will increase accordingly—doubling for whatever equity he contributes from his own pocket, and increasing by 50% whenever the stocks' value increases. If the margin requirement is 50% (that is, if the financial institution does not raise the requirement above the minimum 50%), then the buying power for any SMA will be double the SMA balance.

PORTFOLIO MARGIN ACCOUNTS AND DAY TRADING ACCOUNTS

Portfolio margin accounts are a type of margin account where the initial margin requirement differs according to the particular risk of the portfolio. Whereas Regulation T requires all margin accounts to have an initial margin requirement of at least 50%, portfolio margin requirements can be much lower, perhaps between 15% and 20%. However, while the margin requirement is low, customers wishing to have a portfolio margin account must have a specific (and high) absolute amount of equity, usually $150,000. The portfolio margin is calculated according to the Options Clearing Corporation's (OCC's) **Customer Portfolio Margin system**. **Day trading accounts** are especially risky margin accounts used to make a very high number of trades per day, making a profit or loss off of the small upticks and downticks in the daily price. Because of the extremely risky nature of day trading, the rules with respect to margin trading are a bit different when it comes to clients who wish to day trade. For one thing, day traders must always have at least $25,000 in equity in their account if they wish to day trade. If they don't meet this requirement, they are not allowed to day trade. And, unlike regular margin traders, their buying power isn't twice the SMA; instead, it is four times the equity in their account above the twenty-five percent maintenance minimum, which is called maintenance margin excess.

IMPORTANT TERMS

Credit balance: The credit brokerage refers to how much the customer has contributed to or received in his account.

Debit balance: The debit balance refers to how much the customer has borrowed from the brokerage firm.

Exempt securities: Exempt securities are not required to be registered under the Securities Act of 1933. These include securities issued by the federal government or its agencies, municipal bonds, securities issued by banks, savings institutions, and credit unions, public utility securities, and securities issued by nonprofit, educational, or religious organizations.

Hypothecation: Hypothecation is the name given to the practice of using stocks as collateral for loans. Stock market investors selling on margin give permission for the brokerage to do this when they sign their margin agreement.

LMV: Long market value (LMV) is the current value of the stocks the investor bought on margin. This should not be confused with the value at time of purchase, but always refers to the current value.

Loan value: Loan value is the difference between the margin requirement for an account and the total cost. If a client opened up a margin account and wished to buy 100 shares of stock X at $20 per share, and if the margin requirement for the account were 50%, then the client would have to pay $1000 in cash, and the difference—the loan value—would be $1000.

Margin: Margin refers to any borrowed money that is used to purchase something (in this context, to purchase securities).

Margin calls: Margin calls occur when equity in a margin account goes below a certain maintenance level. (Official rules say that investors must maintain at least twenty-five percent equity in their position; many brokers have higher requirements that that, usually around thirty-three percent.) If this occurs, the brokerage house will issue a margin call to the investor, telling the investor to deposit enough funds or stocks to get back to the minimum. The investor must do so immediately, or the firm will begin selling stocks out of the investor's account to raise the money.

Marginable securities: Marginable securities are securities that can be used as collateral for margin trades. Stocks listed on the New York Stock Exchange and on the NASDAQ exchange are marginable. Certain Over the Counter stocks can also be bought on margin, or used as collateral. Mutual funds and newly issued stocks can't be bought on margin, but can be used as collateral once 30 days have passed. Options (except for LEAPS) and most OTC stocks can't be bought on margin, or used as collateral.

Portfolio margin: Portfolio margin seeks to analyze the risk for a portfolio taken as a whole in the determination of margin requirements. Portfolio margin usually leads to significantly lower margin requirements.

Rehypothecation: Rehypothecation refers to the practice of a brokerage firm using the same stocks as collateral for a loan from a bank, though the commingling of stocks from the accounts of two different customers is prohibited, unless they've both given written permission. The brokerage house may not pledge more than 140 percent of a customer's debit balance.

SMAs: Special memorandum accounts (SMAs) refer to the amount of purchasing power in the account. When stocks purchased on margin increase in value, SMA is created. For every dollar the value increases, fifty cents of SMA is created, because of the fifty percent margin requirement. The customer can then use the value of the SMA to purchase other stocks or withdraw cash without selling the original stocks bought on margin. It is much like a line of credit. Investors are always free to increase their SMA by depositing cash in their account.

SMV: Short market value (SMV) is the current price of stocks a short seller has sold. Do not confuse this with the price of the stock at the time of the original transaction. SMV is always the current value of the stock, and is always fluctuating.

Investment Information and Recommendations

PROHIBITED ACTIVITIES FOR BROKERS

Brokers are legally prohibited from engaging in a number of behaviors designed to unduly benefit themselves or hurt others:

- They are not permitted to **spread market rumors** in order to influence other people to buy or sell a security. This is because market transactions ought to be based on real facts and knowledge.
- They are not permitted to engage in **front-running**, which is when a broker makes a trade due to his foreknowledge of a block trade (a trade of 10,000+ stocks) before it is reported.
- They are not permitted to engage in **churning**, which occurs when a broker participates in excessive trading on a client's behalf only to obtain extra commissions.
- They are not permitted to engage in **commingling**, which is the combination of a customer's fully-paid securities and his margined securities, or the combination of a customer's securities with a firm's securities.
- They are not permitted to **prearrange trades**, which would be an agreement between a broker and a customer to buy back some security at a given price.
- They are not permitted to **guarantee against losses**, since that would be frankly misrepresenting the riskiness of investments.
- They are not permitted to **pay for referrals** by compensating others (whether with cash or something else) for finding, introducing, or referring a client.
- They are not permitted to make **unsuitable recommendations**, which is simply to say that they ought to recommend good investments. If this is serious enough, customers can sue brokers for failing in their obligations.

SOURCES OF MARKET AND INVESTMENT INFORMATION

Since brokers are obligated to make good recommendations to customers, they need to ensure that their sources for **market and investment information** are credible. For the most basic data they can acquire, such as exchange quote and trade-related data from the market, the data is sure to be reliable, and the main issue is simply whether they interpret the data correctly to make good recommendations. However, for data that can be acquired from news outlets, the internet, and other less reliable sources, brokers should exercise more caution.

TRACE, NASDAQ, AND RATING AGENCIES

TRACE stands for the Trade Reporting and Compliance Engine. It is a program developed by FINRA to facilitate the reporting of various trades by brokers. The specific trades reported through TRACE involve over-the-counter secondary market transactions in eligible fixed-income securities. Brokers who are FINRA members are obligated to use TRACE for reporting such transactions. **NASDAQ** stands for the National Association of Securities Dealers Automated Quotations. Following the New York Stock Exchange, it is the second largest stock exchange in the world. **Rating agencies** are independent entities which provide independent opinions on the worthiness of value of various assets, stocks in particular.

RESEARCH REPORTS, PRICING SERVICES, AND PRODUCT-SPECIFIC PERIODICALS

Research reports are documents prepared by investment research teams for brokerage firms or investment banks (or by individual analysts in such teams). Research reports can cover a wide array of topics. **Pricing services** are, quite simply, entities which provide different prices for stocks and other tradable assets. **Product-specific periodicals** are publications released to provide information on particular products or investment strategies.

TRF, EMMA, AND MIG-1 RATINGS

A **Trade Reporting Facility (TRF)** is a service used to facilitate automated trade reporting and reconciliation, specifically for trades which are not made on an exchange. TRFs are available for use by FINRA members. **Electronic Municipal Market Access (EMMA)** is an online source of information for municipal bonds. EMMA is free of charge and geared towards nonprofessional investors. **MIG-1 ratings** are the best ratings which can be received according to Moody's system of municipal bond credit ratings. Brokers should pay careful attention to such ratings.

SOURCES OF DATA ON BUSINESS CONDITIONS, BUSINESS ACTIVITY, AND CORPORATE PROFITS

Since a broker should clearly not be concerned only with the changes in prices for stocks and other investments, but ought to be aware of the underlying causes for such investments, he needs to have **good sources of information** on business conditions, business activities, and corporate profits. Information on these topics can come from a wide variety of sources, such as media outlets, but the more easily accessible the sources are, generally speaking, the more careful the broker should be about using them. A broker can also find good data by studying business indices and statistics, as well as U.S. government sources, in order to gain a better perspective on various business and economic data.

INVESTMENT RISK
CALL RISK, CAPITAL RISK, AND CREDIT RISK

Call risk is the chance that a callable bond will be called, causing the bondholder to lose the stream of interest payments left until maturity. Because bonds are generally called when interest rates are going lower, the bondholder will have a hard time getting a comparable interest rate with the money received if the bond is called. To mitigate this risk, in addition to the call premium that is paid, callable bonds usually have a call protection feature—a period of time during which the issuer may not call the bonds, usually five to ten years in duration. **Capital risk** is the risk of losing all the capital one has invested, particularly for options and warrants. Such securities have expiration dates, and therefore investors can lose all their money at those dates. Purchasing investment-grade bonds can help reduce this risk. **Credit risk** is the risk for a creditor that principal and interest on a loan he has given will not be paid back to him on time. Bond rating agencies (e.g. Moody's, Standard & Poor's, and Fitch) help investors to properly rate bond investments for their credit risk.

CURRENCY RISK, INFLATIONARY RISK, INTEREST RATE RISK, AND LIQUIDITY RISK

Currency risk is the risk that investments will be harmed through changes in currency exchange rates. This type of risk is a problem for international investors. **Inflationary risk** is the risk that investments will substantively decrease in value due to the devaluation of the dollar through inflation. **Interest rate risk** is the risk that investments will be harmed through fluctuations in interest rates. This type of risk particularly affects bond and mortgage holders. **Liquidity risk** is the risk that an investor will not be able to liquidate his assets when he wishes. The investor may want to sell some particular asset, but there may not be much of a market at a price that the investor finds worthwhile.

SYSTEMATIC MARKET RISK, NONSYSTEMATIC MARKET RISK, AND POLITICAL OR LEGISLATIVE RISK

Systematic market risk is the risk intrinsic to the market taken as a whole or to a market segment. It is the risk that is unavoidable in some capacity, the risk that cannot be diversified away. Since nothing is certain with investments, there will always be some market risk inherent in the system. **Nonsystematic market risk** is the risk associated with specific firms, rather than with the market as a whole. This type of risk, unlike systematic market risk, is diversifiable. **Political or legislative risk** is the risk that investments could be harmed through some political events or unrest, whether domestically or abroad.

PREPAYMENT RISK, REINVESTMENT RISK, AND TIMING RISK

Prepayment risk is the risk that an investment which depends upon some stream of fixed income in the future (such as a bond) will have its principal repaid earlier than expected. This would reduce the overall expected gain on the investment. **Reinvestment risk** is the risk that interest or dividends which one receives from different investments have to be reinvested at a lower rate of return. **Timing risk** is simply the risk that an investor might make some transaction at the wrong, failing to minimize his losses or maximize his gains.

INVESTMENT RETURNS

DIVIDENDS, INTEREST, AND TAX-EXEMPTED INTEREST

A **dividend** is a portion of the company's profit that is returned to shareholders. A dividend can come in the form of cash, in which case a check is sent to the owner or to the owner's brokerage account. When dividends are paid in cash, they are considered income, and taxes must be paid on them during the tax year they're received. Dividends can also be in the form of additional shares of stock given to shareholders. These are not taxable until they're sold, just like all stocks. Because this type of stock dividend increases the number of outstanding shares, it decreases the market value of each share, but does not affect the total market value of the company. **Interest** is the fee charged for the use of another's money. It is often expressed as an annual percentage rate (APR). Interest can also be simple or compound; compound interest periodically adds the outstanding interest to the principal, thus increasing the rate at which interest generates. **Tax-exempted interest** is interest income that it not subject to federal income tax. Municipal bonds provide tax-exempted interest.

CAPITAL GAINS, CAPITAL LOSSES, AND RETURN OF CAPITAL

Whenever an investor sells a security for more than he paid for it (the security's cost basis), the investor has received a **capital gain**. If the investor held the security for more than a year, then it is considered a long-term capital gain, and is given favorable tax treatment; it is only taxed at 15 percent. If the investor held the security for less than a year before the sale, it is considered a short-term capital gain, and is taxed at the investor's regular income tax rate, which for most people is higher than 15 percent. If the investor sells a security for less than its cost basis, then he or she has a **capital loss**. If, after adding up all the investor's capital gains and capital losses for the tax year, it turns out that the investor has a net capital loss, he or she may use that capital loss to offset taxes against earned income, up to a limit of $3,000 a year. If an investor has an investment returned to him in part or in whole, such that he is not gaining anything beyond the original investment, then it is a **return of capital** (which is very different from return *on* capital). This is not taxed or considered as income, because it is simply a return of the original investment.

REQUIRED DISCLOSURES FOR SPECIFIC TRANSACTIONS
OFFERING DOCUMENTS, PROSPECTUSES, AND RED HERRINGS

Offering documents are disclosures provided by issuers of securities providing specific and detailed financial information concerning both the issuer and the offering itself. **Prospectuses** are formal documents which brokers are legally required to file with the SEC. They provide information about investments being offered for sale to the public, giving information so that investors can make intelligent and informed decisions. Stocks and bonds have two types of prospectuses, preliminary and final. **Red herrings** are preliminary prospectuses. They are called such, not because they are misleading (as are "red herrings" in logic and rhetoric), but because they include a statement in red lettering on the cover declaring that they are preliminary, and thus that some items might be subject to change.

STATEMENTS OF ADDITIONAL INFORMATION, MATERIAL EVENTS, AND CONTROL RELATIONSHIPS

Statements of additional information, sometimes abbreviated as SAIs, are supplementary documents which are added to prospectuses for mutual fund offerings. These statements provide further details on the fund, although they are not strictly necessary for investors to make informed decisions, and therefore they are not legally required by fund companies to include. (However, they must provide such information for free to customers upon request.)

Material events are any events which substantively impact a prospective investor's decision to invest or not. These can be economic events, political events, or anything else. Brokers should be aware of these and report them to customers as is appropriate. In order to avoid conflicts of interest and thereby protect customers, brokers are required to disclose any **control relationships** they have with the issuer of securities, bonds in particular. Although the initial disclosure can be merely verbal, before a transaction actually goes through, the customer must be informed in writing of the control issue. This usually takes place at confirmation.

COSTS AND FEES ASSOCIATED WITH INVESTMENTS
BREAKPOINTS, ROAS, AND LETTERS OF INTENT LOIS

Mutual funds have portfolio managers who get paid a certain percentage, and in order to encourage investors to invest more, this percentage decreases for higher investment amounts. The point at which the percentage decreases is the **breakpoint**. (Brokers and dealers are forbidden from making "breakpoint sales": sales that seek to maximize commission income by encouraging investors to invest just below the breakpoint.) **Rights of accumulation (ROAs)** are closely related to breakpoints. Investors can receive the reduced sales charge (the percentage paid to the portfolio manager) if the dollar amount of investments purchased, when combined with the fund investment they already possess, surpasses the breakpoint level. **Letters of intent (LOIs)** can be signed by investors to permit them to receive the desired reduction in the sales charge immediately, so long as they pay the remaining amount needed to reach the breakpoint within a given time period.

COMMISSIONS, MARKUPS, NET TRANSACTIONS, SHARE CLASSES, AND FEE-BASED ACCOUNTS

When a broker facilitates an investment transaction for you and then charges you some fee for providing that service, he is receiving a **commission**. However, when he does not merely facilitate a trade, but actually acts as a principal—trading securities using his own account—then the profit he makes on such a transaction will occur from an increased price on the security over the price at which he obtained it: a **markup**. If you take an investment transaction and deduct the commission or fee paid to the broker, you are left with the **net transaction**: what the transaction is when considered by itself. When investing in shares, one can purchase different kinds of shares, organized into different **share classes** based on the privileges and rights associated with those shares. Firms can charge different fees based on different share classes. **Fee-based accounts** differ from other accounts—commission-based accounts—since fee-based accounts compensate the advisor based on a percentage of the client's assets, rather than as a commission for transactions facilitated.

SIPC

The **Securities Investor Protection Corporation (SIPC)** was set up by Congress to protect investors in case their brokerage firm goes out of business. Broker/dealers pay fees every year to the SIPC, which are then set aside to compensate customers of brokerage firms that go under. Each customer is protected up to $500,000, although no more than $250,000 of this can be for cash holdings. And it is important to note that each account is not covered up to $500,000—if a customer has more than one account, that customer's total coverage is still only $500,000. Additionally, joint and group accounts only count as one customer.

FDIC

The **Federal Deposit Insurance Corporation (FDIC)** is a corporation of the U.S. federal government established by the Glass-Steagall Act of 1933. Its goal is to protect customer deposits in banks from bank failure, or bankruptcy. The FDIC insures deposits of up to $250,000 per customer per bank, but only for member banks. Therefore, it is important for depositors to ensure that the banks where they place their deposits are insured by the FDIC.

ANNUAL GIFT TAX EXCLUSION, LIFETIME GIFT TAX EXEMPTION, AND UNIFICATION OF GIFT AND ESTATE TAXES

Gift taxes have an annual exclusion amount of $15,000 for 2020. This means that a person can give gifts to anyone (or any number of people), up to $15,000 per person, without incurring any federal gift tax. Gifts given to U.S. citizen spouses do not count towards this $15,000.

Gift taxes also have a **lifetime exemption amount**. If a person gives gifts in excess of the annual exclusion amount, then those excess gifts will still not be federally taxable so long as they do not exceed the lifetime exemption amount, which is $11,580,000 for 2020. If a person gives $16,000 worth of gifts in a year, and if the annual exclusion amount is $15,000, then the extra $1,000 in gifts will reduce the lifetime exemption amount by $1,000.

Such a large lifetime exemption amount may seem inconsequential for most people, but it is relevant in two ways. First, the lifetime exemption amount might decrease to $1,000,000 in the future. Second, tax law contains a **unification of gift and estate taxes**, such that the lifetime exemption amount for gift taxes is unified with estate taxes. Specifically, if someone gives gifts in excess of the annual exclusion amount (and thus credits those excess gifts against the lifetime exemption amount), the exemption amount for estate tax will be reduced as well—the amount of assets he can transfer to others upon his death, apart from federal taxation, will be reduced by whatever amount by which his lifetime exemption amount for gift taxes is credited.

TAX CONSIDERATIONS FOR THE GIVING OR BEQUEATHING OF SECURITIES

If securities are given to someone else as a gift, then they have the same **tax implications** as any other gift which is given: there is an annual exclusion amount ($15,000 for 2020) and a lifetime exemption amount ($11,580,000 for 2020). In determining capital gains and losses for securities given, the recipient of the securities should assume the cost basis of the donor, that is, the price which the donor paid for the securities himself, even if the securities have since increased in value.

However, if the securities have decreased in value from the date of their original acquisition, the cost basis for them should be their cost basis at the date the securities are given. However, when securities are bequeathed rather than given, the cost basis on the date of the bequeather's death is the relevant one, irrespective of any changes in the securities' value.

Orders and Transactions

SECURITIES QUOTE TOPICS

BIDS, ASKS, SPREADS, FIRM QUOTES, AND SUBJECT OFFERS

Bids are prices which dealers (or others) are willing to pay for particular security. **Asks** are prices at which dealers (or others) are willing to sell a particular security. The **spread** is the difference between the bid and the ask price for a particular security. **Firm quotes** are price quotes on a particular security which guarantee a bid or ask price up to the amount that is quoted. (These can be contrasted with nominal quotes.) **Subject offers** are offers to sell a security, but they are merely presented to give others information and thereby incite a counteroffer. They merely present information without officially placing a security on the market for sale.

BOND QUOTES, THE OTCBB, WORKOUT AGREEMENTS, AND FAST MARKETS

Bond quotes are the prices at which bonds are trading. They are ordinarily stated as a percentage of the respective bond's par value. The **OTCBB** stands for the **Over-the-Counter Bulletin Board**, which is an electronic service used for trading over-the-counter equity securities. The OTCBB is provided by the National Association of Securities Dealers (NASD).

Workout agreements are agreements mutually entered into by a lender and a borrower where the terms of a loan in default are reworked to avoid the borrower's foreclosure or liquidation. Workout agreements involve some kind of relief for the borrower, and they can be beneficial to the lender by ensuring that the borrower will still be able to repay his debt.

A **fast market** is a condition of a stock exchange where the exchange experiences a high degree of volatility in prices and heavy trading. This can lead to problems for many investors, since quotes may not reflect the price of a stock whose price is rapidly fluctuating, and since brokers may not be able to facilitate customer orders as customers demand.

TYPES OF ORDERS

Buy orders are as simple as their name implies: they are orders for a broker to purchase some security. **Sell orders** are likewise simple; they are orders for a broker to sell a security to someone else. **Short selling orders** are orders to sell a security which the investor does not own, done with the assumption that the share can be purchased back at a lower price.

Market orders are plain and simple orders to buy or sell a stock, with no restrictions on the price. A market order is executed immediately, and it takes priority over all restricted types of orders. A market buy order will be filled at the lowest available ask price, and a market sell order will be filled at the highest available bid price. **Limit orders** are orders which specify a maximum buying price or minimum selling price that the investor will accept. **Stop orders** are orders to purchase or sell a security if it passes by some price, done either to lock in profits or to cut off losses.

ORDER TICKET

An **order ticket** must be filed for every stock trade and must include: the account number of the client; the execution price; the time the order was received; the time the order was executed; the representative's ID number; whether the order is cash or margin; whether it is a market, day, or good-till-canceled order; whether the trade was solicited or unsolicited; whether it is a discretionary account; the stock or bond symbol; the number of shares or units; and what sort of trade it is (buy, sell short, etc.).

SHORT SALES

Short sales—that is, when a customer borrows securities, sells them, and seeks to buy them back at a lower price, returning the securities to the lender and pocketing the profit—have special rules governing them, encapsulated in **Regulation SHO**. Regulation SHO demands that all relevant instances must be marked as short sale. Furthermore, the regulation requires brokerage firms to set its own rules for locating, borrowing, and delivering any securities which are intended to be sold short. Such firms must be able to locate and deliver the security on the delivery due date before any short sales occur.

STRATEGIES

Short selling consists of borrowing stocks, selling them, and then hoping to replace them later at a lower price. Unlike most stock market transactions, which involve two parties, short selling involves three parties—the short seller, the buyer, and the individual or corporation that loaned the stock to the short seller. Short selling can be done through **speculation**, that is, watching for the market to experience fluctuations at which point one can make a high-risk investment, banking on a big change in stock price. However, many investors use short selling as an opportunity for **hedging**, or reducing risk. This can be done in different ways, one of which might be to systematically eliminate the industry risk by doing short sell transactions with shares of competing companies in the same industry.

EASY-TO-BORROW, HARD-TO-BORROW, AND FAILURE TO DELIVER

Easy-to-borrow securities are available to be borrowed for short-selling transactions; the delivery of these securities is assured. These securities are stated on a list, the "Easy-to-Borrow List," which is used by brokerage firms and updated every 24 hours. Securities are categorized as easy-to-borrow generally due being highly accessible and having a high number of shares outstanding. **Hard-to-borrow** securities are just the opposite; they are not very accessible or attainable for use in short-selling transactions. **Failure to deliver** occurs when a brokerage representing the seller of a security doesn't deliver the security to the brokerage representing the buyer, or if the brokerage does deliver the security, but it is not in good delivery form. If a failure to deliver occurs, the buyer's broker may buy the security on the open market and charge the seller's firm for the difference. If, after ten days after settlement, the seller still hasn't delivered the security, the seller's broker must buy them on the open market.

BEST EXECUTION OBLIGATIONS

Any firm which provides investment services has a duty for the customers' well-being as well as its own profit, and thus these firms are required to ensure the best possible execution for their customers' orders. These obligations are called **best execution obligations**. Firms are required to seize opportunities where they can attain better prices for investors' desired securities than the current quote, and they should also seek to increase the likelihood and speed of executions.

SOFT DOLLAR ARRANGEMENTS

Soft dollar arrangements are set up between broker-dealers and investment advisers, where the investment advisers receive benefits (e.g. research) in exchange for directing trades towards the broker-dealer. They are opposed to **hard dollar arrangements**, which are ordinary transactions of cash.

CUSTOMER CONFIRMATIONS

Customer confirmations are notices of a customer's transaction(s) that must be delivered to the customer at or before the settlement date of the transaction. This is ordinarily three business days after the trade date. **Customer confirmations** must include

- the account number of the customer
- the ID number of the registered representative
- the trade date
- the type of transaction (bought or sold—BOT or SLD)
- number of shares or the par value of bonds in the transaction
- the yield (if bonds are transacted)
- the CUSIP ID number
- the dollar price of the security transacted
- the total amount of money paid or received, excluding commission
- the commission total
- the net amount, that is, the amount the customer paid or received when the commission is taken into account, and when accrued interest is taken into account for bonds

GOOD DELIVERY

Good delivery involves the requirements that must be met for a security in a transaction to be transferred to a buyer. A **security certificate** meeting these requirements is ready to be transferred "on good delivery." Otherwise, the trade cannot be settled. Some of the general requirements for good delivery are that the certificate must be in good physical condition (i.e. not mutilated), that the certificate must have an endorsement that the exact number of securities (whether shares or bonds) must be delivered, and that the correct currency denomination for the certificates must be delivered.

REQUIREMENTS FOR BONDS

Bearer bonds (a.k.a. coupon bonds), which are not registered to particular individuals, but are as tradable and liquid as dollar bills, must be delivered with all the related unpaid coupons—the interest payments—attached to them in order to be in good form. **Registered bonds**, which *are* registered to particular individuals, must have par values in multiples of $1,000, not to exceed $100,000, in order to be delivered in good form.

REQUIREMENTS FOR STOCK

To be delivered in good form, stock certificates are required to be denominated in ways relating to a **round lot**, that is, 100 shares. The certificates must be denominated in multiples of 100 shares (100, 200, 300, etc.), divisors of 100 shares (100, 50, 25, 20, 10, 5, etc.), or units adding up to 100 shares (30+70, 37+59+4, etc.). Trades of fewer than 100 shares are termed **odd lot trades**, and discrete components of trades which are fewer than 100 shares can be termed **odd lot portions**. These are not required to meet this particular good delivery requirement. For example, in a trade of 430 shares, if the trade were comprised of two 200-share certificates and a 30-share certificate, the trade would be in good delivery form, since the two 200-share certificates would be multiples of 100, and since the 30-share certificate would be exempt as an odd lot portion. However, if the trade were comprised of one 300-share certificate and two 65-share certificates, then it would not be in good form, since, while the 300-share certificate is valid as a multiple of 100 shares, the two 65-share certificates do not meet any of the requirements and are not exempt as an odd lot portion.

Book-Entry Securities and the Direct Registration System

Securities used to be represented mostly by physical certificates, but **book-entry securities** (also called book-entry receipts) are recorded merely electronically. These securities can be recorded in the **Direct Registration System**, a method of storing and trading shares. Trading electronically has the benefits of increased convenience, reduced time spent for trades, and decreased administrative costs. Good delivery for book-entry securities carries with it different requirements than for physical certificates (e.g. a different requirement regarding mutilated certificates), according to the different nature of the transactions.

Due Bills

Because of the way dividends are paid, and the lag between the date of record and the payment day, many times the present owner of a share of stock will not be the person who's actually entitled to the dividend. But that doesn't necessarily mean the dividend will automatically be sent to the rightful owner. Mistakes are made, and sometimes the dividend is sent to the present shareholder, and not to the owner of record. If this happens, it is the responsibility of the owner of record's firm to contact the firm of the shareholder who received the dividend, and present a **due bill**, which simply points out the mistake and requests that it be promptly corrected.

Actions When the Customer Dies

When a customer or client dies, the response on the part of the brokerage is pretty straightforward and simple. As soon as the brokerage has been notified of the death of the account holder, they must mark the account "**deceased**" and cancel all open orders. Any power of attorney in place is revoked, also. The assets in the account are then frozen, and left in place, until the brokerage received instructions from the estate of the client.

When, As, and If Issued Transactions

When, as, and if issued transactions—also called **when issued (WI) transactions** for short—are transactions which involve securities that are authorized for sale but not yet issued. If a new issue of securities has not yet had a public offering, investors can still be sought to purchase the securities, and if they purchase the securities prior to the date of issuance, then the orders are "when issued" orders. These orders are **conditional orders**, because the offering may change the terms of the transactions, or even not occur at all.

Cash Settlement

Using cash settlement, which is also known as **same day settlement**, the seller must deliver the securities, and the buyer must pay for the securities, on the day the trade is executed. If the trade takes place before 2:00 p.m. ET, then settlement must take place by 2:30 p.m. If the trade takes place after 2:00 p.m., it must be settled within thirty minutes.

T + 1, T + 2, and T + 3

The **settlement date** in securities trading is the day that the trades actually settle, or securities change hands, as opposed to the **execution date**, which is the day the trade goes through. If a trade's settlement date is one business day after the execution date, then T + 1 applies; if two days, then T + 2; and if three days, then T + 3. T + 2 is shorthand for regular way settlement. T + 2 is called **regular way settlement** because most securities trades, but not all, settle this way. Stocks, corporate and municipal bonds, and securities issued by agencies of the federal government all settle regular way.

ASSIGNMENT OF STOCKS

For a stock or bond certificate to be **negotiable**, it must be **assigned**—that is, each certificate must have the original signature of the owner of record. If there are joint owners, then the signature of each owner is required. The signature can either be on the certificate signature line, or it can be on a stock or bond power of substitution. A **power of substitution** can be for any amount of shares of a particular security, but can only be for one security.

DK

Trades between dealers are submitted to the **Automated Confirmation Transaction Service (ACT)** via electronic means. On some occasions, the terms that one side submits won't match the terms the other side submits, either because of an error in input, or because one side misunderstood the terms, such as price, number of shares, etc. In this case, the party will receive a **DK notification**, which is short hand for "Don't Know," and the parties must reconcile the discrepancy.

EX-RIGHTS SHARES OF STOCK

Some stocks have certain rights associated with them, such as the right to buy shares from a corporation at a discount or before the issuance date. Sometimes shares of stock will no longer have these rights attached to them, and when that is the case, the stocks are **ex-rights shares** and worth less. The rights can be gone for whatever reason, whether they are expired, transferred to someone else, or already exercised.

RECORD DATES AND EX-DIVIDEND DATES

Customers can purchase securities around the time when a company is declaring or paying dividends for their stockholders. To determine who will be entitled to receive the dividends depends on particular dates surrounding the transaction. The **record date** is the date when the corporation looks over its own records to identify its shareholders, and thus to identify the recipients of dividends. However, since the settlement date for securities transactions is generally three days after the execution date, only those securities purchased at least three days before the record date will receive dividends; otherwise they go to whoever held the securities previously. Because of this, the date which is two days before the record date is the **ex-dividend date**. On this date, since the security is recognized as not entitling the buyer to a dividend, the purchase price of the security is reduced by the value of the dividend.

OATS AND TRF

The **Order Audit Trail System (OATS)** is an automated computer system which is owned by the National Association of Securities Dealers (NASD) and which tracks information for securities transactions, such as quotes, orders, and other information. By tracking the progress of a transaction from the initial order to the final completion (or cancellation) of the order, the system permits audits for such orders to more easily take place.

REAL-TIME TRADE REPORTING

Since the value of securities depends heavily upon the actual market trades which are occurring, it is crucial that trades be reported quickly for others to review the relevant information and come to informed conclusions for their own investment decisions. This shows the importance of **real-time trade reporting,** which requires market makers, and sometimes non-market makers, to report trades immediately following the completion of the transaction. Ordinarily the report time is within ninety seconds.

IMPORTANT TERMS

All-or-none orders: All-or-none orders are similar to fill or kill orders, but with no immediate time limit. The broker has all day to try to fill an all-or-none order. In other words, like a fill or kill order, a partial fill is not acceptable. But, unlike a fill or kill order, the trade doesn't have to be filled immediately or cancelled. All-or-none orders are usually day orders, but can also be good-till-cancelled orders.

At-the-open orders -On occasion, especially when there's been news on a company overnight, an investor will want to buy the stock at the opening price. The investor will place an at-the-open order, which means he is willing to buy at the opening price. But the order must reach the specialist before the market opens, or it is cancelled.

Day orders: Day orders are orders to buy or sell a security which will lose validity (expire) if the transaction is not made within the same day.

Fill or kill orders: Fill or kill orders occur when the client tells the broker that the broker must immediately fill the entire order at the price the client is looking for (or a better one). If the broker can't fill the entire order immediately, the order is automatically cancelled. Partial fills, or delayed fills, are not acceptable. Fill or kill means all or nothing, and right now.

GTC orders: Good till cancelled (GTC) orders are orders which are valid until the customer specifically cancels them (as opposed to expiring after a given period of time or when a security reaches a certain price).

Immediate or cancel orders: Immediate or cancel orders are somewhat similar to fill or kill orders. The customer specifies a minimum acceptable price, and wants immediate execution of the order. However, unlike fill or kill orders, partial execution is acceptable on these orders. If only a partial fill is feasible, then that part of the trade is executed, and the rest is cancelled.

Market-on-close orders: Market-on-close orders are along the same lines as at-the-open orders, but for the close of the day. On the New York Stock Exchange, market-at-close orders must be placed twenty minutes before closing, and then they will be filled at whatever the closing price happens to be.

Not held orders: Sometimes an investor will give the broker the discretion to choose the best price, and time, at which to execute a trade. Because the investor is not holding the broker to a particular price or time, these orders are called not held (NH) orders. All not held orders are day orders only, and cannot be placed with a specialist.

Options: Options are contracts to buy or sell a security in the future, where one person has the right to execute the transaction, and another has the obligation to do so upon the other's exercising of his right.

Professional Conduct

OUTSIDE BUSINESS ACTIVITIES TO REPORT

Registered representatives are required to disclose **outside business activities** which would betray an "**adverse interest**" against the representative's own employer. RRs are permitted to execute trades for people employed at other firms, but they must exercise "**reasonable diligence**" to ensure that such trades do not unduly harm their own employers. In case a RR does have an interest in an account at another firm, that firm is obligated to notify the RR's employer in writing, deliver duplicate documents for the account, and notify the RR of it doing those two things. This must be done before any transactions are conducted for the account. Outside business activities can include personal investment accounts which the RR holds elsewhere than his own firm.

PRIVATE SECURITIES TRANSACTIONS

Private securities transactions are transactions where the broker sells a security not recognized or ordinarily sold by his own broker-dealer and/or receives compensation for the transaction. Such transactions are regulated, since registered representatives are forbidden from using their own brokerage firm as mere fronts for less safe transactions. If a broker engages in a **private securities transaction** which departs from established regulations (such as FINRA Rule 3040), then the broker commits the crime of "**selling away**."

REGULATION OF INSIDER TRADING

Insider trading includes those transactions done by individuals who have access to special, non-public information for a company (or by individuals who receive such information). Because of the risks associated with **insider trading**, legislation exists to regulate it. For example, SEC regulation FD (which stands for "fair disclosure") demands that companies intentionally disclosing material information to someone must also make the information public. If the disclosure is unintentional, then the company is still required to "promptly" make a public disclosure of the information.

INFORMATION SECURITY

Since registered representatives are required to handle a great deal of important proprietary and personal information, it is important for them to take significant steps in developing **information security.** This can be as simple as safeguarding laptops with security and password protection, as well as encrypting one's email interactions.

REGULATORY BODIES
SEC

The **Securities and Exchange Commission (SEC)** is an agency of the U.S. federal government which is primarily responsible for the regulation of the securities industry and stock and options exchanges. It was formed in 1934 by Franklin D. Roosevelt during the Great Depression. The SEC has the authority to file civil and criminal suits against those who violate SEC rules. All broker-dealers are required to register with the SEC.

FINRA

The **Financial Industry Regulatory Authority (FINRA)** is a self-regulatory organization (SRO). It is accountable to and under the oversight of the Securities and Exchange Commission (SEC), and it governs securities trading and investment banking firms. The FINRA promulgates rules and regulations for these firms and their employees and associates, and it enforces the rules. FINRA also settle disputes between member firms and settles disputes between customers from the general public and firms. Anyone who trades securities must be registered with FINRA.

HANDLING CUSTOMER COMPLAINTS

Complaints, to be official, must be in writing. FINRA has different proceedings for handling customer complaints: formal and informal. The customer making the complaint decides whether to pursue formal or informal proceedings. If the customer decides to pursue **formal proceedings** to resolve his complaint, then the complaint must be resolved according to FINRA's code of procedure. According to this, the **District Business Conduct Committee (DBCC)** maintains first jurisdiction over complaints, and if the customer is dissatisfied with the DBCC's handling of the issue, he can appeal the outcome to the FINRA Board of Governors and even up to the Supreme Court. If the customer decides to pursue **informal proceedings**, then the complaint can be resolved according to FINRA's **code of arbitration**. According to this, at least two arbiters will participate in an informal hearing, and their decision will be binding and not open to appeal. Arbitration can be pursued not only by customers, but by any members of FINRA, including complaints that RRs might have with broker-dealers. **Mediation** is also available for complaints, where an independent third party provides a nonbinding resolution to the matter.

ARBITRATION PROCESS

The **arbitration process** is initiated when a party files a **Statement of Claim**, after which the other party has 45 days to respond. The next step is a hearing, although if both parties agree, they can meet with a mediator to try to come up with an acceptable solution. If that doesn't work, a hearing takes place with several arbitrators selected from both inside and outside the securities industry. The ruling of the arbitration panel is final.

SIMPLIFIED ARBITRATION

Any dispute between a customer and a member firm of the FINRA, or between two member firms, must be handled through **arbitration**. This involves one party filing a claim, giving the other party 45 days to respond, possibly trying to work out a mutually agreeable settlement with a mediator, and then having the case go to a panel of arbitrators whose decision is final. If the dispute involves less than $50,000, simple arbitration is used. Under simple arbitration, the timeline of the process is shortened, and a single arbitrator, instead of a panel, hears and decides the case.

MSRB

The **Municipal Securities Rulemaking Board (MSRB)** is a self-regulatory organization (SRO) tasked with developing rules for banks and securities firms to follow whenever they underwrite, sell, purchase, or recommend municipal securities. The MSRB is subject to SEC oversight, and while it generates rules for firms to follow, it is not authorized to enforce violations of such rules.

CBOE

The **Chicago Board Options Exchange (CBOE)** is not only an options exchange—the largest options exchange in the United States—but also a self-regulatory organization (SRO). The CBOE creates rules for options exchanges and enforces them.

BC/DR PLANNING

Though the two terms can be distinguished, **business continuity and disaster recovery (BC/DR) planning** is generally considered as one process by which a firm, in this case a broker-dealer, takes actions to resume the firm's ordinary operations in the case of a significant disrupting event. Plans for these kinds of situation must be in writing, approved by a principal, and include several preventative measures, such as the availability of backup data, alternative communication for a firm with its regulators, customers, and employees, a backup location for employees to work, and a means by which to give customers access to their securities in case of a disaster.

Primary Marketplace

Bringing New Issues to Market

CAPITAL MARKET AND MONEY MARKET

Although they have similar sounding names, the phrase "the capital market" and the phrase "the money market" are two different concepts. The **capital market** consists of medium-term and long-term securities; these are used to finance the operations of governments, corporations, banks, brokerages, etc. These instruments have maturities longer than one year. The **money market** refers to short-term securities used to finance the operations of governments, corporations, banks, brokerages, etc. Money market securities have maturities of one year or less.

FUNCTIONS OF CAPITAL MARKETS

Capital markets serve many beneficial **functions**:

- They mobilize savings into profitable investments.
- They encourage savings in the first place, since savings will have a profitable outlet.
- They increase economic growth, because capital is more efficiently employed.
- They provide stability in securities prices, since capital is more widely available to investors, thus reducing speculation in the long run.

INVESTMENT BANKING FIRMS

Investment banking firms are any institutions (broker-dealers, particularly) which help issuers of securities to raise money for themselves. They assist the issuers in deciding all the facts related to the securities' issuance (which securities, what quantity, what price). **Investment banking firms** often also underwrite the issue of the securities.

UNDERWRITING SYNDICATES

After an issuer (such as a state or local government body) has announced plans to issue bonds, the next step is to find an **underwriter**, someone willing to bring the securities to the public on the issuer's behalf. Because of the large sums of money and the financial risk involved, a **syndicate** (a group of firms that have banded together in order to lower their individual risk and investment) often performs the underwriting. Members of the syndicate must sign a syndicate agreement as part of a syndicate contract, or agreement among underwriters. The contract contains the official terms: how much each firm is obliged to underwrite, how long the obligation lasts, the person officially in charge from each member firm, and so on.

SELLING GROUPS FOR UNDERWRITING SYNDICATES

If an underwriting syndicate need additional assistance in selling securities, they can recruit other brokerage firms that are not components of the syndicate itself. These firms constitute **selling groups**. Members of selling groups do not purchase shares from the issuer, although they perform the service of selling them to the public. Because they are not responsible to the issuer for unsold shares, they receive a smaller commission per share sold.

SPREAD IN UNDERWRITING BONDS

When shares are issued for an underwriting syndicate to sell, they're sold to the syndicate at a certain price. The syndicate hopes to make money by turning around and selling the shares to the public (individual and institutional investors) at a higher price. The price the public pays is the **re-**

offering price. This is part of what makes underwriting a share so difficult: a syndicate has to be the lowest bidder and to sell the shares at a price that the public wants but still make a profit. The difference between the re-offering price (at which the shares are sold to the public) and the price at which the shares are bought from the issuer is the **spread**. This spread can be subdivided into the syndicate manager's fee and the takedown.

FACTORS OF A WINNING UNDERWRITING BID

Syndicate members will look at the proposed bond and crunch the numbers to determine the selling price and terms necessary for them to both sell the bonds and make a profit. Their profit comes from the **spread**, or the difference in the price they pay the issuer for the bonds and the price at which they sell the bonds to the public. In addition, they receive a **management fee** for each bond sold. Syndicate members then write the **scale**, which determines the actual price for each series of bond. They then submit their bid at the lowest price at which they think they can make a profit. The bid with the lowest net interest cost to the issuer is the winner. Syndicates must be very sure of their numbers, because they can't back out of a winning bid, even if it turns out they calculated wrong and will lose money.

BLUE SKY LAWS

Blue sky laws are state laws designed to protect investors from fraud in securities transactions. **Blue sky laws** require all securities offerings and sales, brokerage firms, and brokers to register with the customer's home state. The security issuer is thus responsible to register not merely with the SEC but with each state where the securities are sold.

REGISTRATION STATEMENT PARTS

When an investment company files a **registration statement** with the SEC, it consists of two parts. The first part is the **prospectus**. This is the information that every potential investor in the company must be provided with before they're allowed to purchase the company's shares. The prospectus is also known as a summary prospectus, or an NI-A prospectus. The second part is the information that must be on file with the SEC and available for public inspection, but is not required to be provided to all potential investors. It is also called the **statement of additional information (SAI)**.

COOLING-OFF PERIOD AND DUE DILIGENCE MEETINGS

Issuers of securities are required to file with the SEC for the new offering. At the date of filing, a **cooling-off period** commences, at the end of which the issue is either cleared or rejected for public sale. The cooling-off period lasts at least twenty days, and during it, underwriters can advertise for the offering and solicit (nonbinding) indications of interest. Syndicate members are permitted to leave the underwriting agreement within the cooling-off period, but forbidden once the period has ended. Near the end of the cooling-off period, the underwriter holds a meeting to give information for the new offering to syndicate members, selling groups, brokers, institutions, and any other interested parties. This is the **due diligence meeting**, designed to ensure that all material information related to the offering is disclosed to potential investors.

PRELIMINARY PROSPECTUS AND FINAL PROSPECTUS

The **preliminary prospectus** must be submitted along with the registration statement for the issuance of new securities, as the preliminary prospectus is required to be available to potential investors during the cooling-off period. This prospectus includes the general but important facts regarding the securities issuance, but does not include the public offering price or the date when the issue will first be sold. Preliminary prospectuses are also called red herrings because they include a statement in red lettering on the cover declaring that they are preliminary, and thus that some items might be subject to change. The **final prospectus** is prepared near the end of the cooling-off period. It includes the public offering price, as well as the underwriter spread and the date when the securities will be available (the delivery date).

STABILIZING BIDS

Stabilizing bids occur when underwriters, following an initial public offering, bid to repurchase the issued securities at the offer price. This is done in order to stabilize the secondary market price of the issued securities. **Stabilizing bids** are not forbidden, but they are regulated; if an underwriter wishes to do a stabilizing bid, he must first notify his regulatory authority.

PENALTY BIDS

Penalty bids are bids to purchase securities which have recently been issued in an initial public offering. These bids carry with them a penalty on the condition that the purchaser resells the securities in a specified amount of time, though the penalty disappears after that duration passes. The purpose of **penalty bids** is to prevent "flipping" IPO securities, that is, seeking to resell them quickly based on a fluctuation in price and gain a profit. This penalty may sometimes be borne entirely by the client of a broker, but ordinarily requires the broker to forfeit any commission he gained back to his underwriting syndicate.

OVERALLOTMENTS

Overallotments are options for underwriters to sell additional securities within an initial public offering, normally no higher than 15% of the original issuance. **Overallotments** may be exercised for different reasons. If the securities have a high demand and/or are trading at a price higher than the initial price, then the overallotment option might be exercised to raise additional capital. However, they can also be used if the security price drops too low; the underwriters can seek to increase the security's trading price by repurchasing them at the lower price, thereby decreasing the supply, and then still have other securities to sell at a higher price. Overallotments are also called *greenshoe options*, based on their origination with Green Shoe Manufacturing.

TOMBSTONE ADVERTISEMENTS

Tombstone advertisements are ads in newspapers to proclaim an announcement of new securities for sales, receiving their name due to their austere, black-and-white appearance, looking like a tombstone. **Tombstone advertisements** are given during the cooling-off period for the securities (being the only allowed ads during that period), and therefore they are not offered for sale. They merely provide information concerning the basic facts of the securities to be issued, and they generally inform potential investors of how to obtain a prospectus for the securities.

SHELF REGISTRATION

Shelf registration occurs when a company fulfills registration requirements for securities a long time ahead of the actual time of the securities' issuance, up to three years. If market conditions are not favorable to the issuer for securities he would issue at that time, he can invoke shelf registration so that when market conditions improve, he can issue the securities quickly. Issuers can also invoke **shelf registration** to register securities for more general, undefined future offerings. Shelf registration is formalized in *SEC Rule 415*.

Initial Public Offerings

SECURITIES ACT OF 1933

The **Securities Act of 1933** can also be called the Truth in Securities Act, the Paper Act, the Full Disclosure Act, the Prospectus Act, or the New Issues Act. It was enacted by Congress in response to the 1929 stock market crash, and it regulates new issuances for corporate securities, requiring any issuers to fully and truthfully disclose information for the new issue of securities.

REGISTRATION STATEMENT REQUIREMENTS

When a company files a registration statement with the SEC, so that it may publicly issue its securities, the **registration statement** must include the following information:

- issuer's name
- description of issuer's business
- names and contact information of the issuer's control persons (officers, directors, and >10% owners of the company's securities)
- the purpose of raising the money with the issuance
- the company's capitalization
- the company's complete financial statements
- legal proceedings being filed against the company, if material

STATEMENT OF ADDITIONAL INFORMATION

All information that an investment company is required to provide to investors before they purchase shares in the company is provided in the prospectus. However, some investors and members of the public may desire additional information about the company beyond what's provided in the prospectus. This additional information, such as the history of the company, or a detailed financial profile, is in the **statement of additional information (SAI)**, and must be provided to potential investors upon request. These days, the SAI is commonly provided on the company website.

FILING DATE AND EFFECTIVE DATE FOR SECURITIES REGISTRATION

The filing date is the date when the (hopeful) issuer of securities files the requisite registration statement with the SEC. This **filing date** initiates the cooling-off period, which is at least twenty days long. The **effective date** is the date when the cooling-off period ends, that is, once the securities are cleared for public sale.

PRE-FILING PERIOD FOR SECURITIES-TO-BE-ISSUED

The **pre-filing period** is the entire time before the issuing company files to register the securities-to-be-issued with the SEC. During this period, offers to sell the securities are restricted. The regulations forbid all oral or written "offers to sell," but this term has a very broad meaning. It does not refer to offers in the sense of contract law, but refers to any attempts to increase or incite interest among possible buyers—in other words, any attempt to get people interested at all. This restriction exists to prevent issuing companies from "jumping the gun" in advertising the securities. However, the important of full, public disclosure presses the other way, encouraging companies to reveal information. For this reason, securities law has exemptions to the release of information for securities-to-be-issued, such as *SEC Rules 137, 138*, and *139*. (These rules apply to the cooling-off and post-registration periods as well.)

Cooling-off Period for Securities-to-Be-Issued

Within the **cooling-off period**, the period between the initial filing of securities to be registered with the SEC and their approval (also known as the "filing period"), offers to sell the securities are more widely permitted. While brokers may not make offers in the sense of contract law—that is, offers which legally bind the other party to purchase—they can still seek indications of interest. This is done through **tombstone advertisements**, which are the only allowed types of ads during the cooling-off period.

Discuss What Information May Be Released for Securities in the Post-Registration Period.

During the **post-registration period**, securities are allowed to be offered as normal. There are still normal regulations governing securities sales, but nothing additional for this period. For example, written offers to sell and confirmations of sales must be qualifying prospectuses, and no security can be delivered for sale unless a qualifying prospectus attends or precedes it. The post-registration period can also be called the *post-effective period*, since it follows the effective date, when the securities are approved for public sale.

Regulation A Offerings

Regulation A offerings are any offerings of securities which are worth $5 million or less within a twelve-month period. Due to the smaller size of these offerings, the offerings are exempt from the more stringent registration requirements for other securities. **Regulation A offerings** need only a simplified or abbreviated registration statement. Moreover, an **offering circular** must be given to potential investors in the issued securities. The name for these offerings arises from the fact that SEC Regulation A governs offerings of this sort.

Securities Exempted from Registration

Some securities are **exempt** from the registration requirements applicable to other securities per the Securities Act of 1933. This is due either to the **credit standing** of the issuer, which is perceived to be high, or to the **authority** belonging to a government regulatory agency. (In the case of fixed annuities, they are exempt because the insurance company guarantees them.) The exempt securities include the following:

- securities issued by the federal government or its agencies
- municipal (local government) bonds
- securities from banks, savings institutions, and credit unions
- public utility securities
- securities issued by nonprofit, educational, or religious institutions
- fixed annuities and insurance policies
- notes, bills of exchange, bankers' acceptances, and commercial paper with an initial maturity of at most 270 days

Transactions Exempted from Registration

In addition to specific securities being exempted from **ordinary registration requirements**, certain transactions can be exempted as well, including the following:

- intrastate offerings
- Regulation A offerings
- Regulation D offerings

- Regulation S offerings
- private (non-public) offerings

SECTION 3(A)(11) OF THE SECURITIES ACT OF 1933, INCLUDING RULE 147

The exemption from registration for intrastate offerings is codified in **Section 3(a)(11)** of the Securities Act of 1933, including *Rule 147*. The rule required that, for the offering to qualify as exempted, the issuing company must be incorporated in the state where it is selling the securities, it must conduct 80% of its business in that state, and all its customers must be residents of that state. These securities would not be exempted from state-level registration, however.

Private Placements

RULE 144

Rule 144 is an SEC rule governing the sale of restricted, unregistered, and control securities. (*Control securities* refer to securities that effectively give the owner control over the entity.) **Rule 144** establishes five requirements which must be met for the securities to be permissibly sold:

- A specific holding period must pass. This can involve the seller to wait between six months and twelve months before being allowed to sell.
- An "adequate" amount of information concerning the securities' past performance has been publicly disclosed.
- The amount of securities to be sold is no more than 1% either of the outstanding shares or of the average weekly trading volume over the previous four weeks.
- A seller desiring to sell over 500 shares or $10,000 must file a form with the SEC prior to making the sale.
- Other requirements for ordinary trades have been fulfilled.

RULE 144A

Rule 144a is an SEC rule which provides exemptions from ordinary registration requirements for specific securities transactions. **Rule 144a** transactions must be private resales of at least $500,000 units of restricted securities, and they must be made with a *qualified institutional buyer (QIB)*, which generally refers to an institution with at least $100 million in assets to invest. An institution's status as a QIB depends upon its presentation of specific documents to the SEC, including audited financial statements.

- This rule permits securities to be more liquid than otherwise, since there are fewer restrictions on their ability to be transferred. In fact, one particular purpose of the rule is to encourage foreign institutions to sell their securities in U.S. markets.
- This rule is distinct from rule 144; the two should not be confused.

REGULATION D OFFERINGS

Regulation D provides the rules by which securities can be exempted from the ordinary SEC registration requirements. The purpose of this is to aid smaller companies who could not afford to pay for all the registration fees. The exemptions also improve the rate at which these smaller companies can raise funds for themselves. **Regulation D** offerings are also called *private placements*. They can be given to a maximum of 35 "unaccredited investors," as defined according to the regulation.

REGULATION S OFFERINGS

Regulation S offerings are offerings exempt from ordinary SEC registration requirements, particularly for entities seeking out foreign investors. The two main requirements for **Regulation S offerings** are (1) that the securities must be offered in a legitimate offshore transaction, as defined by Regulation S (including that the transaction cannot be done with a U.S. citizen, even one who lives outside the U.S.); and (2) that the entity cannot attempt to directly sell the securities in the United States.

Municipal Securities

COMPETITIVE SALES AND NEGOTIATED SALES

Competitive sales occur when underwriters make proposals to purchase a new issue of securities, with the securities going to the underwriter (or the underwriting syndicate) offering the lowest bid. This can also be called a public sale or a competitive bid. **Negotiated sales** differ from competitive sales, for they occur when the issuer simply selects an underwriter (or syndicate) to whom to sell the new issue of securities. This can also be called negotiated underwriting. Both competitive sales and negotiated sales are means of **primary financing**—that is, obtaining financing within the securities' primary market.

PUBLIC OFFERINGS, PRIVATE PLACEMENTS, AND ADVANCE REFUNDING

Public offerings occur when an entity sells shares to the public for the purpose of raising funds. **Private placements** occur when an entity sells share to a small number of specific investors, again for the purpose of raising funds. Investors in private placements are usually larger ones, such as banks and mutual funds. **Advance refunding** is used for debt securities, issuing bonds at a lower rate in order to pay off bonds outstanding. It is often used for municipal bonds, giving governmental entities an opportunity to delay their required debt payments.

OFFICIAL STATEMENTS FOR MUNICIPAL BOND SECURITIES

Official statements of a municipal bond issue must be signed by an officer of the issuer, and they must contain all the information prospective investors will need to evaluate the bond. **Official statements** will also include the terms of the offering; a summary; the purpose toward which the funds raised will be put; the authority to issue the bonds; any collateral or security; a detailed description of the issuer, including credit rating; the actual construction plan; the results of a project feasibility study; details of the indenture; legal proceedings affecting the bond; tax status of the bond; and financial statements, legal opinion, and consultant reports. An official statement for municipal bonds is similar to a prospectus for other securities. Municipal bonds also have a *preliminary official statement*, which is roughly equivalent to a preliminary prospectus for other securities.

NOTICES OF SALE

Notices of sale are announcements made by municipal entities to declare that the entity is now accepting bids from underwriters (or underwriting syndicates) to purchase the issue of a new bond. **Notices of sale** should include the following:

- amount and kind of bonds
- purpose for selling the bonds
- interest payment dates and maturity schedule
- bond counsel that prepared the legal opinion
- location and time for bids to be delivered
- good faith deposit (a refundable deposit displaying intent to purchase)

NORMAL ALLOCATION PRIORITY IN BOND UNDERWRITING

When a bond issue is oversubscribed, the syndicate must use **allocation priorities** to determine who gets the opportunity to purchase the bonds and who doesn't. First priority goes to presale orders. These are orders that were placed even before the syndicate was announced as the winning bidder, which means that these customers didn't even know the terms of the offering, but wanted to buy the bonds based on past history of their dealings with the underwriter and/or issuer. Next priority goes to group net orders, which are orders placed after the syndicate wins the bid, and they don't specify that any particular member of the syndicate will receive the takedown. Next are designated orders, which are orders in which the customer specifies that they want a certain member of the syndicate to receive credit for the order. The lowest priority goes to orders from members for themselves, or a related account.

PROHIBITED ACTIVITIES FOR A MUNICIPAL SECURITIES BUSINESS RELATED TO POLITICAL CONTRIBUTIONS

To ensure that traders in the municipal securities industry are not engaging in "**fraudulent and manipulative acts and practices**," the MSRB prohibits brokers and dealers from doing business with municipal securities issuers if they have made any political contributions to officials of those issuers. Moreover, brokers and dealers are obligated to disclose their political contributions and related information to the public. The more specific and exhaustive rules governing political contributions are found in *MSRB Rule G-37*.

MANAGER'S FEE, TAKEDOWN, CONCESSION, AND REALLOWANCE FOR AN UNDERWRITING SYNDICATE

The spread for an underwriting syndicate is composed of two factors, the manager's fee and the takedown. The **manager's fee** is the profit earned by the syndicate manager, and is generally the smallest of fees for the share's sale. The **takedown** is the profit earned by the members of the syndicate; since they are assuming the risk to sell the securities they purchased from the issuing company, they deserve most of the profits. Whenever underwriters employ selling groups to assist the selling of their securities, they give a percentage of the takedown to the selling groups; this percentage is the concession. The remainder of the takedown is the **additional takedown**. Firms not part of the syndicate or a selling group can still profit through the selling of an issuing company's securities. Any portion of the takedown earned by these companies is the **reallowance**.

EASTERN AND WESTERN UNDERWRITING SYNDICATES

There are two different ways to assign the financial obligations of syndicates. The first is the **Western-style syndicate**. Under this arrangement, the financial obligations are divided between the firms, and each firm is only held responsible for selling its own allocation of bonds. Under an **Eastern-style syndicate**, each firm receives an allocation, but any unsold bonds are the responsibility of the entire syndicate, and they are divided proportionally. So even though a member firm sells all its allocation, it may be required to purchase unsold bonds from other allocations.

UNDERWRITING A MUNICIPAL BOND ISSUE

The first way of underwriting a municipal bond issue is a **negotiated underwriting**. When this method is used, the municipality selects one investment banker to do the underwriting. Revenue bonds are typically done through a negotiated underwriting. The underwriter and the issuer work together on the details, such as interest rates and price. Most general obligation bonds use a process called **competitive underwriting**, in which bids are taken from several different sources, and the underwriting is awarded to the lowest qualified bidder.

The Secondary Market

BROKER AND DEALER

A **broker** is a person or institution which acts as a middleman between the buyer of a security and the seller of a security. The broker makes his profit by charging a sales charge, or *commission*, for arranging the transaction. Brokers do not own any products for which they arrange transactions, but simply facilitate the transferal of ownership from a seller to a buyer. A **dealer** is a person or institution which sells its own inventory to buyers (like a used-car dealer). A dealer charges a *markdown* when he purchases inventory, lowering the price he pays for the inventory; and he charges a *markup* when he sells it, increasing the price the customer pays for it. Furthermore, dealers sometimes intend for the inventory to appreciate in value while they hold it.

- Whether a firm is acting in the capacity of a broker or dealer must be disclosed on the receipt of trade, or the confirmation. Commissions need to be disclosed, but not necessarily markups or markdowns.
- Firms are prohibited from acting as both a broker and a dealer in the same transaction. Either a commission can be charged, or a markup or markdown, but not both.

DESIGNATED MARKET MAKERS

Designated market makers (DMMs), also called *specialists*, seek to keep the trade of some particular security active, fair, and orderly in a stock exchange. **Designated market makers** will have the security in inventory, and will also post bid and ask prices for it. DMMs are broker-dealers. Designated market makers are obligated to help the market move smoothly, but their ability to do that can also be used to wrongfully manipulate the market. Needless to say, DMMs are prohibited from market manipulation.

EXECUTION OF ORDERS

Designated market makers have a specific arrangement by which they execute orders in a particular sequence. Orders are executed by priority, parity, and precedence:

- **Priority** refers to the fact that the highest bid and lowest ask prices are the first ones to be executed.
- **Parity** refers to the chronological priority of orders. If multiple orders are placed at the highest bid or lowest ask price, then the orders arriving first are executed first.
- **Precedence** involves the size of orders. Where priority and parity do not break the tie, then the larger orders receive higher priority.

MARKET MAKER REPORTS

FINRA regulations require that **market makers** must file reports during designated hours of their last sales. These reports must include the price, size, whether it was a buy, sell, or cross trade, and the NASDAQ symbol. These reports must be filed within ninety seconds of the transaction. In addition, market makers must file a daily report on the total numbers of shares they traded that day in the stocks they're making a market for.

Equity Securities

OTC MARKET

The **over-the-counter (OTC) market** is also known as the *second market* (not to be confused with the secondary market, which encompasses all the various ways of trading stock besides new issues). It consists of a nationwide network of brokers and dealers connected by phone and computer who trade non-listed stocks from their offices. NASDAQ, Bulletin Board, and Pink Sheet stocks comprise the second market, with the most prominent distinction being between NASDAQ issues and non-NASDAQ issues.

PINK SHEETS

Pink sheets are publications providing bid and ask prices for over-the-counter (OTC) securities on a daily basis. **Pink sheets** also provide information for the market makers who provide such prices. Pink sheets are prepared by the *National Quotation Bureau*, and they receive their name from their having historically been printed upon pink sheets of paper. Since pink sheets deal with the OTC market, they involve securities for companies who do not need to file with the SEC. Companies trading on pink sheets will have their stock symbol end in the suffix *.PK*.

OTCBB

The over-the-counter bulletin board (OTCBB) is a regulated electronic medium for trading **over-the-counter (OTC) securities**, displaying quotes, recent sale prices, and volume information. Stocks trading on the OTCBB include the suffix OB in their stock symbol, and they are generally considered riskier than stocks trading on the NASDAQ exchange.

THREE-QUOTE RULE FOR BULLETIN BOARD STOCKS

For bulletin board stocks and pink sheet stocks traded on the OTC, there may not always be much indicated **trading interest** on the part of market makers. So, when a broker or dealer gets a trade order for a bulletin board or pink sheet stock, the broker or dealer must first check and see if there are at least two market makers making firm quotes for the security. If not, the broker or dealer must consult at least three other brokers or dealers to come up with a price.

AUCTION MARKETS

Auction markets are arrangements where prospective buyers and prospective sellers compete with another to make bids and offers. Securities traded in **auction markets** will naturally be traded according to the highest bid and lowest ask price. The execution of orders in auction markets involves matching compatible bids and asks. Examples of auction markets include the Philadelphia Stock Exchange (NASDAQ OMX PHLX), NYSE Euronext, NYSE MKT LLC (formerly NYSE Amex Equities), and NYSE Arca.

NYSE

The **New York Stock Exchange (NYSE)** is the biggest stock market by total market value in the country, and it is often referred to as the "big board." In general, older, larger, and more established company's shares are traded on the NYSE. The **Dow Jones Industrial Average** is an index based on thirty of the largest and most heavily traded stocks on the NYSE. Much of the trading on the NYSE still occurs on the actual floor between human beings bidding against each other in person.

NYSE MKT LLC

One of the world's foremost equities exchanges is the NYSE MKT, or **NYSE MKT LLC**, formerly the American Stock Exchange (AMEX) and, after that, NYSE Amex Equities. It is designed for small-capital companies. Like the NYSE it handles stocks of companies from all over the United States. The regulations under which the NYSE MKT operates are typically somewhat more lenient than those governing the NYSE, so it therefore has a larger representation of stock issued by smaller companies. It is also known as "the curb."

LISTING REQUIREMENTS FOR EXCHANGES

Different exchanges have different requirements which companies must fulfill before being permitted to participate in trading on the exchange. These are called **listing requirements**, or *listing standards*. These requirements are entirely up to the discretion of the exchanges, not regulated by the SEC. The standards include both financial and non-financial requirements. The requirements can be based on stock price and the number of publicly traded shares and shareholders, among other considerations.

NASDAQ

The **National Association of Securities Dealers Automated Quotations (NASDAQ)** is an electronic market that handles more volume than the NYSE, although the market value of the NASDAQ is lower than that of the NYSE. NASDAQ consists of the NASDAQ National Market, for better-known companies, and the NASDAQ Capital Markets, or Small Cap, for newer, smaller enterprises.

ACCESS LEVELS

For any sort of informed securities trade, the potential buyers and sellers need trustworthy information. However, when trading in the NASDAQ, everyone does not receive the same amount of information. Instead, the information is revealed according to three different **access levels**.

NASDAQ LEVELS 1, 2, AND 3

NASDAQ dealers and brokers are all connected by computer, and NASDAQ uses a computerized quotation system to display quotes on the OTC. **Level 1** quotations are much like NYSE quotes, in which the highest bid and the lowest ask among firm quotes from market makers are displayed. This information is available to the general public. Beyond Level 1 information, approved customers have access to **Level 2** quotes, which, in addition to the more accessible information, also show who the market makers are for the stock, their firm quotes for the stock, and the size of the lot they're quoting. **Level 3** is for market makers only, and includes the ability to enter or change their quote.

SEC ORDER HANDLING RULES

The SEC has a number of regulations governing trades on the NASDAQ, including various **order handling rules**. These rules, as the name implies, cover how to handle different orders. Two such rules are the Limit Order Display rule and the Quote rule. The **Limit Order Display rule** requires market makers to include better-priced limit orders in market maker quotes (i.e. better-priced than whatever the market makers' bid or ask price is). The goal is to provide investors with the lower price. The **Quote rule** requires public quotes to be displayed for the securities on which market makers (or specialists) are making markets. The goal for this rule is to increase transparency.

GENERAL LISTING REQUIREMENTS

A company that wishes to trade on the NASDAQ must meet these **general listing requirements**:

- The company must have at least 1,250,000 publicly-traded shares, not counting shares owned by officers, directors, or owners of >10% of the company.
- At the time of listing, the regular bid price needs to be $4. (Sometimes $3 and $2 prices are permitted, if other criteria are fulfilled.)
- Three market makers must exist for the stock.
- The company must abide by NASDAQ corporate governance rules 4350, 4351, and 4360.
- The company must have a minimum of 450 round lot shareholders, 2200 shareholders total, or 550 shareholders total with an average trading volume of 1.1 million in the previous year.

LISTING STANDARDS

In addition to fulfilling NASDAQ's general listing requirements, a company also must fulfill the requirements for one of NASDAQ's three listing standards. According to **listing standard #1**, it must have a minimum of $11 million in pre-tax earnings over the previous three years, and a minimum of $2.2 million over the previous two years. The last three years cannot include a year with a net loss. According to **listing standard #2**, it must have a minimum of $27.5 million in cash flow over the previous three fiscal years. No year of those three can have a negative net cash flow. Furthermore, revenues for the previous fiscal year must be $110 million at minimum, and average market capitalization for the previous year (not fiscal year, necessarily) must be $550 million at minimum. **Listing standard #3** is similar to #2 but has an exception. The three-year cash flow requirement can be waived if the company maintains an average market capitalization of $550 million at minimum over the previous year (twelve months, not fiscal year). Revenues in the previous year fiscal year also must be $90 million at minimum.

ECNs

Electronic communication networks (ECNs) are systems which aim to facilitate more direct trading between traders and brokerage firms. ECNs allow orders to be executed without a third party, especially orders executed by a market maker. ECNs are often utilized by institutional investors who do their own trading of massive quantities of shares twenty-four hours per day. The three biggest ECNs for stock trading are Island, Archipelago, and Instinet.

DARK POOLS OF LIQUIDITY

For some orders, the volume of securities traded can be hidden from public knowledge. This is usually done by institutional investors, to keep their trades secret from other (competing) institutional investors. These types of trades are said to involve **dark pools of liquidity**, since the actual trades are concealed or cloudy.

Debt Securities

SECONDARY MARKET FOR MUNICIPAL SECURITIES

The **secondary market** for municipal securities consists of the transactions for those securities after they have been initially issued by the government body issuing the bond. (Transactions to purchase bonds directly from the issuer comprise the primary market.) The different types of orders and offerings in this market depend on whether the bond is sold at a discount, at a premium, or at par. These terms depend upon the relation between the bond's coupon rate (the stated interest rate on the bond) and the bond's current yield (the effective rate of interest, given the actual expected cash inflows and the current market price). If the coupon rate is greater than the current yield, then the bond sells at *premium*; if the coupon rate is lower than the current yield, then it sells at a *discount*; and if they are equal, then it sells at *par*.

BROKER'S BROKER

Most brokers deal with the general public, and primarily with individual investors. However, some municipal bond brokers don't deal with individual investors or the general public at all. They deal only with other municipal brokers, and large financial institutions, such as banks. A broker in this category is known as a **broker's broker**. Because he's dealing with companies who haven't sold all the bonds they've been assigned, confidentiality is very important, and a broker's broker never reveals the names of his clients and customers.

GOVERNMENT AGENCY BONDS

Government agency bonds are not the same as U.S. Treasury or municipal bonds, but pertain to agencies of the federal government. (**Government agency bonds** also can pertain to quasi-governmental agencies, which are privately operated though either being originally part of the federal government or being sponsored by the federal government.) They are not guaranteed in the same way that Treasury securities are. Actual federal agencies authorized to **issue debt securities** are the Farm Credit Administration and the Government National Mortgage Association (GNMA, or Ginnie Mae). Quasi-governmental agencies authorized to issue debt securities are: Federal Home Loan Mortgage Corporation (FHLMC, or Freddie Mac), Federal National Mortgage Association (FNMA, or Fannie Mae), and Student Loan Marketing Association (SLMA, or Sallie Mae). Except for Ginnie Mae, securities offered by these agencies are not backed by the full faith and credit of the U.S. government, so they pay higher interest than Treasury securities, though lower interest than private bonds.

CORPORATE BONDS AND HIGH-YIELD BONDS

Corporate bonds are bonds issued by corporations. Whereas Treasury bonds can be backed by the full faith and credit of the U.S. government, corporations do not have that guarantee, and thus generally have higher interest rates. Since the riskiness of the bond is inversely related to the interest rates, **high-yield bonds** are bonds with lower credit ratings than usual corporate bonds (below a "BBB" S&P rating and below a "Baa" Moody's rating). These are called "junk bonds," although they are still popular among investors worldwide.

REPURCHASE AGREEMENT

Some financial institutions raise cash through a **repurchase agreement**. This entails selling some of their securities, usually for a fixed amount of time, after which they agree to buy them back. The securities become the collateral, making it a very safe loan for the lender. This way, the financial institution doesn't have to sell the securities to come up with cash. Not all repurchase agreements, or repos, come with a fixed maturity date. Some are left open, in which case the lender has the right to demand repayment at any time. Whether fixed or open, if the borrower defaults, the lender has the right to sell the securities. Repurchase agreements are sensitive to interest rates—if they rise sharply, the lender's collateral loses value.

COMMERCIAL PAPER

Commercial paper refers to short-term, unsecured promissory notes issued by corporations to cover cash shortages brought on by various factors, such as large accounts receivable or seasonal business fluctuations. Maturity on **commercial paper** is generally within 90 days, but can range anywhere from 1 to 270 days. There are two kinds of commercial paper. *Direct paper* is sold directly by the financing institution to the public, without going through dealers. *Dealer paper* is any commercial paper marketed through dealers.

CDs, BROKERED CDs, AND JUMBO CDs

Certificates of deposit (CDs) are financial instruments offered by banks, having a specific term (such as six months or one year) and usually having a fixed interest rate. Due to the decrease in accessibility for money, banks generally have higher interest rates on CDs. **Brokered certificates of deposit** are CDs which are not purchased directly from a bank, but instead mediated by a brokerage firm (or from some other entity besides a bank). These CDs are generally pricier. **Jumbo certificates of deposit** are CDs with a minimum face value of $100,000. These are, of course, ordinarily purchased only by large institutional investors, and they are considered to be low-risk.

BA

A **banker's acceptance (BA)** is commonly used in international transactions. It is the corporate equivalent of a post-dated check, and can have limits of 1 to 270 days. A banker's acceptance is better than a regular postdated check, however, because the holder has the goods being traded as collateral in case the bank underwriting the acceptance goes under. Bankers' acceptances are bought and sold in the money market. They sell at a discount and mature at face value.

ARSs

Auction-rate securities (ARSs) are a form of debt security where the interest rate is determined by a Dutch auction. (A *Dutch auction* is a "reverse" auction, where the auctioneer begins with a high price and keeps lowering it to some minimum price. The first bidder wins.) These debt securities typically have a long-term maturity, but in practice are treated as shorter-term, since the interest rate is periodically (e.g. monthly) reset through another Dutch auction.

ABSs

Asset-backed securities (ABSs) are securities which are backed with some sort of asset as collateral. The collateralized asset may be loans, leases, receivables, royalties, and other things. **Asset-backed securities** offer an alternative for many investors to corporate bonds.

Other Securities

ELKSs

Equity-linked securities (ELKSs) are hybrid securities, partly involving debt and partly involving equity. Fundamentally, they are debt securities which will behave like normal debt securities if a specified stock maintains a specific level of performance, but if that stock drops below the minimum performance level, then the investor receives an amount of stock instead. For instance, suppose that an ELKS is purchased which is linked to a company whose stock is trading at $20 per share, and suppose that the minimum percentage is 80%. If the share price drops below $16 (80% of $20) at any time before the maturity date of the ELKS, then the investor will receive a predetermined quantity of shares at the maturity date, rather than a repayment of the cash principal. Since ELKSs are riskier, they tend to have a higher coupon rate than convertible debt, which is a different kind of hybrid security.

ETNs

Exchange-traded notes (ETNs) are hybrid securities which serve as a mixture of bonds and exchange-traded funds (ETFs). As their name implies, they are traded on an exchange, although they also have a maturity date like bonds. But with ETNs, the repayment of principal at the maturity date is modified according to the day's market index factor. (Further, the repayment is reduced by investing fees.) The value of an ETN, however, is not simply based on the market index, but also depends on the creditworthiness of the debtor company, since ETNs are unsecured debt instruments. Unlike ordinary bonds, ETNs do not have periodic coupon payments.

HOLDRs

Holding company depository receipts (HOLDRs) are essentially bundles of stocks traded as singular units, printed on a single stock certificate. The groupings by which stocks are bundled can be according to sectors, industries, or other classifications. HOLDRs provide the benefit of diversification without the fees of multiple transactions. HOLDRs were created by Merrill Lynch.

OTC Options

Over-the-counter (OTC) securities are securities traded apart from an exchange. Since they do not abide by any particular exchange rules, OTC options can come in a variety of forms and contain unusual features. OTC options thus are characterized by both increased flexibility and increased risk.

ADR

An **American Depository Receipt (ADR)** is a financial instrument created so that the stocks of foreign companies can be bought and sold on stock markets in the United States. Each ADR represents a certain number of shares of a foreign company, usually somewhere between one and ten shares. Each individual share is known as an *American Depositary Share*. ADRs are bought and sold just like other common stocks listed on the exchanges, and ADR owners have the same rights as other stock holders, including voting and receiving dividends, which are paid in dollars. An ADR is technically owned by a bank, which handles the ADR, and is held in the buyer's name. An ADR can fluctuate in value due to changes in currency rates.

Sovereign Debt

Sovereign debt is a governmental debt security, though it is issued by a foreign national government. It is issued in the foreign country's currency and serves the purpose of funding that country's growth. **Sovereign debt** has two primary risks: first, since it is usually aiding a developing country, the possible instability of the country lowers the chance of repayment; and second, because the debt is in a foreign currency, there is always the foreign currency exchange risk.

EXCHANGE RATES AND CURRENCY TRADING

An **exchange rate** is the relationship between any two currencies, and it reflects how many units of one currency are required to obtain one unit of the other currency. They change daily, and many different factors can affect them. This constant change in the exchange rate is known as the float. If the dollar is going down in value with respect to another currency, it is depreciating; it will take more dollars to buy one unit of the other currency. When the dollar is getting strong, it is appreciating, and can buy more of the other currency. Because of the nature of exchange rates, and due to their constant fluctuation, **currency trading** can be quite profitable. But it is very risky, and not suitable for the average investor. Exchange rates which change according to the supply and demand fluctuations within the market are *floating* exchange rates, whereas exchange rates pegged by the government as the official rate are *fixed* exchange rates. One of the ways in which exchange rates are modified is through the intervention of central banks. A central bank will either buy or sell a particular currency in order to alter the value of its nation's currency against some foreign currency.

SPOT MARKETS AND FORWARD MARKETS

The difference between spot markets and forward markets deals chiefly with time. **Spot markets** are markets where goods are exchanged for cash and immediately delivered. There is no delay to the purchases, and contracts are effective at once. **Forward markets**, on the other hand, are markets involving agreements for future transactions (including future delivery), though with a price set at the time of the agreement.

EXCHANGE CONTROLS

Since national governments have a vested interest in what their currency's exchange rate is, they will sometimes erect **exchange controls** in order to modify the rate as they see fit. This can include banning (or restricting) the use of another currency within their country, banning their own citizens from even possessing another currency, fixing exchange rates (rather than permitting them to float), and controlling the quantity of a foreign currency which is imported or exported. Generally speaking, financially weaker countries are more prone to implement exchange controls.

EURODOLLARS, EUROBONDS, AND EURODOLLAR BONDS

When U.S. dollars are deposited anywhere in the world outside the United States, they are called **Eurodollars** (even if they're not in Europe). The important thing to remember is that they're in American dollars, and not the currency of the bank where they're deposited. Likewise, a **Eurobond** is any long-term debt instrument that's sold in a country other than the one whose currency it is in. A **Eurodollar bond** is a U.S. bond, denominated in American currency, which is sold anywhere outside the United States. The U.S. government doesn't issue Eurodollar bonds, but many foreign governments do, and so do some state and local governments in America, as well as foreign and American corporations.

Factors Affecting Markets

BUSINESS CYCLE STAGES

The first phase of the business cycle is **expansion**. During expansion, business conditions are good, and economic activity is plentiful. There are plenty of jobs, and stock prices, house prices, and wages are generally on the up-trend. This phase can continue for years, but eventually it will stop, and the high point will be looked on as the second phase of the business cycle, the **peak**. After an economy has peaked, economic indicators and trends gradually go on the downswing due to less investing and spending. This is the third phase of the cycle, called **contraction**. The period of contraction is also known as a *recession*, or if it is severe enough, a *depression*. The last phase of the cycle, the **trough**, occurs when the downtrend stops and levels off. Eventually the cycle will start all over with a new period of expansion.

LEADING AND COINCIDENT INDICATORS

Economists use a variety of ways of measuring how the economy is doing, and seeing where the economy is in the business cycle—whether expansion, peak, contraction, or trough. Some of the main measures are called **leading indicators**. They're called leading indicators because they tend to predict where the economy is headed, not where it is actually at. Changes in leading indicators can signal a recession or an expansion. Some leading indicators are the number of new houses being constructed, the amount of inventory the manufacturers of durable goods have on hand, and the stock market, though there are others too. There also are **coincident indicators**, which reflect the current status of the economy by varying directly with economic shifts.

LAGGING INDICATORS

Besides leading indicators, another set of numbers to confirm the trend are called **lagging indicators**, because it takes a while after economic conditions have changed for them to reflect the change, but once they do, it is more proof that the economy is either improving or declining. Lagging indicators include but are not limited to earnings and profits of major corporations, rising or falling numbers of unemployment compensation claims being filed, rising or falling wages, and a change in the ratio of credit to income on the part of consumers.

YIELD CURVES

Yield curves are graphs representing the interest rates for various bonds of the same credit rating but with different maturity dates. The x-axis displays the maturity date while the y-axis displays the interest rate. A common yield curve compares U.S. Treasury debt for maturities of three months, two years, five years, and thirty years. Such a curve, since it represents the risk-free rate for debt securities, then serves as a basis of comparison for other bond yields. **Yield curves** are utilized in forecasting economic changes, especially economic growth and output.

KEYNESIAN ECONOMIC THEORY

Keynesian economic theory is named for John Maynard Keynes, a very influential economist of the twentieth century. Keynes taught that continued demand is what keeps the economy going, as demand for products leads to more businesses being opened, more jobs created, more money loaned, rising wages, etc. Based on that belief, he said it is the job of the federal government to keep the economy going by spending tax money on government projects designed to stimulate certain sectors of the economy or to stimulate the economy as a whole. In Keynesian theory, big government spending is not only good, but actually necessary, for a healthy economy.

MONETARIST ECONOMIC THEORY

Monetarist economic theory is the brainchild of economist Milton Friedman. Friedman taught that inflation and deflation do not randomly occur, but are the direct result of the amount of the money supply. When there is not enough money in circulation, prices fall. When there is too much money in circulation, people have more dollars to bid against each other for goods and services, so prices rise. Therefore, Friedman felt it is the job of the federal government to carefully regulate the money supply, so as not to cause disruptions in the economy, and that the government should otherwise stay out of the market. Monetarists believe that the money supply should increase, but only gradually. This is intended to keep demand for goods and services without increasing the risk of huge rates of inflation.

EFFECTS OF INFLATION ON BOND INTEREST RATES

Since inflation decreases the purchasing power of a currency, it causes the future cash flows of a bond (both the periodic coupon payments and the repayment of the principal at maturity) to be less valuable. In response to this lower demand, investors will require a **higher bond yield**—more attractive interest rates—in order to justify their purchase. In other words, the inflation risk causes investors to demand more compensation for their investment. In addition to inflation, bond yields are affected by the creditworthiness of the issuer of the bonds and by prevailing market interest rate. The worsened returns from fixed-income securities like bonds are reduced when investors choose instead to have investments which more naturally hedge against inflation risk, such as stocks and inflation-indexed bonds.

NORMAL, INVERTED, AND FLAT YIELD CURVES

Yield curves, in showing the relationship between bond interest rates and maturity dates, can take different shapes. A healthy economy will be reflected by a **normal yield curve**, where the yield (interest rate) increases as the bond's maturity increases. However, with an **inverted yield curve**, bonds with longer maturities are displayed as having a lower yield rate. This generally signifies a future recession. Yield curves which show minimal to no difference between short-term and long-term yields are **flat yield curves**. These can signify a change from recession to economic health or vice versa.

INTEREST-RATE-SENSITIVE STOCKS

Interest-rate-sensitive stocks are shares of stock whose value is extremely sensitive to changes in interest rates. The price of these stocks will fluctuate widely, for instance, with a modification in the risk-free rate. These stocks will have large beta factors according to the capital asset pricing model. Their sensitivity to interest rate changes can be due to the type of industry of which they are a part and to the degree to which the company operates off of debt.

DEFENSIVE INDUSTRIES

Defensive industries are those sectors of the economy that sell products that people tend to buy no matter what the state of the economy is. Two big **defensive industries** are food products and tobacco products. Companies in these industries are generally safer investments in bear markets, since the demand for their products is pretty steady and predictable. For the same reason, they are seen as less-than-ideal investments in bull markets because people don't tend to buy any more of these basic products, meaning there's no reason to expect large changes in earnings or profits.

CYCLICAL INDUSTRIES

Cyclical industries are the opposite of defensive industries. The prospects for companies in these industries tend to rise and fall right along with the business cycle. Generally speaking, they're great investments in bull markets and bad places to be in bear markets. **Cyclical industries** tend to sell expensive durable goods, such as automobiles, or the raw materials used to produce durable goods.

FRB

The **Federal Reserve Board (FRB)** plays one of the biggest, if not the absolute biggest, roles in determining the state and direction of America's economy. As a network of regional banks operating under the authority of the federal government, the FRB makes decisions that can have huge and immediate impacts on the stock markets and other areas of business. They set interest rates, and determine by how much, if any, the money supply will be increased.

FOMC

The **Federal Open Market Committee (FOMC)** is the actual means by which the Federal Reserve Board controls the money supply. They do this by either buying securities from banks or by selling securities to banks. Buying securities creates more money in the money supply, and is thought to stimulate the economy. Selling securities to banks takes money out of the money supply, and is thought to slow the growth of the economy, thereby preventing inflation from getting out of hand.

OPEN MARKET OPERATIONS

Open market operations consist of transactions to buy or sell government securities for the purpose of altering the amount of money in the bank system. Buying government securities places more money into the system, thus causing market growth, while selling securities causes contraction.

MAIN INTEREST RATES

There are four important interest rates to know. The first one is the **federal funds rate**. It is the rate the country's largest banks charge each other for overnight loans in the amount of one million dollars and higher. It is the most volatile rate, and short-term interest rates throughout the economy are usually pegged to it. The **prime rate** is the one most people are familiar with: it is the rate banks charge their safest customers—large corporations with excellent credit. The prime rate moves up and down with the money supply set by the Federal Reserve Board. The **discount rate** is the interest rate the Federal Reserve Board charges to Federal Reserve Banks for short-term loans. The **broker loan rate** is what banks charge brokers and dealers when they lend them money for their customer's margin accounts. It is also known as the call loan rate, or call money rate.

DISCOUNT RATE

The discount rate is the interest rate that the Federal Reserve Board charges its member banks for short-term loans. When the Fed changes the **discount rate**, the change ripples out into the economy, and little changes can have big effects. When the discount rate is lowered, it costs banks less to borrow money from the Fed and from each other, and so they can charge lower interest to their customers, which tend to stimulate more people and companies to borrow money. Raising the discount rate has the opposite effect.

RESERVE REQUIREMENTS

Reserve requirements are specific ratios established by the Federal Reserve which specify how much of customer deposits each commercial bank must hold in its reserves rather than lend out. By changing these requirements, the Federal Reserve can alter rates for borrowing and interest, since there will be a greater or smaller supply of money available to be lent out to customers.

BOP

The **balance of payments (BOP)** for a country keeps track of all the inflows and outflows made for that country in a given time period. This involves a record of all the transactions made between the country and all others, tracking the dollar amount of all imports and exports, financial transactions included. A positive balance of payments indicates a net inflow of money, and a negative balance indicates a net outflow. The BOP is more comprehensive than the *balance of trade (BOT)*, which includes only tangible imports and exports. The BOP also includes intangible exchanges, such as financial transactions, in the calculation.

EFFECTS OF EXCHANGE RATES ON SECURITIES MARKET

There are two basic ways in which exchange rates affect the securities market. First, changes in exchange rates directly affect the value of securities for foreign companies. Second, changes in exchange rates affect the cost for domestic businesses to do business abroad, thereby altering the value of those businesses' securities in the market. **Exchange rates** can themselves be affected by the prevailing market interest rates in different countries. A high interest rate in one country will attract lenders to lend money there, thus increasing foreign investment and increasing the exchange rate. The opposite occurs with lower interest rates.

Market Analysis

MARKET SENTIMENT AND MARKET MOMENTUM

Market sentiment refers to the prevailing attitude of investors in a market towards particular securities. **Market sentiment** presupposes crowd psychology, or the tendency of people to act in some sort of conformity with the group. Market sentiment is reflected by the actual activity of the stock: rising prices signal a bullish sentiment and falling prices a bearish sentiment. **Market momentum** is a particular measure of market sentiment. It is a calculated by multiplying the trading volume for particular securities by the change in a given market index.

MARKET INDICES

Market indices are numbers reporting an aggregate value from the combination of several securities' individual values. **Market indices** are valued at a given date and presented in comparison to their base value from some earlier date. The securities which compose the market indices are selected so that the indices can report the market's performance as a whole. A prominent example of a market index is the S&P 500 Index.

VOLATILITY

Volatility is the degree to which a security's price has fluctuated (or will fluctuate) within a given time period, whether it has increased or decreased. **Volatility** can be distinguished between *historical volatility (HV),* which measures the changes in a security's price over a prior time period, and *implied volatility (IV)*, which is the estimated degree of volatility for a security's price in the future—what various market factors imply about the security's potential behavior. *Options volatility* is the application of volatility measures to options transactions. The premiums for options is related directly to the volatility for the underlying security; higher volatility increases the option premium, and vice versa.

PUT-CALL RATIO

The **put-call ratio** is a comparison of the total trading volume of put options in the market to call options. This ratio is utilized to analyze market sentiment, determining whether that sentiment is bearish or bullish. Since the buyer of a put option gains the right to sell a security in the future, a higher put-call ratio generally signals a bearish market, where investors desire to sell their securities before the price drops further. The opposite is the case for a lower ratio.

SHORT INTEREST

Short interest is the number of shares which investors have sold short but not yet closed out—that is, the number of shares which investors have borrowed and sold, but have not yet repurchased (to return the shares to the lenders). Since the purpose of selling short is to sell the borrowed security at a higher price at which it is later repurchased, a high number of total securities sold short in the market shows that investors believe the market price for many securities will drop. As such, short interest is one way to measure market sentiment. Expressed mathematically, short interest will be measured as the percentage of shares sold short in comparison to the total number of shares outstanding.

INDEX FUTURES

Index futures are a type of futures contract which correspond to a particular market index. The relation between the index and the price at which the futures contract is fixed may vary among different types of **index futures**, but they all are similar in their correspondence to a market index.

Portfolio managers will often use index futures as a hedge against risks in their other investments. Many index futures are linked to the S&P 500 Index.

THE BOND BUYER AND MUNIFACTS

The Bond Buyer and *Munifacts* are the two main sources of information on **municipal bonds**, both for new issues and for the trading market for already issued bonds. *The Bond Buyer* comes out every day, and is the authoritative source of municipal bond information. Every Friday it publishes the total volume of bond offerings expected to come to market in the next 30 days, which is known as the 30-day visible supply, and the placement ratio index, which is the percentage of last week's offerings that actually sold. *The Bond Buyer's* companion publication is *Munifacts*, which is delivered by wire to terminals in offices and contains bond news and price information.

BOND BUYER INDICES

Just as the S&P 500 Index is an index commonly used in understanding the stock market, there are a number of **bond indices** to help in understanding the bond market. *The Bond Buyer* presents a number of these helpful indices:

- The *20-Bond GO Index* (also called "Bond Buyer 20" or the "20 Bond Index") is an index based on the average yield of twenty municipal general obligation (GO) bonds, all of which have A ratings or better, with twenty years until their maturity date.
- The *11-Bond GO Index* (also called "Bond Buyer 11" or the "11 Bond Index") is an index derived from the 20-Bond GO Index. Eleven bonds are taken from the twenty bonds comprising the 20-Bond GO Index, only those with AA ratings or better, and an index is based on them.
- The *25 Revenue Bond Index* (also called the "RevDex") is an index representing the average yield for twenty-five different revenue bonds, all of which have A ratings or better, with thirty years to maturity.
- The *Municipal Bond Index* (also called the "40-Bond Index") is an index representing the average price of forty highly traded general obligation and revenue bonds, all of which have A ratings or better, with twenty years as their average maturity.

Technical Analysis

TECHNICAL ANALYSTS

Whereas fundamental analysts work on determining which securities to purchase, **technical analysts** work on determining the proper time to purchase a given security. This is done through an analysis of various stock patterns, both for the market as a whole and for individual stocks, with the presupposition that stocks' past activity is an indicator for its future activity.

TREND LINES, SAUCERS, AND INVERTED SAUCERS

Though stocks may fluctuate seemingly unpredictably in a short period of time, they tend to have a definite pattern, a **trendline**, over longer spans of time. If the stock price is gradually increasing over time, then it is in an uptrend, and if the opposite is the case, then it is in a downtrend. **Saucers** are a particular type of trendline involving an initial decrease in stock prices followed by an increase. Because the stock first dips before increasing, it looks like a flattened "u," or a saucer. The reverse is the case with **inverted saucers**; they initially increase and then drop in price.

HEAD-AND-SHOULDERS AND INVERTED HEAD-AND-SHOULDERS PATTERNS

Head-and-shoulders patterns are more complicated than saucers. They involve three peaks in the stock price, with the second one being the highest (just as a head is higher than two shoulders on each side). The other two peaks are roughly the same "height," though not necessarily. Between each peak, the stock price dips to some minimum and then rises up to the next peak. After the third peak, the stock price decreases. **Inverted head-and-shoulders patterns** are the opposite, having three troughs rather than three peaks, and signaling a stock price increase at the end of the fluctuation.

BEARISH AND BULLISH TRENDS

In all of these trends, the **final activity** of the stock is crucial in determining whether the pattern signifies a *bearish* or a *bullish* trend. For example, saucers and inverted head-and-shoulders patterns both increase at the end of their fluctuation, so they indicate bullish trends; but the head-and-shoulders pattern and the inverted saucer are both bearish signs, since they decrease at the end.

CONSOLIDATION, SUPPORT LEVELS, RESISTANCE LEVELS, AND BREAKOUTS

Consolidation occurs when a stock's trendline is relatively flat over a significant period of time, when its price remains within a particular and narrow trading channel or trading range. When this pattern is plotted on a graph, the minimum price at which the stock is exchanged within this time period is its **support level**, while the maximum price is its resistance level. If a stock price exits this channel—whether decreasing below the support level or increasing above the resistance level—then a **breakout** is occurring: the stock is leaving its previous horizontal trend and beginning a new one.

ACCUMULATION/DISTRIBUTION INDEX

The **accumulation/distribution index** is utilized in technical analysis in order to gauge market momentum at a given time. The goal is to determine whether stocks are being purchased (accumulated) or sold (distributed), and this is done through an analysis of the stock's price and its volume flow. The particular formula is as follows:

A/D = [(close – low) – (high – close)] / (high – low) x period's volume

Close = closing price

Low = low price

High = high price

The goal of this formula is to spot a divergence between the volume flow and the stock price, thus signifying that a current stock trend is about to end.

OVERBOUGHT AND OVERSOLD STOCKS

Stocks are **overbought** if their prices have increased beyond their true value, being unjustifiably increased by speculation or other artificial causes. If a stock is overbought, then it has likely reached its peak price and will be declining soon, in which case it would be wise to sell. Similarly, when stocks are **oversold**, their prices are artificially lower than their true value, so the proper course of action is to buy. One possible indicator for this is by comparing the pattern of stock prices in relation to a significant market index, such as the Dow Jones Industrial Average or the S&P 500.

MOVING AVERAGES

Since stock prices fluctuate to a notable degree on a daily basis, it can be difficult to track long-term patterns of stock price. To solve this, various **moving averages** of stock prices are used, giving an average price of the stock for a given time period, and then plotting those average prices over a period of time to smooth out the stock's price pattern. There are different kinds of moving average which emphasize different factors in their calculation. A **simple moving average (SMA)** is the most common method, calculated by taking the sum of all the closing prices for a given time period and dividing it by the number of instances used.

For instance, a five-day SMA will take the previous five days' closing prices and divide it by five. A **linear weighted average** places more weight on more recent stock prices within the specified time period. For instance, a five-day linear weighted average might multiply the most recent closing price by five, the next by four, the next by three, etc., and then divide the whole sum of those multiplied prices by the sum of the multipliers (in this case, 5+4+3+2+1=15). This average is the least common method used. An **exponential moving average (EMA)** also places more weight on more recent stock prices, but uses a smoothing factor that is understood to be more efficient than the linear average in responding to stock price changes. The calculation is more complicated, so most traders complete the calculations electronically.

Fundamental Analysis

FUNDAMENTAL ANALYSTS

Technical analysts try to determine when to buy a security by tracking its price patterns over time, but **fundamental analysts** focus on information concerning the company itself in order to determine the intrinsic value of ownership in the company (stock), which is then compared to the stock's actual price. The type of information analyzed by fundamental analysts includes its management, its financial statements, its industry, the overall economy, and competitor companies.

ANNUAL REPORT

An **annual report** is intended to comprehensively summarize a company's activities for investors (and others) over the past year. (*Interim reports* are reports issued more frequently.) Annual reports include financial statements (such as income statements, balance sheets, and statements of cash flows), notes to the financial statements, accounting policies, statements and reports from management, directors, chairmen, and/or auditors, material risk disclosures, and other information.

DEPRECIATION, DEPLETION, AND GOODWILL

Depreciation refers to the systematic decreasing of an asset's value over its useful life. It would not be proper for an asset like a building or a machine to be recorded at its historical cost and then removed in its entirety from the balance sheet when it is discontinued, so its book value must be steadily lowered over the course of its useful life. **Depletion** refers to the systematic decreasing of natural resources as they are extracted over time, such as timber or oil. Since natural resources do not have a fixed useful life, the strategy for allocating depletion costs over time is different, and usually is calculated by dividing the total cost by the estimated total resource to give a depletion charge per unit of resource. The total cost includes acquisition of asset, exploration costs, development costs and restoration costs following extraction. **Goodwill** is recorded as an intangible asset on a company's balance sheet, and refers to the general value of the company in excess of its assets' book value. For instance, goodwill would include the value of having a well-known brand name, skilled employees, good customer relations, and other things.

BALANCE SHEET

A balance sheet is a monetary representation, meeting the standards of generally accepted accounting principles, of assets, liabilities, and owner's equity for a given date. The **balance sheet** is intended to show what a company possesses at a given point in time (assets) and of those assets, what the company owes (liabilities) and what it owns (equity). Thus, for a balance sheet, it should always be the case that assets = liabilities + equity.

ASSETS

Some different kinds of assets are current assets, fixed, assets, and intangible assets:

- **Current assets** are a company's most liquid assets. Current assets are one of the major considerations when determining a company's value. They include any cash on hand and everything the company owns that will be converted into cash in the next year, such as accounts receivable, money market funds, inventory, etc.

- **Fixed assets** are what a company owns that couldn't quickly be sold to raise cash, such as plants and equipment. These things aren't very liquid, as there is usually not a big market for them, and they often aren't worth much due to depreciation. But they do have some value, and could conceivably be sold for some amount eventually.
- **Intangible assets** are nonphysical assets, which include patents, intellectual property rights, trademarks, goodwill, and other things.

LIABILITY

Liabilities are the debts and obligations of a business, and are listed on the balance sheet by due date and current or long-term status:

- **Current Liabilities** – Debts that must be paid in the short-term, generally within a year. Usually presented in order of payment due date or priority of payment.
- **Long-Term Liabilities** – Business debts that are due over the longer term, which is generally considered longer than one year.
- **Valuation Accounts** – Similar to valuation accounts for assets, these are associated with the original liability, i.e., not separate assets or liabilities. The changes, such as discounts on bonds, affect the amount of the liability.

OWNER'S EQUITY

Owner's equity is the remaining interest in assets after liabilities have been deducted. Originally created by the investments of the owners, **owner's equity** can increase by the addition of investors and decrease when it is distributed amongst its investors. It can also fluctuate because of business operations. When there is a sole owner, owner's equity is called *proprietor's equity*. In a partnership, equity accounts are set up for each partner, allowing for individualized accounting of investments, income, or withdrawals. When a corporation is formed, accounts are determined by their source. Minimum contributed capital is determined by incorporation regulations or state law. **Retained earnings** are a result of accumulated earnings minus losses and dividends and are considered a resource to use when growing the business.

LIFO AND FIFO METHODS

When determining the value of its inventory, a company can choose to use either the first in, first out (FIFO) method or the last in, first out (LIFO) method. Using the **LIFO method**, when a company sells a product from its inventory, it calculates the cost of that sale based on the newest item in its inventory. For instance, if 600 objects were purchased on Jan. 1 at $10 apiece and 400 more on Feb. 1 at $12 apiece, and if there were 750 objects remaining on Feb. 15, then the inventory value would be (600 * $10) + (150 * $12) = $7,800. Using the **FIFO method**, when a company sells a product from its inventory, it calculates the cost of that sale based on the oldest item in its inventory. For instance, given the above example, the inventory value on Feb. 15 would be (400 * $12) + (350 * $10) = $8,300.

STRAIGHT-LINE DEPRECIATION VERSUS ACCELERATED DEPRECIATION

Except for real estate, pretty much all physical property owned by a company depreciates (loses value over time) due to obsolescence and wear and tear. There are different ways to reflect this depreciation, but two general approaches. In the **straight-line method**, the cost of a physical asset is divided by the number of years of expected useful life. So if a company buys a new machine for five million dollars, and its useful life is estimated at 20 years, the company could use straight-line depreciation and depreciate $250,000 a year for each of the 20 years. Or the company could use **accelerated depreciation**, and write off larger amounts in the first years of owning the property and smaller amounts in the later years of its use. Accelerated depreciation can come in different

74

forms, particularly the *double-declining balance (DDB) method* and the *sum-of-the-years'-digits (SYD) method.*

INCOME STATEMENT

A company's **income statement** reports its revenues and expenses for a given period of time, showing how the *revenues* result in a given net income, thus indicating the success or failure of a company's profitable activities. The *expenses* listed on the income statement include all the charges against the revenues, such as write-offs and taxes. The main components can be listed as follows:

Net Sales

– Cost of Goods Sold (CGS)
– Operating Expense
– Interest Expense
= Taxable Income
– Taxes
= Net Income
– Dividends
= Retained Earnings

INTERMEDIATE CALCULATIONS

Besides net income (also called **net profit**), there are a number of intermediate income calculations made on an income statement. In order, these include:

- *EBITDA* – earnings before interest, taxes, depreciation, and amortization
- *EBIT* – earnings before interest and taxes
- *EBT* – earnings before taxes

The name of the calculation tells where it is located on the income statement. EBITDA appears before operating expenses are subtracted (since those include depreciation and amortization), but after cost of goods sold is subtracted. EBIT appears before interest expense is subtracted, and EBT appears before taxes are subtracted.

LIQUIDITY

Liquidity is a company's ability to quickly convert its assets into cash. Several different measures can serve to analyze **liquidity**:

- *Working capital* = current assets – current liabilities
- *Current ratio* = current assets / current liabilities
- *Quick assets* = current assets – inventory
- *Acid test ratio* = (cash + A/R + short-term investments) / current liabilities

CAPITALIZATION RATIOS

Capitalization refers to a company's equity plus its long-term debt. **Capitalization** is a measure of how solid a company is financially. There are several ratios used to calculate this from various perspectives. One is the *debt-to-equity ratio*, which is found by dividing total liabilities by shareholder equity. The second ratio is the *bond ratio*, which is calculated by dividing long-term bonds payable by total capitalization. The third is the *common-stock ratio*, which is found by dividing the total equity held by shareholders of common stock by the company's total capitalization. The last ratio is the *preferred-stock ratio*, which is calculated by dividing the equity owned by holders of preferred stock by the total capitalization. When companies have a lot of

75

leverage—that is, when a great portion of their capitalization is financed by debt—the risk of bankruptcy increases for that company. Obviously, this risk is an important factor of consideration for potential investors.

STATEMENT OF CASH FLOWS

A **statement of cash flows** is responsible for communicating to readers the amount and uses of cash funds for a business over a time period. It is divided into three sections: operating, investing, and financing. The *operating* section involves all those cash flows tied up with the company's main operations, that is, the same activities which are used to determine net income. The *investing* section tracks the cash movement for transactions involving securities (available-for-sale and held-to-maturity) and property, plant, and equipment, in addition to collections and sales on purchased loans. The *financing* section includes cash from the repayment of debts, the payment of dividends, the issuance of stock, and any other finance activities (such as derivatives).

INVENTORY TURNOVER RATIO

Inventory turnover is a ratio of cost of goods sold divided by the average inventory (beginning inventory plus ending inventory divided by two). If the number is low, it represents slow-moving items, which is a bad sign for business. If the inventory is perishable, such as food, then the inventory turnover ratio should be high. The **inventory turnover ratio** is an indicator of how hard the inventory is working for the business.

PROFIT MARGIN

Profit margin is the ratio of a company's net profit (i.e. net income) to the revenue (i.e. net sales) for a given time period. Generally, a lower profit margin means that an investment in the company will be riskier. **Profit margin** can be a helpful measure for comparing companies within the same industry.

BOOK VALUE PER SHARE

Book value per share is the measure of how much each share of stock would actually be worth if the company were to be sold to satisfy creditors. **Book value per share** is an important figure for more conservative investors. Book value per share is determined by subtracting all liabilities (such as creditors and preferred stock holders, since they are paid before holders of common stock) from the total value of all tangible assets. This is the book value, or *net asset value (NAV)*, of the company. What's left over is divided by the number of shares of common stock outstanding, and the result is the book value per share. The NAV can also be divided by the number of bonds a company has, to arrive at the *net asset value per bond*.

INTEREST COVERAGE RATIO

A company's **interest coverage ratio** shows how easily a company can pay the interest expense on its outstanding debt. It is calculated by dividing the earnings before interest and tax (EBIT) by the interest expense for a given period. A lower number for this, such as 1.5 or less, signifies a heavy debt burden that the company must deal with. This ratio can also be applied to particular kinds of interest expense. For instance, the *bond interest coverage ratio* equals the EBIT divided by the total bond interest expense.

EPS

Earnings per share (EPS) refers to the allotment of a company's income for each share of outstanding stock. The formula for it is as follows:

EPS = (net income – preferred dividends) / avg. shares outstanding

Another variation of earnings per share is *fully diluted earnings per share*. As the name implies, this number spreads the company's income across more shares, thus lowering the amount per share. This dilution occurs by assuming that every source of stock conversion (e.g. stock options and convertible bonds) is used to purchase stock. These stocks are then added to the number of shares outstanding in the ordinary EPS formula.

P/E Ratio, the Dividend Payout Ratio, and ROE

The **price/earnings (P/E) ratio** is calculated by dividing the current price of a share of stock by the company's current earnings per share. A stock with a high P/E ratio is considered expensive, all other things being equal, and a stock with a low P/E ratio is considered a bargain, all other factors being equal. The **dividend payout ratio** measures the company's earnings which are paid out to stockholders. It is calculated by dividing the dividends by the net income for a given period. Or, equivalently, it is calculated by dividing dividends per share by a company's EPS. **Return on equity (ROE)** measures how much income the company makes based upon its shareholder's equity. It is calculated by dividing net income by shareholder's equity (which excludes preferred shares). This also can be called *return on net worth (RONW)*.

Nominal Yield and Current Yield

Yield is the value of the interest payments received from a bond compared to the bond's value. There are several ways to measure a bond's yield. The **nominal yield**, also known as the *coupon yield*, is the interest rate with which the bond was sold. However, as market conditions change, and interest rates go up and down, the value of a bond goes up and down in inverse proportion to interest rates. So **current yield** is a more accurate measure of bond value, and it is determined by dividing the coupon rate by the current market price.

Municipal Securities Analysis

GO BONDS

General obligation (GO) bonds are issued to pay for improvements that benefit a community, but don't produce income. They are also known as *full faith and credit issues*, because they are repaid from tax revenue raised by the issuing government entity. The merits of a GO bond depend greatly on whether the community of the issuer is likely to be able to raise the funds to pay back the interest and principal. Are property values high? Is the local economy strong and diversified? Is the population growing, or at least stable? How much debt does the issuer have now, and can he manage this new obligation? Do they plan to issue any further debt soon after this issue? What are the sources of the tax revenue, and do they look likely to remain consistent until maturity? These are the types of considerations to make when evaluating GO bonds.

RATIOS TO MEASURE MUNICIPAL DEBT

The following are the major ratios used in measuring **municipal debt**:

- *Net debt to assessed valuation*: The municipality's debt divided by the value of the purchased property, as assessed for tax purposes. The lower the better, preferably 5% or below.
- *Net debt to estimated valuation*: Similar to the above, but based on estimations, not actual assessments, which vary.
- *Taxes per capita*: Are citizens paying a high tax burden already?
- *Debt per capita*: Is government debt per person high or low?
- *Collection ratio*: How much of the taxes owed are actually collected?
- *Coverage ratio*: How many years' worth of annual revenue will it take to cover the debt? This is calculated as revenues/debt, and it can be based on net or gross revenue, but usually net.

Also, though not a ratio, it is important to look at the municipality's *debt trend*: Is the taxing authority adding to or reducing its debt, generally speaking?

REVENUE BONDS

Governments issue **revenue bonds** to finance projects and facilities that are expected to generate enough revenue to pay bondholders back without resorting to tax money. Since they are backed not by a government's ability to tax, but by the expected revenue stream generated by the proposed facility or project, careful analysis must be done to ensure that the project will be able to generate enough income to repay bondholders. Is there a legitimate need for the project, and will enough people use it to make it worthwhile? Are there other facilities nearby that serve the same purpose that will draw revenue away from the project? If not, are there plans to build any competing projects? Will the facility bring in enough money to pay for itself and repay investors? These are the types of considerations to make when evaluating revenue bonds.

When assessing revenue bond prospects, there are a number of important factors to consider:

- **Feasibility studies** are analyses of the strengths and weaknesses of the activity being financed by the revenue bonds. It is important to know whether the revenue bonds are funding a sensible operation. Municipalities are required to have these studies for revenue bonds, and they hire their own consultants to carry them out.
- **Financial reports** are also required to be provided by the municipalities. These are subject to external audits, which help to provide assurance of the information's reliability to potential investors.

- **Catastrophe clauses** are clauses stating that if a catastrophic event destroys a facility designed to produce funds for repaying the revenue bonds, then the insurance gained from such an event will repay bondholders.

FLOW OF FUNDS

The **flow of funds** explains how a municipality uses the revenue it generates. The revenues normally are distributed to pay various expenses in a particular order:

1. *Operation and maintenance* – payments to maintain the facilities and pay the employees
2. *Debt service* – repayment of bond principal and interest
3. *Debt service reserve* – savings for future debt repayments
4. *Reserve maintenance fund* – savings for future maintenance payments
5. *Renewal and replacement fund* – payments to renovate or update facilities and to replace old equipment
6. *Surplus fund* – payments for miscellaneous expenditures

When a municipality distributes funds in this order—covering operation expenses before repaying bond debts—it is called a *net revenue pledge*, since the municipality pledges to repay investors from net revenue. If the pledge is to pay investors before operations expenditures, then it is called a *gross revenue pledge.*

COVENANTS

Covenants are promises made by the bond issuer, legally binding him to certain courses of action in order to better protect investors. Because the purpose is to protect investors, these are specifically called protective covenants. Examples of such covenants are as follows:

- Rate covenants are promises to charge adequate rates, so that sufficient revenue is generated to repay bond principal and interest.
- Maintenance covenants are promises to preserve and repair the facilities.
- Insurance covenants are promises to appropriately insure the facilities.

Other protective covenants can restrict the issuer from paying a certain amount of dividends to shareholders, or from issuing newer and higher-priority debt.

CREDIT ENHANCEMENTS

Credit enhancements are actions taken by a municipality or company to improve its creditworthiness. This can be accomplished with insurance, collateral, the guarantee of a third party, or internal changes that demonstrate the entity is better able to repay debts.

Equity Securities

AUTHORIZED STOCK, ISSUED STOCK, AND OUTSTANDING STOCK

Authorized stock is the maximum number of shares that a company has been approved to sell on the market. They may sell them all immediately, or hold them back for sale at a later date, or for other purposes, such as employee stock options. Holding stocks back is fairly common, and authorized shares often exceed the actual shares issued for sale on the market. Once all authorized shares have been sold, or issued, the company may not sell any more shares without getting approval from current stockholders, because the company charter must be amended. **Issued stock** is the number of shares that have ever been sold and held, even if they have since been repurchased by the company or retired. **Outstanding stock** is the number of shares that are currently held by investors and tradable in the market. If no shares have been repurchased or retired, then issued stock = outstanding stock.

TREASURY STOCK

Shares that have been issued and sold are sometimes bought back by the company. The stock that is bought back from the market and held by the company is known as **treasury stock**. The corporation may hold the stock for future use, such as employee stock options, or they may retire it for good. Stock buybacks are usually seen as an indicator of a company's belief in the strength of its value, and are often followed by an increase in share value, as investors will interpret the buyback as a sign of strength. Even if the share price remains the same, the earning per share should go up, since the number of shares outstanding that will share in company earnings has been reduced. The rights that apply to outstanding stock still on the market, such as *voting rights* and *dividend rights*, don't apply to treasury stock.

PAR VALUE FOR STOCKS

The **par value** for a stock is the value stated on the stock certificate. This is the requirement which the company is legally obligated to pay a shareholder in exchange for ownership in the company, no matter how worthless the stock certificate might be on the open market. Consequently, the par value for stocks tends to be very low, $1 or even $0.01 per share, in order to lower the company's obligation in the event of stock devaluation. Predictably, stocks with a par value are known as *par value stocks*, and stocks lacking a par value are known as *no par value stocks*.

LIMITED LIABILITY

In sole proprietorships or partnerships, the owners of the business are fully responsible for the liabilities which their business incurs to various creditors. There is a connection between the assets they personally own and their business, so that if their business goes under, creditors can lay claim to other assets besides what they have invested in the business. This is *unlimited liability*. By contrast, **limited liability** entails that investors are not liable for all of the debts which a corporation has, but are liable only to the extent of their investment. While investors can then partake of the benefits of the company's growth, they are not subject to enormous harm if the company has severe debts or even bankruptcy.

STOCK CERTIFICATE

A **stock certificate** is a piece of paper stating how many shares of the stock a person owns. It also includes the name of the company, the investor's name, and the CUSIP number. CUSIP stands for Committee on Uniform Securities Identification Procedures. This is a unique identifier of stocks and bonds, much like a serial number, and it can be used to identify the rightful owner of these

80

instruments if they're lost or stolen. To sell stocks, the owner of the shares must sign the back of the certificate, or a stock power, giving the right to his broker to make the transfer.

ESCROW RECEIPTS

When investors transact option contracts, the contract depends upon the fact that one of the investors has the underlying security and will have it for a specific time period, up to the last time when the other investor can exercise the option. When investors want better proof that the other man indeed possesses the underlying security, they can seek an **escrow receipt**, a bank's guarantee that the option writer has the security and that it is easily deliverable.

ENDORSEMENTS, TRANSFER AGENTS, AND REGISTRARS

Endorsements refer to the signing of some document which effectively permits for some money or asset to be transferred to a different person. A **transfer agent** is a person or institution that acts on behalf of a corporation to keep track of investors and their activities, including account balances and account transactions. Transfer agents also help with the mailing and canceling of stock certificates, and deals with any problems investors may have, such as lost stock certificates. Whenever transfer agents facilitate the transfer of a stock from one shareholder to another, there are *specific transfer procedures* which they must follow, as outlined by the SEC. **Registrars** are similar to transfer agents, working with them to keep track of stockholders and bondholders. The primary objective for registrars is to ensure that the number of outstanding shares do not surpass the quantity of authorized stock for the company.

PREEMPTIVE RIGHTS

A **preemptive right** is the right of a shareholder (though not of just any shareholder) to maintain his current percentage of share ownership in case the corporation decides to issue more stock. If a company decides to issue more stock, the company must give these privileged shareholders first crack at buying the shares before the company offers the shares to the general market (and usually below market price). Current shareholders will receive a *subscription rights certificate*, which will spell out the terms and conditions of the offer, such as the date, price, and how many shares they're entitled to buy based on their current ownership.

RIGHTS OF COMMON STOCKHOLDERS

Common stockholders can have varying rights associated with their stock ownership. They can have *preemptive rights*, which privilege them to purchase shares of a new offering before the public; they can have a *pro rata share of dividends*, in which they receive dividends proportionally to their stock ownership in the corporation; they can have *access to corporate books*, where they gain information about the corporation's operations to which the public (and other shareholders) are not privy; and they can have various *voting powers* to influence the direction of the corporation.

VOTING POWERS FOR COMMON STOCKHOLDERS

Common stockholders can have varying levels of **voting powers**. While most preferred stock does not include voting rights, most common stock does. Common stockholders generally get one vote for each share they own per issue to be decided. For instance, a stockholder owning 1,000 shares in a corporation, voting for candidates to fill 5 different positions on the board of directors, will have a total of 5,000 votes to expend. However, corporations can facilitate different kinds of voting, which explain how these votes can be expended. *Statutory voting* requires the stockholder to split up his votes evenly among the issues being voted on. For instance, the above shareholder will have 1000 votes maximum to expend on each of the 5 different positions being filled. *Cumulative voting*, on the other hand, does not require stockholders to split up their votes evenly. They are free to distribute their votes as they please. For instance, the above shareholder, if he wanted, could use all 5,000 of his votes on one particular candidate running for a singular position on the board of directors. Since it is often inconvenient for all common stockholders to physically attend annual corporate meetings, they can still exercise their voting rights by hiring **proxies**, agents legally enabled to vote on the stockholders' behalf.

DIVIDENDS

A dividend is a portion of the company's profit that is returned to shareholders. A **dividend** can come in the form of cash, in which case a check is sent to the owner or to the owner's brokerage account. When the company announces dividends, there will be some dollar amount per share distributed to shareholders. When dividends are paid in cash, they are considered income, and taxes must be paid on them during the tax year they're received. Dividends can also be in the form of additional shares of stock given to shareholders. These are not taxable until they're sold, just like all stocks. Because this type of stock dividend increases the number of outstanding shares, it decreases the market value of each share, but does not affect the total market value of the company.

IMPORTANT DATES

A corporation must let the stock exchange know that it is getting ready to pay a dividend. The day it announces this is the **declaration date**. When it makes this announcement, it will declare a record date and a payment date. The **record date** must be at least ten days after the declaration date. Whoever is the owner of record of shares on the record date will be entitled to the dividend. To be considered the owner of record, a stock buyer must purchase the stock before the ex-date, which is two days before the record date. In other words, the owner must purchase the stock at least three business days before the record date. The **payment date** is generally three to four weeks after the record date.

STOCK SPLITS

A **split** is a change in the number of shares of stock outstanding. The most common split is the *forward split*, which increases the number of shares outstanding, with a corresponding adjustment in share value. For example, in a 2-for-1 forward split (the most common type of split), a shareholder will receive two shares for every one they own, and the price of each new share will be half that of the former share price. Forward splits are done in most cases because a stock price has gotten so high that the cost of trading the stock has become prohibitive. More investors will be willing to buy the stock at a lower price. Forward splits are usually considered a sign of confidence on the part of the company, and it is not uncommon for share prices to rise after a forward split occurs. A *reverse split* is the opposite—the number of shares outstanding is reduced in order to raise the price of each share, so a person who owned two shares before now owns one (in a 1-for-2 split). Reverse splits are usually considered negatively, and it is common for the price of a stock to drop after one takes place.

SPINOFFS

A **spinoff** occurs when a corporation "spins off" (or splits off) one of its divisions/sections, making it a separate entity altogether and endowing it with particular facilities and assets. When this occurs, shareholders in the original corporation also receive stock in the spinoff entity. Spinoffs can increase the value of stocks previously held in the one corporation before the spinoff, since it gives investors the option to choose whichever section of the company they think will be more profitable.

PENNY STOCKS

Penny stocks are shares of very small publicly traded companies, generally traded as over-the-counter stocks, not on major exchanges. **Penny stocks** are prone to speculative and volatile price changes and manipulation, thus being very risky. They are also characterized by **illiquidity**; that is, they are difficult to trade to others. Because of this, a broker must acquire his customer's written consent before facilitating any penny stock transactions for him.

TRANSACTION RULES

There are special rules accompanying **penny stock transactions**. A broker wishing to facilitate such a transaction is required by the SEC to give the customer a document outlining the risks of penny stock investments, the market price for the stock, and the compensation the brokerage firm will receive for executing the transaction. Brokerage firms also must send monthly statements to penny stock investors, disclosing the value of their penny stocks.

TYPES OF PREFERRED STOCK

CUMULATIVE PREFERRED STOCK AND PARTICIPATING PREFERRED STOCK

Cumulative preferred stock is preferred stock that gives the stockholder the right to missed dividend payments from the company. Should the company miss a dividend payment to owners of cumulative preferred stock, the company must make up the payment at a later date, as it stays on the books as a debt until paid. This is opposed to *straight (or non-cumulative) preferred stock*, which has a fixed dividend payment (like cumulative preferred stock), but if the company misses any payments, they are not made up later. **Participating preferred stock** entitles the stockholder to a portion of the profits that remain after dividends and interest have been paid by the corporation. These are so called because they permit stockholders to participate further in the company's profits. Participating preferred stockholders also have special rights should the corporation liquidate.

CONVERTIBLE PREFERRED STOCK AND CALLABLE PREFERRED STOCK

Convertible preferred stock consists of shares that can be converted into common stock if the owner so chooses. The conversion price is preset, and convertible preferred shares tend to rise and fall in value along with common shares because of this feature. They also usually have lower dividend payments than other preferred stocks. **Callable preferred stock** consists of shares that the company reserves the right to buy back at a future date at a specific price. When a company calls a preferred share, it will pay a premium over the stated price to make up for loss of future dividends. This can also be called *redeemable preferred stock*. Callable preferred stock is ordinarily covered by a *sinking fund provision*. In the same way that corporations can repurchase bonds with a sinking fund, the same can be done for their repurchasing of preferred stock.

ADJUSTABLE-RATE PREFERRED STOCK

Normal preferred stock pays dividends at a fixed rate, but **adjustable-rate preferred stock** has the level of dividend payment change periodically. These payments are altered according to a benchmark, usually the risk-free rate on U.S. Treasury securities. Despite the fact that these types of stocks can change in their return, they are generally acknowledged to be more stable than preferred stocks with a fixed rate.

COMMON STOCK AND PREFERRED STOCK

The vast majority of stocks issued are **common stock**. Some corporations issue a limited number of preferred stocks. Holders of **preferred stock** do not have voting rights under most circumstances. But there are financial benefits to owning preferred stock instead of common stock. If a company goes bankrupt, preferred stock owners take precedence over common stock holders when it comes to distributing whatever assets are available. And preferred stock usually comes with a fixed dividend paid on a regular basis, so that even if the owners of common stock don't receive a dividend, preferred stock owners will. And because the dividend is fixed, owners of preferred stock can depend on a regular income. Because of these differences, the prices of preferred stocks tend to rise and fall with relation to interest rates, and not with other factors that affect the price of the common stock.

Capital Gains and Losses and Holding Periods

Capital gains occur when an asset (usually a security) is sold for a price greater than the price at which the investor purchased it. Similarly, **capital losses** occur when the investor loses money on the sale of the asset. Capital gains and losses are subject to federal, state, and local taxes. The taxation depends upon the **holding period** of the security, that is, how much time passed between when the asset was purchased and when it was sold. If the holding period is one year or less, then any capital gain or loss is classified as *short-term*, and gains are consequently taxed as if they were ordinary income (i.e. by the investor's tax bracket). *Long-term* capital gains or losses occur for holding periods exceeding one year. Long-term gains have a lower tax rate than most income rates, being taxed at 15% maximum.

Taxation for Dividends

When dividends are distributed as cash, they are subject to **taxation** as well. And just as capital gains can be taxed less if they are classified as long-term, so also dividends can be taxed differently, depending on whether they are qualified or non-qualified. **Qualified dividends** are dividends which can be taxed at the (lower) long-term capital gains rate. To count as qualified dividends, they must be disbursed by a U.S. corporation or a qualifying foreign corporation, and they must be held by the investor for at least 60 days within the 121-day period that begins 60 days prior to the ex-dividend date. **Non-qualified dividends** are taxed at the investor's ordinary income rate. Starting in 2013, however, all dividends will be taxed at the ordinary income tax rate, thus rendering the qualified/non-qualified distinction negligible.

Capital Losses Offset Capital Gains

While investors are taxed on **capital gains**, the amount of capital gains on which they are taxed can be reduced by their **capital losses**. An investor with $10,000 in long-term capital gains and $5,000 in long-term capital losses during the year will have to pay taxes only on $5,000 worth of long-term capital gains. Only short-term losses can offset short-term gains, and only long-term losses can offset long-term gains. Besides offsetting capital gains, capital losses can also offset **ordinary income** if there are no capital gains left to offset. However, ordinary income can be offset by a maximum of $3,000 per year, with the remaining balance being carried forward to the next year. For example, if an investor had long-term capital gains of $5,000 and long-term capital losses of $15,000 for the year, then he would pay no taxes on the capital gains, deduct $3,000 from his ordinary income, and carry the remaining $7,000 balance to the next year, which can offset future capital gains or income.

Tax Implications for Stocks Acquired Through Conversion

If stock is acquired through **conversion**, such as by exercising the conversion feature on convertible bonds, then any gain or loss acquired through the conversion is not immediately relevant to capital gains or losses. Instead, the **basis** of the stocks is equal to the value of the debt at the point of conversion. This basis is then the reference point for determining future capital gains or losses on that stock. For example, if a convertible bond with a basis of $1,000 is converted into 20 shares of stock selling at that date for $55 apiece, then the basis of the stock investment will still be $1,000 (effectively $50 per share), and the investor will recognize no capital gain or loss at that point. (That is, he will not recognize a gain of $100 at the date of conversion, even though the stock is valued at $1,100 and the bond at $1,000.) However, if the investor were to then sell the stocks at $60 per share one year later, then that would be taxable event upon his capital gain of $10 per share sold. The **holding period** for the stock begins at the date of the debt issuance, not at the date of conversion.

STOCKS' COST BASIS

The **cost basis** (or *tax basis*) for stocks is the reference point to be used when determining one's capital gains or losses. If your stock's cost basis is $5,000 and you sell it for $5,500, then you have a capital gain of $500. Cost basis will often be listed as **cost basis per share**. The cost basis for stock is not ordinarily the purchase price of the stock. When buying stock, the basis will be increased by fees and commissions paid to the broker or dealer.

GIFTS AND INHERITANCE

Stocks acquired as **gifts** will have a basis equal to the donor's basis unless they have decreased in value since the donor acquired them. In that case, their new basis is their value at the time of donation. If they have increased in value since the donor acquired them, the basis for the gift recipient will still equal the donor's basis. Stock acquired by **inheritance** will have a basis equal to the value per share at the point of the bequeather's death. All securities acquired by inheritance are automatically taxed as long-term.

EFFECT OF DIVIDENDS

If **dividends** are gained on stock and then reinvested in the stock, the dividends are still treated as income, in which case their reinvestment increases the cost basis of the stock by the amount reinvested. Moreover, all reinvested dividends are still taxable.

ISOs AND NSOs

Incentive stock options (ISOs) are employee stock options which carry tax benefits with them, whereas **nonqualified stock options (NSOs)** are ones which don't. When an employee has an NSO, he will have to pay taxes on the gain he acquires when he exercises it, even though he receives no cash in the transaction. For example, if a stock option entitles an employee to 20 shares at $20 per share, and the market value of the shares at the date he exercises the option is $25 per share, then, with an NSO, he would have to report income of $100 (20 shares x $5/share) and pay income tax on it. The cost basis of his investment would then be $500 (20 shares x $25/share), and any capital gains or losses would be determined against this basis. But with ISOs, any taxes are deferred to the time when the stock is sold. When the employee exercises the stock, he is to use the exercise price as his cost basis (in the above case, $20/share), and the only tax he has to pay is on any capital gains he might have. The sale of an ISO must occur at least two years from the granting of the option and one year from the exercising of the option, however, or the tax benefits will be forfeited due to a *disqualifying disposition* of the stock.

AVERAGE BASIS METHOD FOR MUTUAL FUNDS

Mutual funds make the calculation of capital gains and losses to be much trickier, since the customer is often unaware of all the securities transactions executed by the fund manager. One common method is the **average basis method**. According to this method, the total money paid for shares is divided by the total number of shares to give the investor an average basis per share. Then, whenever he sells any shares, the basis is lowered accordingly: the quantity of shares decreases, but the basis per share remains the same. If an investor purchased 100 shares for $15/share two years and 100 shares for $20/share last year, then if he sold 150 shares today, the cost basis to which he would compare the selling price would be $2,625 (150 shares x $17.50/share). The remaining cost basis on his other 50 shares would be $875 (50 shares x $17.50/share). It can be difficult to determine whether capital gains are short- or long-term with average basis methods. To solve this, there used to be *average cost single category (ACSC)* and *average cost double category methods (ACDC)*, but ACDC has been discontinued by the IRS since April 2011.

FIFO, LIFO, AND SPECIFIC SHARE IDENTIFICATION

With the **first in, first out (FIFO) method** for valuing one's stocks, given a list of how many shares were bought or sold on which day (and at what price), the investor assumes for simplicity's sake that any shares sold are the oldest ones he possesses. If he bought 100 shares at $15 per share two years ago and 100 shares at $20 per share last year, then if he sells 150 shares today, it will be as if he sold $2,500 worth of shares: (100 shares x $15/share) + (50 shares x $20/share). $2,500 would be the basis against which he compares the selling price to determine capital gains or losses. Under the **last in, first out (LIFO)** method, the newest stocks are assumed to be the ones sold. In the above example, the cost basis of the sold shares would be $2,750: (100 shares x $20/share) + (50 shares x $15/share). **Specific share identification** involves the most work, since the investor (or mutual fund manager) must keep track of the buying and selling prices for every transaction of stock at the time it was transacted. The benefit of this is that it tends to reduce one's taxes. Other methods are *high cost, first out (HCFO)* and *low cost, first out (LCFO),* where the basis is determined by the relative prices of the acquired shares, not the time at which they were purchased.

WASH SALES

The IRS generally permits investors to offset investment gains with capital losses up to $3,000 a year. However, a capital loss may not be used to offset gains if the investor, within thirty days after taking the loss, then buys the same security, or one that is "*substantially identical*," which would include warrants, rights, options, and convertible bonds in the same stock. If the investor purchases the same security or a substantially identical one within thirty days of the loss, it is considered a **wash sale,** and cannot be factored in with net capital losses to offset gains or income.

RIGHTS OFFERING

In a **rights offering** (also called a *rights issue*), a company will issue the right to purchase additional stocks to current stockholders in the company. The company will set a predetermined number of shares and price per share, giving shareholders the right to purchase such shares in the future, sometimes within a set time period. Since rights offerings can give an incentive for shareholders to purchase further stock, they are often used as a means to raise capital for the company.

WARRANTS

Warrants are the right to buy a stock at a specified price, which is almost always higher than the price the stock is trading at when the warrant is issued. If the stock price rises above the warrant price, the **warrant** becomes very valuable, much like a call option, as the warrant owner has the right to purchase stock below the market price. The owner may choose to exercise the warrant and buy the stock, may sell the warrant, or may continue to hold it hoping the stock goes even higher, until the expiration date. Most warrants are good for five years.

ANTI-DILUTION PROVISIONS

With options and convertible securities, their main value derives from the fact that stocks can be purchased for a price lower than the market price. Because of this, holders of options and convertible securities would dislike any additional issuance of stock, which would dilute the value per share by spreading out the total equity of the company over more shareholders. Consequently, certain options and convertible securities will have an **anti-dilution provision** (or *anti-dilution cause*), which guarantees that the company will not dilute shares through further stock issuance.

ADRs

An **American Depositary Receipt (ADR)** is a financial instrument created so that the stocks of foreign companies can be bought and sold on stock markets in the United States. Each ADR represents a certain number of shares of a foreign company, usually somewhere between one and ten shares. Each individual share is known as an American Depositary Share. ADRs are bought and sold just like other common stocks listed on the exchanges, and ADR owners have the same rights as other stockholders, including voting and receiving dividends, which are paid in dollars. An ADR is technically owned by a bank, which handles the ADR, and it is held in the buyer's name. An ADR can fluctuate in value due to changes in currency rates.

Debt Securities

TREASURY BILLS

Treasury bills (T-bills) are short-term obligations issued by the United States Treasury Department of the federal government. Like zero-coupon bonds, **Treasury bills** don't pay interest, but are sold at less than face value, and the buyer collects face value at maturity. They are one of the main ways of funding the operation of the federal government, and they are sold in amounts ranging from $1,000 to $1,000,000. They have maturities of 4, 13, or 26 weeks. Their prices are quoted in yield, which means that on paper the bid will be higher than the ask. Gains from Treasury bills are taxed only at the federal level.

TREASURY NOTES

Treasury notes (T-notes) are medium-term obligations issued by the United States Treasury Department of the federal government. Unlike T-bills, **Treasury notes** do pay interest, paying every six months. Proceeds from Treasury notes are used to fund the intermediate operations of the federal government. Their maturities range from one to ten years. They may also be refunded at maturity, with a new note instead of payment. T-notes are quoted as a percentage of par in increments of 1/32. Gains from Treasury notes are taxed only at the federal level.

TREASURY BONDS

Treasury bonds (T-bonds) are long-term obligations issued by the United States Treasury Department of the federal government. The proceeds from them help fund the long-term operations of the federal government. Like T-notes, **Treasury bonds** pay interest every six months. They are issued with maturities of ten to thirty years. For five years, from 2001 to 2006, the federal government stopped issuing thirty-year bonds. But due to popular demand by investors, the sale of thirty-year bonds was re-instituted in January of 2006. They are quoted as a percentage of par in 1/32 increments. Gains from Treasury bonds are taxed only at the federal level.

TREASURY RECEIPTS AND STRIPS

Brokerage firms and other financial institutions may purchase Treasury notes and Treasury bonds and put them in trust. They then sell the receipts, or rights to individual interest or principal payments, to other investors. These are called **Treasury receipts**. However, unlike the original treasury bonds and notes, Treasury receipts are not backed by the full faith and credit of the U.S. government. **STRIPS** stands for *Separate Trading of Registered Interest and Principal Securities.* STRIPS are much like Treasury receipts, except that since the government has authorized stripping the securities into separate components, STRIPS are backed by the full faith and credit of the U.S. government.

TIPS

Treasury Inflation Protection Securities (TIPS) were created to attract investors by offering protection against rising inflation, which erodes the value of fixed-income securities. Every six months, the interest rate paid on TIPS is adjusted to reflect changes in the *Consumer Price Index (CPI)*. When inflation is rising, the interest payment paid on TIPS rises; if the CPI were to drop, interest payments would be lowered. Because of this built-in protection, TIPS are sold at lower interest rates than other government securities. Any raise in interest paid due to the adjustment is taxable in the year the adjustment is received.

Yield to Maturity, Yield to Call, and Yield to Worst

A bond's **yield to maturity (YTM)** is how much return the bondholder will earn annually by holding the bond all the way to its maturity date. If it is the original owner of the bond, this is the coupon rate, or nominal yield. But if the bondholder bought the bond on the market, the yield to maturity (YTM) will depend on whether he bought the bond at a discount or at a premium. (Very few bonds trade at par.) Bonds bought at a discount will have a higher YTM, and bonds bought at a premium will have a lower YTM. Yield to maturity is also called basis.

Yield to call (YTC) is the bondholder's return if the bond is called before it matures. **Yield to worst (YTW)** is the lowest possible yield for a bond without the issuer defaulting. It is obtained by calculating the YTM and the YTC for all the call dates and selecting the lowest.

Discount Yield

The **discount yield** of a bond is the return to a bondholder for short-term bonds and T-bills sold at a discount. The calculation for discount yield assumes 30-day durations for months and 360-day durations for years.

Ginnie Mae Pass-Throughs

Ginnie Mae pass-throughs are mortgage-backed securities whose repayment is guaranteed by the Government National Mortgage Association (GNMA) and thus backed by the full faith and credit of the federal government. Ginnie Mae (the GNMA) does not purchase or sell any of these securities, but simply guarantees their repayment.

Fannie Mae, Freddie Mac, and Sallie Mae

Fannie Mae is the *Federal National Mortgage Association*, or *FNMA*. It is a publicly-traded company aimed at increasing homeownership among Americans with low to middle incomes by expanding the secondary mortgage market. **Freddie Mac** is the *Federal Home Loan Mortgage Corporation*, or *FHLMC*. It is very similar to Fannie Mae (and thus called Fannie's "little brother"), expanding the secondary mortgage market. The main difference between the two is that Fannie generally purchases mortgages issued by banks whereas Freddie generally purchases mortgages issued by thrifts (i.e. savings and loan associations).

Sallie Mae is the *Student Loan Market Association*, or *SLMA*. It is a publicly-traded company that manages student loans, both by providing them and by buying them from other lenders.

GSEs

Government-sponsored enterprises (GSEs) are privately-owned corporations that make borrowing easier for different groups of people (e.g. homeowners or students). Because they serve this public function, GSEs have the backing of the federal government. Examples of GSEs are Fannie Mae, Freddie Mac, Sallie Mae, Ginnie Mae, and others.

CMOs

Collateralized mortgage obligations (CMOs) are issued by private financial institutions. They are bundles of private mortgages, much like the pass-throughs that are put together by the various federal agencies. Although marketed by private companies, CMOs are usually secured with financial instruments from Ginnie Mae, Freddie Mac, and Fannie Mae, and so are rated AAA. Mortgages are bundled by maturity dates into groups called **tranches**. In a standard CMO, all tranches receive interest payments every month, but only one tranche at a time receives principal payments.

Main Characteristics

CMOs are considered very safe because they're tied to mortgages guaranteed by the federal government, although they are not themselves backed by the government. Their yield is higher than that of government securities, and payments are received monthly, instead of every six months. There is a big market for CMOs, so they're usually quite easy to sell, although this isn't true of all of them. The more complex ones tend to have lower liquidity. **Prepayment** is a risk, and some varieties of CMOs have other risks that make them unsuitable for less experienced or less wealthy investors. All investors must sign a **suitability statement** saying that they understand the risks of CMOs before purchase.

CDOs

Collateralized debt obligations (CDOs) are similar to CMOs, also being subdivided into tranches bearing different degrees of risks and maturities. The main difference is that they are backed by debts other than mortgages, such as loans or bonds.

Bond Indentures

For any bond, the interest rate, frequency of interest payments, maturity date, characteristics of the bond (e.g. convertibility, callability), and the principal amount need to be disclosed in a contract between the bond issuer and the bond buyer. This contract is called an **indenture**.

Flat Trades for Bonds

A **flat trade** for a bond occurs if the bond is traded to another investor without accrued interest being included in the price. This can occur either because no interest has actually generated, or because the bond is in default. -Compare this with the meaning of "flat trades" for equity securities, which has the related meaning of "breaking even." A stock trades flat if it is sold for the same price at which it was purchased.

Taxation of Bonds

Bondholders' income normally comes from the periodic interest payments of the bond. However, discounts and premiums make things slightly more complicated. For tax purposes, any discount on a bond has to be **accreted** (*increased*) on a straight-line basis over the bond's term; the annual accretion amount is then added to the investor's reported income on the bond. The opposite occurs for bonds purchased at a premium. Premiums are **amortized** (*decreased*), with the annual amortization amount being subtracted from the investor's reported income. For example, suppose an investor purchased at 95 a 10-year bond with a face value of $1,000 and stated rate of 6%. The discount of $50 would be accreted at a rate of $5 per year, and so the bondholder's reported income for each year would be $65 ($60 interest + $5 accretion). Bonds that are originally issued at a discount are unsurprisingly called **original issue discounts (OIDs)**.

Taxation of Municipal Bonds

Gains from investments on municipal bonds are ordinarily not taxed. **Taxable municipal bonds** can be issued if the purpose of the bond revenue has no clear public benefit, but most municipal bonds are tax-exempt. This means not only that coupon payments are not taxed, but also that gains from original issue discount (OID) bonds are tax-exempt as well. Accretion on the discount of municipal OID bonds is treated as tax-exempt interest income. Discounts on municipal bonds purchased in the secondary market are not even accreted. These are the only bonds whose discounts are not accreted.

CAPITAL GAINS AND LOSSES ON BONDS

Accretion of **bond discounts** and amortization of **bond premiums** affect not only reported income but also capital gains and losses on bonds. For example, suppose a bondholder purchased at 95 a 10-year bond with a face value of $1,000 and stated rate of 6%. Suppose this bondholder sold the bond to another investor for 105, 5 years after the bond's issuance. If so, the capital gain on the sale would be $75—the difference between $1,050 (the selling price) and $975 (the $950 buying price plus $25 accretion over five years).

TERM BONDS AND SERIAL BONDS

Any particular bond always has a particular maturity date, but bond issuers can attempt to strategically issue bonds of different durations for the sake of financing their own activities. **Term bonds** are bonds of the same issuance which have the same maturity date, whereas **serial bonds** mature at different (though regular) intervals.

Corporate Bonds

BOND

A bond is a debt instrument, or debt security. Unlike stockowners, investors who purchase **bonds** receive no ownership in the company and no voting rights. Bonds are issued by private companies, by the federal government, and by state and local governments (municipal bonds) to raise money for various projects, or for operating expenses. The value of bonds fluctuates with interest rates, and not with the success of the company or the stock market. Should a company go bankrupt, bond owners are compensated before stockholders if there are any assets to be liquidated. For this reason, bonds are called *senior securities*.

BOND RATINGS

Many bonds are rated by **bond rating companies**. The three best known are *Moody's*, *Standard & Poor's*, and *Fitch*. These companies assign ratings to bonds based on their evaluation of the creditworthiness of the bond issuer. They evaluate such things as how much debt the company has and the company's ability to manage it, how much cash flow the company can reasonably expect, and the history and performance of the company and its managers at handling debt. As a company's circumstances change, their bond rating can be upgraded or downgraded.

CALL PROVISIONS ON BONDS

Call provisions are arrangements on bonds stating that the bond issuer has the right to purchase back and retire the bond. These provisions ordinarily establish a timeframe when the call can occur, including details on the price and accrued interest paid to the bondholders. Bond issuers will call bonds if the market interest rate is lower than the bond rate, so that they can refinance their bonds to pay less interest. Due to the risk this places on bond investors, bonds with call provisions have a higher yield. A particular type of call provision is a *make whole call*, whose aim is to properly compensate bond investors for future interest revenues they do not receive because of a bond call. With a make whole call provision, the bond issuer will be required to pay a lump sum equal to the net present value (NPV) of the future interest payments at the time of the call.

SECURED BONDS

Secured bonds are bonds backed by some collateral, such that if the issuer defaults, the bond investor has claims on the collateralized asset. *Mortgage bonds* are bonds secured by a mortgage on property owned by the issuer. The issuer would then have to liquidate this asset to repay the bondholder if he defaults. *Equipment trusts* are bonds issued by transportation companies backed by the assets they employ, such as trucks or airplanes.

Collateral trusts are bonds backed by financial assets, such as stocks and other bonds. *Guaranteed bonds* are bonds backed by the promise of a firm besides the issuer, ordinarily a parent company. In the case of trusts, the collateralized assets are under the authority of a third-party trustee.

UNSECURED BONDS

Unsecured bonds differ from secured corporate bonds because there is no collateral behind them, which means they're riskier than secured bonds. The two main types of **unsecured corporate bonds** are debentures and subordinated debentures. Holders of *debentures* are treated like other business creditors in the event of liquidation due to bankruptcy; they collect only if any assets remain after employees, taxes, and secured creditors are paid. But they do come before holders of *subordinated debentures*. Because of this, subordinated debenture investments usually have higher rates of return to make them more attractive to investors.

ZERO-COUPON BONDS AND STEP-UP BONDS

Zero-coupon bonds don't pay interest. Instead, their price is heavily discounted from face value. When the bond matures, bondholders receive the full face value, but they gain no interest in the meantime. **Zero-coupon bonds** cost much less to purchase, but are extremely sensitive to changes in interest rates. Small changes in interest rates can have a huge impact on zero-coupon bonds (much more so than on regular bonds), since the present value of the bond is based entirely on the maturity-date payment and not on any coupon payments. Because the investors profit simply from the principal increase, these are also called *capital appreciation bonds*. **Step-up bonds** are bonds whose interest rate increases over the term of the bond. The bond contract specifies how the coupon payments grow over time.

CONVERTIBLE BONDS

Convertible bonds are bonds that can be converted into a stated quantity of shares of the issuing company's stock. This makes them attractive to investors because they combine features of both financial instruments—they pay interest, which is regular income, and they can also appreciate if the company's stock appreciates. If the stock goes up, the holder of a convertible bond can choose to convert them to stocks, or sell the bond on the market, and receive a premium to reflect the appreciation of the stock. Some **convertible bonds** give the issuer the right to *force conversions*, forcing bondholders to convert their convertible bonds into stock. Companies who force conversions usually do so to refinance their bonds if a lower interest rate is available.

PARITY, CONVERSION RATIO, AND PARITY PRICE FOR CONVERTIBLE BONDS

Parity occurs when a convertible bond is trading on the market for the same price as the stock to which it can be converted. The **conversion ratio** gives the number of shares a convertible bond may be converted into. It is calculated by the following formula:

Conversion ratio = (par value of bond) / (conversion price of stock)

For instance, for a bond with a par value of $1,000 and a conversion price of $20, the conversion ratio would be 50 shares. Since the **parity price** of the bond is the price equivalent to the value of the underlying stock, its formula is as follows:

Parity price = (market price of stock) x (conversion ratio)

For instance, if the conversion ratio is 50 shares, and if the stock is trading on the market at $22/share, then the parity price of the bond would be $1,100 (a premium of $100 over par).

ARBITRAGE TRADING

Arbitrage is a highly specialized trading strategy that seeks to take advantages of differences in prices between different securities, different markets, or the same securities in different markets. Sometimes a stock will trade for slightly different prices on two different exchanges; arbitragers will take advantage of this price differential to make a quick profit. Other arbitragers specialize in corporate takeovers—buying the company being taken over and short selling the company doing the takeover. There are many different kinds of arbitrage, but they all require highly technical knowledge, and many of them can be extremely risky. *Convertible bond arbitrage* seeks to capitalize on any discrepancy between a convertible bond and the underlying stock.

Municipal Securities

MUNICIPAL BONDS

There are three main types of municipal bonds, categorized according to the way that the bond repayments can be financed. **General obligation (GO) bonds** are the first type. These are issued to pay for improvements that benefit a community, but don't produce income. They are also known as "full faith and credit issues," because they are repaid from tax revenue raised by the issuing government entity. **Revenue bonds** are issued by governments to finance projects and facilities that are expected to generate enough revenue to pay bondholders back without resorting to tax money. **Double-barreled bonds** are revenue bonds that also have the backing of the taxing authority. They are considered GO bonds, even though they depend primarily on revenue generated from the project for repayment.

LTGO BONDS

Limited-tax general obligation (LTGO) bonds repay the bondholders solely through taxation (as all general obligations do), but contains provisions limiting how much the municipality can increase taxes to repay the bonds. This increases the risk of these bonds and thus increases their return as well.

SHORT-TERM MUNICIPAL OBLIGATIONS

There are a number of different ways for municipalities to fund immediate projects with short-term (one year or less) debt securities, classified according to the means of repaying the debt:

- **Tax anticipation notes (TANs)** are issued for an immediate activity or project, which are expected to be repaid with taxes.
- **Bond anticipation notes (BANs)** are similar to TANs, except that the debts are expected to be paid off through the later issuance of bonds.
- **Revenue anticipation notes (RANs)** are similar to the above two, except that the debts are expected to be paid off through the project's own revenue.
- **Tax and revenue anticipation notes (TRANs)** are expected to be paid off with both taxes and revenues.
- **Grant anticipation notes (GANs)** are issued by municipalities who expect to repay the debts with grants from the federal government.
- **Tax-exempt commercial paper** is a short-term loan which gives the investor (lender) various tax benefits at the local, state, or federal levels.

SPECIAL TAX BONDS AND SPECIAL ASSESSMENT BONDS

Special tax bonds are municipal bonds where bondholders are repaid through a particular tax levied specifically for their repayment. Generally, this tax will be related to the project which the bonds have funded. For example, an excise tax on tobacco might repay bondholders whose bonds funded some public hospital venture. **Special assessment bonds** are municipal bonds where bondholders are repaid through the taxation of the particular community which receives the benefits. For example, if a public playground or park is built in some community, then the property taxes of that community might increase to pay off the bondholders, according to the likelihood that such people would utilize it.

MORAL OBLIGATION BONDS

Moral obligation bonds are municipal bonds where the municipality adds a moral pledge to repay the bondholders, with this pledge backed by a reserve fund established in case of default or any other failure to pay. This is a merely moral obligation, not a legally binding one, yet municipalities have an additional incentive to keep their word, since their credit rating would suffer otherwise.

COP

A **certificate of participation (COP)** grants an investor the right to some lease revenues for a facility that is constructed through a municipal bond issuance. Rather than entitling the investor to the rights of the bondholder, a COP participates in the ownership of the facility and the municipality leases it until all the lease payments are made. COPs provide investors with a solid backup plan if the municipality defaults, for they then can sell or utilize the facility as they see fit.

MANDATORY REDEMPTION SCHEDULES

Mandatory redemption schedules lay out specific dates at which a bond issuer is required to call (redeem) outstanding bonds, either all of the bonds in an issuance or only some. Some **mandatory redemption schedules** require the issuer to call various outstanding bonds when a certain amount of cash is available in a bond sinking fund.

EXTRAORDINARY REDEMPTION

Extraordinary redemption refers to bonds that are called by the issuer due to some event that is both unusual and infrequent. There must be a provision for this kind of **extraordinary redemption** laid out in the bond contract. An example of an event which could permit issuers to call outstanding bonds is a disaster which prevents the construction of, or outright destroys, the project financed by the bonds. Another example is if the interest on the bonds was originally planned to be non-taxable, but bond proceeds must be used in such a way that they are now taxable.

PUTTABLE BONDS

A put is the right to sell something to someone. Some bonds, usually municipal bonds, contain a put option. These are known as **puttable bonds**. A bondholder with a puttable bond has the right, after a specified amount of time, to sell the bond back to the issuer at face value, or **par**. Once the put option date has been reached, the bondholder has the right once a year to sell it back at par, and the issuer has the obligation to buy it back at par. This gives bond buyers added protection against changes in interest rates, and makes their bonds more attractive on the open market.

BOND REFUNDING AND PRE-REFUNDING

Bond refunding is when an issuer sells a new bond issue in order to raise money to redeem a previous bond issue. This is done to take advantage of lower interest rates. **Bond refunding** becomes more likely as bonds get closer to the maturity date. **Pre-refunding** is when the issuer sells a new set of bonds at a lower interest rate, but doesn't call the previous issue of bonds. The proceeds from the sale are placed in escrow and used to buy federal government securities, and the interest received is used to call the previous issue at the first call date. This is also known as advance refunding. Bonds that are pre-refunded have the highest possible bond rating, as the risk of default is virtually nil.

CROSSOVER REFUNDING

Crossover refunding refers to a particular way in which a municipality may issue new bonds to pay off older bonds. When the new bonds are issued, which are called *refunding bonds*, their proceeds are placed in an escrow account (i.e. a third-party account). These proceeds are used to pay off interest payments on the refunding bonds until the older bonds arrive at their maturity date, at which point the proceeds are then used to repay those older debts.

Factors That Affect Bond Liquidity

The following affect **bond liquidity**:

- how well-known or widely owned they are
- the bond *rating* (higher rating → easier trades)
- the *quality* of the bond issuer
- how *mature* the bond is
- how high the *interest rate* is
- whether it is trading at, above, or below *par*
- whether it has any *call features*

Odd First Coupon Bonds

Odd first coupon bonds are bonds whose first coupon comes after an irregular period, either shorter or longer than all the other coupon bonds. Since bonds ordinarily have coupon periods of six months, **odd first coupon bonds** are ones issued in the midst of these six-month intervals. If the first coupon period is shorter than the other periods, the bond has an *odd short first coupon*, and if it is longer, then it has an *odd long first coupon*.

Day-Count Conventions

Day-count conventions are systems used to determine how many days exist between bond coupon payments. This might seem strange, since it would seem to be a simple matter of counting the actual days. But such a method is simply one option—namely, the actual **day-count convention**. A common convention is the *30/360 day-count convention*, which assumes 30 days per month and thus 360 days per year for the sake of simple calculations with uniform periods.

Tax-Equivalent Yield

The tax-equivalent yield is the yield that a taxable bond needs to have before taxes in order to achieve the same return as a nontaxable bond.

Tax-equivalent yield = (desired yield) / (1 – tax rate)

For example, if a nontaxable bond had a yield of 18% and the tax rate were 12%, then any taxable bonds, to be more valuable to the investor, would need to have a yield of 20.45% (18% / 88%).

Federal, State, and Local Taxation for Municipal Bonds

Investors need not pay any taxes on interest income from **municipal bonds**, although they may have to pay state or local taxes, depending on their laws. U.S. territories (including American Samoa, Guam, Puerto Rico, and the Virgin Islands) and federal districts (Washington, D.C.) are triple tax-free regarding municipal bonds. Bondholders don't have any federal, state, or local taxes to pay on interest. Most states, but not all, are triple tax-free regarding municipal bonds for investors purchasing bonds issued within their own state. Despite all these tax exemptions for interest income, *capital gains* from the sales of bonds are still taxable.

Bank Qualified Bonds

Banks like the benefit of tax-exempt interest earned on municipal bonds. But with the *Tax Reform Act of 1986*, banks can't deduct the carrying cost of holding municipal bonds in inventory; that is, they can't deduct the interest expenses which are incurred to purchase or carry those bonds. This tends to negate the benefits of tax-exempt interest income. But there are exceptions to this rule which allow banks to deduct 80% of the carrying cost on particular bonds. Specifically, if the bonds are issued by a qualified small issuer (i.e. an issuer that issues $10 million in tax-exempt bonds or less yearly), issued for some public purpose, and designated as tax-exempt, then they qualify. These types of bonds are often called **bank qualified bonds**.

Managed Investments

Mutual Funds

OPEN-END MANAGEMENT

Investment companies are classified into three separate categories according to the *Investment Company Act of 1940*. Of the three, the most common kind is the **management investment company (MIC)**. There are two types of management investment companies: open-end and closed-end. Open-end MICs are more commonly known as *mutual funds*. They are called open-end because there is no limit to the number of shares that can issue. Unlike closed-end management investment companies (MICs), open-end MICs do not issue a fixed number of shares. When they register with the SEC, they do so as an open offering, which gives them the right to raise more investment capital by issuing and selling shares continuously. In addition, the shares of open-end MICs do not trade on the secondary market. Anyone who wants to purchase shares must buy them directly from the MIC, and the *offering price* is determined by dividing the net asset value of the MIC by the number of shares outstanding and then adding a sales charge. Fractional shares can be bought, not just whole shares. And when a shareholder wants to sell, the shareholder must sell the shares back to the company, not on the secondary market.

BENEFITS OF MUTUAL FUNDS

There are many reasons it makes sense for investors to choose to invest by way of **mutual funds** instead of selecting their own stocks. They may have little or no experience in investing, and can feel bewildered at all the investing options available today. A mutual fund solves this problem. A professional experienced investment adviser uses his knowledge and skill for the investors' benefit. Their investment dollars are automatically diversified, giving them the benefit of reduced risk and opportunities for gains in several areas. The cost to get started is often only a few hundred dollars. A professional custodian protects their investment. In addition, all investors in a mutual fund are on an equal footing, since there's no such thing as preferred stock, and everyone owns the same class of shares. And should the investor decide to liquidate their holdings, the mutual fund is required to buy them instantly.

VALUE FUNDS

Value funds are mutual funds which aim to hold stocks that have an undervalued price and tend to pay out dividends. Since the share prices are undervalued, they are expected to rise in time and give the fund investors capital gains.

GROWTH FUNDS

Growth funds are only suitable for aggressive investors who are comfortable with a high degree of risk. Because growth funds invest in younger, less established companies that are growing fast, the risk with this type of fund is greater than that of investing in an index fund of established companies across the spectrum of the American economy. **Growth funds** are for people who are looking for maximum capital gains and are not interested in income, as the types of corporations in which growth funds invest do not pay dividends.

INCOME FUNDS

Income funds, like index funds, are generally considered more conservative, and are more suitable for investors with a strong aversion to risk. **Income funds** are not designed for capital gains, or for spectacular contrarian plays, but for safe, predictable, steady income. They buy shares of companies who are well established and have been paying dividends for a long time.

COMBINATION MUTUAL FUNDS

Combination mutual funds are a cross between, or combination of, growth funds and income funds. In fact, they are often referred to as *growth and income funds*. Managers of these funds spend some of their money on shares of companies with lots of growth potential, and some of it on well established companies with a strong dividend history. Not as risky as a pure growth fund, and not as conservative as a pure income fund, these funds are popular with investors who are seeking a balanced portfolio.

BALANCED FUNDS

Balanced funds, unlike many mutual funds, invest in both stocks and bonds. For this reason, **balanced mutual funds** are also commonly known as *hybrid funds*. The objective is a balance between capital gains and income. The general mix is 60 percent stocks to 40 percent bonds, although this is not a hard and fast rule, and many fund managers use their own ratio, especially as market conditions change. Balanced funds are considered to be pretty suitable for all investors.

INTERNATIONAL FUNDS

International funds are not usually suitable for investors with low tolerances to risk. **International funds** can post spectacular gains, but the risks attendant to investing in foreign companies is very high. Some funds are made up of shares of companies from around the world, while many of them focus on buying shares of companies in one particular country or region. Many of these countries and regions do not have the economic history and political stability that we enjoy in the United States. Foreign funds are therefore only suitable for investors who understand the risks and are comfortable with them.

SECTOR FUNDS

Sector funds invest in only one area, or sector, of the stock market, or one industry, etc. Many popular **sector funds** are in gold mining stocks, utility stocks, technology stocks, etc. While generally not as high-risk as foreign funds and special situation funds, there is certainly risk attached to investing in a sector fund. It is the risk of putting all your eggs in one basket. Many sector funds pop up only after the sector has had a huge run up, and investors are clamoring to get in on the market. By then, many times market conditions have changed and future investors don't get the same returns, and in fact often experience losses. Sector funds are for investors who know what they're doing, and understand that sector investing may not be the riskiest kind of fund, but it is also not the safest. Sector funds are also called *specialized mutual funds*.

INDEX FUNDS

Index mutual funds are one of the more conservative mutual fund choices. Because these funds deliberately choose stocks to achieve the same performance as a broad based market index, (often the S&P 500), the portfolio will usually achieve roughly the same rate of return as the general market. Generally speaking, there is not much risk with this kind of approach, and there usually is not opportunity for extraordinary profits, although there are obviously exceptions to both of these rules. But many investors like this approach, and because of the much lower number of trades involved in an index fund, costs are often much lower than with other types of funds.

ASSET ALLOCATION FUNDS

Asset allocation funds are generally considered to be less risky than most other types. These funds allocate their assets between stocks, bonds, and cash, depending on market conditions. **Asset**

allocation funds will also adjust the percentages of each allocation as conditions change—it's not necessarily a uniform split among the three. Risk is lessened, but as always, with lower risk comes lower potential gains. For investors primarily concerned with safety, asset allocation funds are a good choice.

LIFE-CYCLE FUNDS

Life-cycle funds are a type of asset allocation fund that change the investment allocation as the investor ages. If the investor is younger, the allocation will involve stocks to increase risk, but as the investor ages, the allocation will involve more bonds to decrease risk. Since this is based on the age of the investor, these funds are also called *age-based funds*.

MONEY MARKET FUNDS

Investors use **money market funds** to park cash while they are out of the market. They receive interest income, and have maximum liquidity, and generally face lower risk than with securities. Money market interest rates are always changing, and the net asset value is always at one dollar, although this is not actually guaranteed. During times of volatility in the stock markets, many investors will look to money market funds for liquidity and capital preservation.

NAV

Net asset value (NAV) is the value of one share of a mutual fund. NAV is always changing, and must be calculated every day at the end of the trading day. Although it is quite a complicated calculation, in principle it is very simple. The fund's total liabilities are subtracted from the fund's total assets, which leaves the net asset value of the fund. That figure is then divided by the total number of shares outstanding, which gives the NAV per share. Usually, when NAV is mentioned, it refers to share NAV, not fund NAV. There are only two things that cause a mutual fund's share net asset value to rise. One is when *new investors* come in and add cash to the mutual fund. The second is when the *value of the securities* in their portfolio goes up. Just the same, there are only two things that drive down a share's net asset value. One is when capital gains and/or income are *paid out* to shareholders. The other is when the value of the *portfolio securities* decreases. The buying and selling of stocks have no effect on net asset value, and when the fund redeems investors' shares, there is no effect on net asset value, because cash is being traded for securities, and vice versa.

FORWARD PRICING AND LATE TRADING

Since the net asset value (NAV) of open-end mutual fund shares is recalculated at the end of each trading day, and since investors wish to buy or sell mutual fund shares during the day, there has to be a sensible way to put a price tag on their transaction. This is done by **forward pricing**: using the next available NAV for each share bought or sold. This ordinarily involves waiting for the NAV to be computed at the end of the trading day. **Late trading** involves purchasing mutual fund shares after the market has closed for the day but still obtaining that day's closing price, not the next day's price. This practice is illegal.

PUBLIC OFFERING PRICE OF A MUTUAL FUND SHARE

A mutual fund's **public offering price** is the price the general public pays, no matter if they buy the share directly from the fund, or from a dealer, or from an underwriter, or a combination of any of the above. Broker/dealers and underwriters get a discount from the public offering price (POP) and they make their money on the difference between what they pay the fund for the shares and what they charge the investing public for the shares.

AUTOMATIC REINVESTMENT OF DISTRIBUTIONS IN MUTUAL FUNDS

Mutual funds must offer **automatic reinvestment of distributions** in order to be allowed to charge the maximum sales charge of 8.5 percent. Additionally, many mutual funds that don't charge the maximum also allow automatic reinvestment of distributions. Normally, investors in mutual funds would receive any dividends and/or capital gains in cash, by a check issued by the mutual fund. However, customers of funds that offer automatic reinvestment of distributions may choose to have their dividends and capital gains automatically reinvested in the mutual fund instead of receiving cash.

FAMILIES OF FUNDS AND CONVERSION PRIVILEGES

Many mutual fund companies offer more than one mutual fund. It is quite common for mutual fund companies to offer many, many choices for investors with different investment goals, or to provide for investors who want to divide their portfolio for balance, diversification, and risk aversion. The group of funds offered by an individual mutual fund company is known as a **family of funds**. Many mutual fund companies allow investors in their fund to transfer their money in and out of different funds in the family without incurring sales charges. This is known as a **conversion (exchange) privilege.**

NO-LOAD FUNDS

Many mutual funds charge a **load**, or *fee*, to investors who participate in the fund. This fee goes to reimburse underwriters and dealers who market the fund to investors. But a mutual fund can choose to distribute its shares to investors without using underwriters and dealers. If they do so, and therefore don't charge a fee to cover their sales expense, they are known as a **no-load fund**. In addition, a 12b-1 fund with a 12b-1 fee of 0.25% or less is also classified as a no-load fund.

12B-1 FEES

12b-1 fees are fees paid annually on mutual funds, ordinarily between 0.25% and 1% of the fund's net assets, to cover marketing and distribution costs for the fund. Their name is based upon the section from the *Investment Company Act of 1940* bringing them into existence. When originally created, the fee was thought to help investors, since the marketing and distribution benefits presumably outweighed the cost of the fee. That assumption is more challenged today, however.

LOAD FUNDS

Load funds may market and distribute their shares through one of two ways: (1) utilizing an underwriter only, who sells the shares to the investing public, or (2) utilizing an underwriter who sells the shares to brokers and dealers, with the brokers and dealers then selling the shares to the investing public. In either case, there is a profit built into the process for all parties between the fund and the investor. This is what the load is for, to cover sales expenses.

FRONT-END LOADS AND BACK-END LOADS

When mutual funds use broker/dealers or underwriters to sell their shares to the public, they must pay for their services. To cover these sales and marketing services, mutual funds charge a fee, called a load. Loads vary fund by fund, but by law they cannot exceed 8.5 percent of the public offering price. Mutual funds that use a **front-end load** charge the fee when the investor buys shares. When a mutual fund charges the fee when the investor withdraws shares (instead of when the investor buys the shares), it is called a **back-end load**. Back-end loads encourage investors to invest for the long-term because the load decreases the longer the investor holds the shares. If investors hold the shares long enough, the load eventually drops to zero. Because of this feature, back-end loads are also known as contingent deferred loads.

CALCULATION OF LOAD

There is a simple way of **calculating a mutual fund's load**. If you know the public offering price, and the net asset value per share, you can subtract the NAV from the POP. This will give you the load in dollars. You then divide that figure by the POP, and you'll have the load expressed as a percentage. Likewise, to determine the public offering price, simply add the dollar amount of the load to the net asset value.

DOLLAR-COST AVERAGING

Dollar-cost averaging is a popular method of investing in mutual funds. **Dollar-cost averaging** occurs when a customer invests a fixed amount of money into a mutual fund on a regular basis— every month, every three months, etc. It is popular because it requires no decision making, and because it allows the investor to buy more shares when the price is lower. On the other hand, if share values don't fluctuate much, but trend in one direction, dollar-cost averaging can be less than ideal. When shares are trending sharply up, the investor's money buys fewer and fewer shares of something that's becoming more and more valuable. Conversely, when the value of the shares is going downhill, the investor is buying more and more shares that are becoming less and less valuable, and the investor has no guarantee that the value will ever turn around and begin rising again.

CLASSES OF SHARES IN MUTUAL FUNDS

Although all mutual fund shares are common stock, and mutual funds do not issue preferred stock, there are three classifications of shares bought by investors in the funds. What separates the three is the amount of the sales charges the investor will pay, and the manner in which the investor pays them. **Class A shares** are bought with a front-end load, and the load can be lowered by investing in large enough amounts to qualify for breakpoints. **Class B shares** are bought with a back-end load, which decreases over time. **Class C shares** are 12b-1 shares.

REDEMPTION OF MUTUAL FUND SHARES

Mutual fund shares are not traded on the secondary market. An investor buys them directly from the company, or one of its underwriters or broker/dealers. When a mutual fund shareholder wants to sell, the mutual fund company **redeems the shares**; that is, the mutual fund company buys the shares back. When shares are redeemed, they are destroyed, as mutual funds are constantly issuing new shares. When a customer notifies the mutual fund company that he wants to sell his shares back, the company must redeem the shares within seven calendar days, except in extraordinary circumstances.

SYSTEMATIC MUTUAL FUND WITHDRAWAL PLANS

Many mutual funds allow investors to withdraw funds on a pre-planned, systematic basis. These methods are called **withdrawal plans**. There are three basic approaches to systematic withdrawal. The first is when the customer wants to receive a *fixed dollar amount* at every interval. In this case, the fund redeems however many shares necessary at the current net asset value to raise the amount of money requested by the customer. The second is where the customer doesn't specify a fixed dollar amount, but rather specifies a *fixed percentage* or number of shares to be redeemed at every interval. Lastly, the customer may choose to redeem shares over a stated amount of time, known as a *fixed-time withdrawal plan*.

RESTRICTIONS ON MUTUAL FUND REDEMPTION

Since mutual funds differ from ordinary stocks, in that shares are constantly being newly issued or destroyed upon redemption, the situation for mutual funds is more vulnerable than for other stock transactions. Consequently, there are various **restrictions on mutual fund redemption** to protect mutual funds from a rapid or sudden redemption of fund shares.

TAXATION OF MUTUAL FUND'S INVESTOR'S PROFITS

The tax rate that a mutual fund investor pays depends on several different factors, and **tax rates** can be quite different, depending on how the profit being taxed was derived. Income from dividends is simply taxed at the 15 percent rate. But realized capital gains are divided into two categories, *short-term* and *long-term.* Long-term capital gains are capital gains realized from the sale of securities held for longer than a year, and they're taxed at the capital gains rate of 15 percent. Capital gains realized from the sale of securities held for less than a year are taxed at regular income tax rates.

Other Investments

CLOSED-END MANAGEMENT INVESTMENT COMPANIES

There are two types of management investment companies (MICs)—open-end and closed-end. **Closed-end MICs** are commonly known as *publicly traded funds*. They are called closed-end because they issue a fixed quantity of shares. Open-end funds have an indefinite number of shares, but closed-end funds have a finite number.

CLOSED-END MANAGEMENT INVESTMENT COMPANIES

When closed-end management investment companies begin trading, they issue a **fixed number of shares** that are available for purchase by the public, issued at the IPO price. These shares then trade on the secondary market, just like other securities. They may also issue preferred stocks and sell bonds. Unlike in open-end funds, in closed-end funds only whole shares can be bought (never fractional shares). The market determines the price of a share of a closed-end MIC. Moreover, while open-end funds always trade their shares at their NAV, closed-end funds, being subject to the forces and influences of the secondary market, can sell with a premium or discount to their NAV.

UITs

One type of investment company is the **unit investment trust (UIT).** Unit investment trusts operate by issuing shares entitling the owner to a portion of the investment portfolio owned by the trust. These shares can't be sold on the market, but only bought back, or redeemed, by the trust itself, and the trust is obligated to purchase them when an investor wants to sell. Unit investment trusts don't have boards of directors, and they don't have investment managers or advisers (and thus no fees for them). They usually invest in government bonds or in mutual funds. Since UITs are not traded on the secondary market and have a finite number of shares that must be redeemed with the original issuer, one of their characteristics is *limited liquidity*.

TYPES OF UNIT INVESTMENT TRUSTS AND CLOSED-END FUNDS

There are a variety of mutual funds depending on the investments which the funds make. These include *growth, income, balanced, sector, international*, and other types of funds. Other investment companies, such as unit investment trusts and closed-end funds, can likewise have these different kinds of funds, even though (open-end) mutual funds tend to have the greatest variety.

ETFs

Exchange-traded funds (ETFs) are types of mutual funds which are, like stocks, traded on an exchange. Many **exchange-traded funds** are designed to track an index, which is a passive type of investing and so requires smaller managing fees. Thus, the advantage of ETFs is that they provide the diversification which comes with mutual funds, the lower fees which come with index funds, and the flexibility of trade which comes with ordinary shares of stock.

REITs

Real estate investment trusts (REITs) are a specialized type of investment in real estate that trade on the stock market, and which have special tax advantages for investors. To qualify as a REIT, and thus to avoid being taxed as a corporation, a trust must (1) derive at least 75% of its income from real estate-related activity, (2) hold at least 75% of its assets in real estate, government securities, or cash, and (3) distribute 90% of its profits to shareholders. That rule is one of the things that make an REIT such an attractive investment. An REIT is organized as a trust, but it is bought and sold just like a common stock on a stock exchange. Shares are sold to raise capital for large real estate projects, usually commercial. Though REITs are like mutual funds in that they pool investors' money and distribute shares, they are unlike mutual funds in that they have a *finite number of shares*. Related to this, while REIT securities are originally issued at their initial public offering (IPO) price, they can also be traded on the secondary market; investors are not limited from purchasing REIT shares directly issued by the issuer. And since REITs can be traded on the secondary market, shares will not simply be priced at their net asset value (NAV), but can move above or below NAV, according to market dynamics and sentiments.

There are three different kinds of real estate investment trusts (REITs):

- *Equity REITs* purchase real estate equity, owning real estate and making profit off of rent revenue or capital gains when the real estate is sold.
- *Mortgage REITs* purchase various debt securities related to real estate, such as construction loans and mortgages. The income from mortgage REITs is therefore based on interest.
- *Hybrid REITs* are combinations of the above two, investing in both equity and debt securities related to real estate.

TAX TREATMENT

Unfortunately for investors, dividends from REITs are often taxed at the same rate as ordinary income. Yet, certain dividends are "**qualified dividends**" and are thus eligible to be taxed at capital gains rates. Furthermore, some portions of dividends can qualify as returns of capital, in which case they are not taxed at all.

FOFS AND HEDGE FUNDS

Funds of funds (FOFs) are investments that invest in other funds, rather than investing directly in securities such as stocks or bonds. It can also be called *multi-manager investment*. **Hedge funds** are private investment funds that are legally restricted to very wealthy individuals, individuals who have an income surpassing the requisite threshold and at least a $1 million net worth. Hedge funds are, in essence, mutual funds for the super wealthy. Hedge funds are similar in structure to mutual funds, but they are dissimilar in that they are unregulated (because private) and thus have a wider array of investment options. Hedge funds are characteristically *very risky and speculative*, using purchases on margin, short sales, and other higher-risk investment strategies to aggressively make a profit. Hedge funds' riskiness seems to contradict their name, since hedging is the reduction of risk—but the reason for the name is that, when hedge funds historically arose, one of their main purposes was to hedge against the risk of a bear market by selling short. Hedge funds have very limited liquidity, often keeping investors' money for at least one year. For tax purposes, hedge funds will be arranged as limited partnerships, so that they will qualify as flow-through entities. The manager of the fund (or an affiliate) will be the general partner, and the investors will be limited partners.

BLIND POOLS

Blind pools are stock offerings or limited partnerships that pool together investment money without having any stated objectives for the fund. The reason investors are willing to invest in **blind pools** is due to the reputation of the individuals or company managing the fund. Some blind pools have a good reputation, but naturally, this is very prone to fraud. Blind pools are also called *blank-check offerings*.

PRIVATE EQUITY

Private equity consists of any equity which isn't quoted on any public exchanges. Private investments might involve funding a private company to develop new technologies, or simply to be more successful in general. **Private equity** also might involve purchasing a public company for the sake of making it private. Private equity often involves investors with enormous amounts of capital.

STRUCTURED PRODUCTS

Structured products are securities which are linked to some other underlying asset, such as another security, a group of securities, a commodity, and index, or something else. **Structured products** can sometimes have a "principal guarantee" feature, which means simply that the principal is guaranteed to return if the investor holds the investment for long enough (e.g. to maturity for debt securities).

Annuities

ANNUITY

Life insurance companies sell **annuities**. Purchasers of annuities are buying a regular payment from the company, guaranteed for life. This guarantee makes an annuity different from virtually all other investments. Purchasers make either a one-time lump sum payment or a series of regular payments, and later they are entitled to regular withdrawals of income payments. Annuities can also have *riders*: provisions built into the policy but purchased as a separate entity, entitling the annuitant to additional benefits other than the usual coverage. For example, a life insurance could have, as a rider, an "accelerated death benefit," which permits the policy holder to receive some of the coverage before death, such as in the case of severe illness. The coverage provided by the company at the policy holder's death would then be reduced by the accelerated amount. But in order to have this accelerated benefit, it would have to be separately purchased as a rider on the ordinary life insurance contract.

FIXED ANNUITY AND VARIABLE ANNUITY

A fixed annuity guarantees a specific rate of return. Investors' premiums are deposited into the insurance company's general accounts. **Fixed annuities** are not considered securities, because all the risk is on the insurance company, not the buyer. **Variable annuities** are considered securities, because the purchaser is taking the risk. With variable annuities, investors' monies are deposited into an account separate from the insurance company's general account, and the company invests these funds. Variable annuities guarantee payments for life, but don't guarantee the amount of the payments or the rate of return on the investment.

SURRENDER CHARGES AND MORTALITY AND EXPENSE CHARGES

Surrender charges are fees paid based upon an undue cancellation of some account or policy, occurring most often with life insurance policies. The **surrender charge** is meant to cover the cost for keeping the account on the books, and therefore is usually waived for individuals who notify the insurance company of the cancellation sufficiently in advance. **Mortality and expense charges** are fees included in variable annuities. When a life insurance company provides an annuity to some customer, the company calculates risks such as the life expectancy of the annuitant and charges a fee based upon these risks.

VARIABLE ANNUITY PHASES

The time during which the purchaser of an annuity is paying into the annuity, up until the time the purchaser begins receiving income payments, is called the **accumulation phase**. The period after payments begin is called the **annuity phase**. The purchase is accumulating units, which are called either *accumulation units* or *annuity units,* and which determine how much the purchaser receives during the annuity phase.

DEATH OF ANNUITY PURCHASER

There is generally a long period of time between the purchase of an annuity and the time before payments begin. If the purchaser should die, in most cases the annuity's **beneficiary** will get all the money the purchaser paid in plus any gains that have accumulated by the day of the purchaser's death. In cases where the account has lost money, the beneficiary will receive the total of what the purchaser paid in. The age of the beneficiary is not a factor, and the beneficiary is not subject to early withdrawal penalties.

PAYOUT OPTIONS OF ANNUITIES

There are three different options that from which annuity owners can choose when deciding how they want to receive their annuity. The first one is the simplest, and is called **life income**. With life income, the insurance company pays the annuitant until he dies; after the annuitant dies, no payments are given to beneficiaries. The second option is **life with period certain**. With this option, the annuitant chooses a period of either 10 or 20 years (the period certain). The annuitant will then be guaranteed payments for life, but if the annuitant dies before the period certain is over, his beneficiary receives payments for the rest of the period certain. The last option is **joint life with last survivor**. With this arrangement, two parties, usually husband and wife, are entitled to one payment, and when the first party dies, the other party receives the payments until his or her death.

MUTUAL FUNDS AND VARIABLE ANNUITIES

In many ways, variable annuities function just like a mutual fund. Money from large numbers of investors is pooled and invested for their mutual benefit in the insurance company's separate account, just as in a mutual fund. Many of these separate accounts are registered as open-end management investment companies. The big difference between **variable annuities** and **mutual funds** is that dividends and capital gains are not distributed to purchasers of variable annuities, and dividends and capital gains accumulate with taxes deferred until payout. Mutual funds distribute these gains and dividends, and their shareholders must pay taxes on the gains immediately.

SEPARATE ACCOUNTS FOR ANNUITIES

Separate accounts refer to specific investment accounts owned by an insurance company. These accounts are isolated from the insurance company's general investments, which means that they are not guaranteed by the insurance company (the investments provide a variable rate of return), although it also means that the investments are safe if the insurance company becomes insolvent.

ACCUMULATION UNITS AND ANNUITY UNITS

When the annuitant is contributing funds into an annuity, he actually purchases particular units. These units are **accumulation units**, and they vary in price; a series of fixed contributions by the annuitant might purchase more units or fewer, depending on the units. The value of accumulation units depends upon the performance of the underlying investments for the annuity. When it comes time for the annuitant to receive payouts (i.e. when the accumulation period has ended), the accumulation units will be converted into **annuity units**, and the annuitant will receive an equal number of annuity units per distribution.

IMMEDIATE PAYMENT ANNUITIES

Immediate payment annuities are annuities purchased with one lump sum, in which case distributions begin to occur immediately. **Immediate payment annuities** are suitable for retired persons who fear they may outlast their retirement savings, but since these annuity payments are cancelled upon the death of the annuitant, they carry the risk, in cases of early death, of significantly decreasing an inheritance.

WAIVER OF PREMIUM

A **waiver of premium** is a provision in an insurance contract which waives the policyholder of any obligation to pay further premiums but still be entitled to the insurance benefits. This waiver kicks in due to some serious disability for the policyholder and usually only after the policyholder has been disabled for some period of time (e.g. six months). To obtain this provision, a policyholder has to purchase it upfront with the insurance contract, and due to the risk, it can afford to the insurance company, policyholders must be sufficiently healthy and young to qualify.

ANNUITIZATION

Annuitization is the process by which an annuity investment is converted into payments. The *fixed annuitization method* takes the total account balance for the annuitant and divides it by a particular annuity factor (which factor is derived from an IRS table) to arrive at an equal payment that cannot later be changed. *The fixed amortization method* takes the total account balance and amortizes it over the annuitant's life expectancy, again using IRS tables. The interest rate to be used in the amortization cannot exceed 120% of the federal mid-term rate. As with the fixed annuitization method, this method fixes the periodic payments so that they may not be changed. The *required minimum distribution method* takes the account balance at December 31 of each year and divides it by the life expectancy of the annuitant, according to the same tables mentioned above. This method allows for different distributions depending on changes in the account balance and life expectancy.

AIR

The **assumed interest rate (AIR)** is the rate of growth, assumed by the insurance company, that is necessary for the underlying investments of an annuity to cover the insurance company's costs and provide the company with its target profit margin. The AIR enters into the calculation to determine an annuitant's periodic income payments.

TAXATION OF ANNUITIES

In the **accumulation period**, any growth on the underlying investment in an annuity has tax-deferred growth. The annuitant does not have to pay any taxes on it until the **distribution period.** The taxes paid on the payouts in the distribution period will be at the ordinary income tax rate. Although gains on investments will largely involve capital gains, tax regulations still require that annuity growth be taxed as ordinary income. The taxable amount will vary according to the nature of the payout. If it is one lump-sum payment, then the annuitant will pay taxes on all the investment growth at that point. If the payouts instead come in a series of periodic payments, then each payment will be considered as partly a return of the original investment (and thus nontaxable) and partly a gain on the investment (and thus taxable). Early withdrawals to annuities (before the age of 59 ½) are subject to a 10% penalty. Certain early withdrawals can be waived from this penalty, however, if they are for qualified reasons (e.g. purchasing a home, disability, or 55 and unemployed) and are distributed in a certain number of substantially equal periodic payments (SEPPs), at least five.

FIXED ANNUITIES

If an annuity gives periodic payments to the annuitant during the annuity's distribution period, then each payment will be considered as partly a return of the original investment (and thus nontaxable) and partly a gain on the investment (and thus taxable). For **fixed annuities** (annuities paying a series of fixed payments), the particular composition of principal and gain (i.e. original investment and gain) is determined by an exclusion ratio, which is calculated as follows:

Exclusion Ratio = Original Investment / Expected Total Payout

Since the original investment is nontaxable, then the percentage of each periodic payment attributable to that original investment will be excluded from taxes, hence the name of the ratio. The **expected total payout** is calculated by multiplying the fixed payment amount by the number of months the annuitant is expected to live, based on IRS tables. For example, if an annuitant paid $100,000 into an annuity with fixed monthly payments of $800 and was expected to live for 23 years, then the expected payout would be $220,800 ($800 x 12 x 23), and the exclusion ratio would be 45.29% ($100,000 / $220,800). Thus, for a given tax year, the 12 monthly payments totaling $9600 would be deducted by 45.29%, or $4,347.84.

Taxes on fixed annuities are generally taught in terms of an "**exclusion ratio**," where the expected payout of the annuity is calculated so that each monthly payment can be broken up between the original investment and the gain on investment, with only the latter being taxable. This can be on the Series 7 exam, so it is important to know. But there is a shortcut: the nontaxable portion for each annuity payment can also be calculated by ignoring the expected payout altogether. Just divide the original investment by the number of expected years in the annuitant's life to get the yearly deduction. For instance, in the example from the other card on fixed annuities, calculate it this way:

$100,000 / 23 years = $4,347.82 (The difference from the other card is due to rounding.)

And if you want the nontaxable portion of each *monthly* annuity payment, simply divide the yearly number by 12 to get $362.32.

VARIABLE ANNUITIES

Since **variable annuities** do not have a fixed monthly payment, calculating the taxable amount for each payment is different than for fixed annuities. One ignores the expected total payout over the life of the annuity, looking simply at the **original investment amount**. The original investment amount, when divided by the life expectancy of the annuitant (in months), gives the amount of original investment attributable to each monthly payment, regardless of how much gain on investment is included in each monthly payment. For example, if an annuitant contributes a total of $100,000 to a variable annuity and has a life expectancy of 23 years, then he will have a yearly tax deduction from his annuity income of $4,347.82 ($100,000 / 23 years), or a monthly deduction of $362.32. On closer inspection, you'll notice that this is simply a shortcut way of making the exact same calculation as for fixed annuities. The formula for taxes on fixed annuities (involving the exclusion ratio) unnecessarily includes the expected payout, when the only relevant variables are the original investment and the life expectancy of the annuitant.

DEATH BENEFITS ON ANNUITIES

If an annuitant dies in the **accumulation period**, then the money will go to the specified beneficiaries, who will have to pay taxes on any gain earned in the annuity up to that point; they will have to pay ordinary income tax rates. If an annuitant dies in the **distribution period**, then the insurance company's obligation to make further payments depends on the nature of the agreement. A "*life-only annuity*" means that payments are made to the annuitant while he is alive, so that the company is not obligated to make any other payments if he dies. A "*term-certain option*" in the annuity requires payments to be made to a specified beneficiary if the annuitant dies before a particular length of time has passed. A "*joint-life annuity*" requires payments to be made to the other person associated with the annuity (usually a spouse), so that the company is obligated to make payments until both parties are deceased. Again, any money received by beneficiaries is subject to ordinary income tax.

Limited Partnerships

DPPs

Direct participation programs (DPPs), also called *direct participation plans*, are flow-through investments. The profits, losses, and income flow through the DPP and to the investors directly. The DPP itself pays no taxes; only the individual investors do. DPPs are organized as limited partnerships, and the two terms are generally used interchangeably. Limited partnerships are generally involved in real estate, oil and gas, or equipment leasing. Limited partners (as opposed to general partners) put up the money, but don't manage the business, and they have limited liability. One drawback of a limited partnership is that it is very difficult for a partner to sell his interest in one. Another is that they're sometimes organized simply to create losses that the partners can use to shelter income from taxation, although doing so is illegal.

GENERAL PARTNERS IN LIMITED PARTNERSHIPS

A **limited partnership** must have at least one general partner and at least one limited partner, although they usually have more. The **general partner** has more responsibilities and liabilities than does the limited partner. The general partner does the actual managing of the business and makes decisions that are legally binding for everyone in the partnership. He may be paid for services as a general partner, and may buy and sell property on behalf of the partnership. The general partner must avoid conflicts of interest with the partnership, and must keep his own funds separate from partnership funds at all times. The general partner may not borrow money from the partnership (although the partnership may borrow from the general partner), and he has a legal responsibility to use the assets of the partnership for the best interests of the partnership. Finally, the general partner is personally liable for all obligations incurred by the partnership.

LIMITED PARTNERS IN LIMITED PARTNERSHIPS

Limited partners, unlike general partners, are not personally liable for obligations incurred by a limited partnership. The **limited partner** cannot make management decisions, but does have the right to sue the general partner if he believes that the general partner is not acting in the best interests of the partnership. Limited partners are allowed to vote on certain partnership matters, and they can inspect the financial records and accounting books of the partnership if they so desire. But their main role is to put up the money, while the general partner actually runs the business.

ACCREDITED INVESTORS FOR LIMITED PARTNERSHIPS

The average man on the street is not qualified to take part in a limited partnership sold by private placement. The government requires that anyone taking part in a privately placed limited partnership have substantial income and/or substantial net worth. According to the SEC, to qualify as an **accredited investor**, a person must either have a net worth of more than one million dollars on his own or together with a spouse, or the person must have had an income of over $200,000 for each of the last two years, plus have a reasonable expectation that he will continue to receive the same level of income.

DISSOLUTION OF A LIMITED PARTNERSHIP

Terms for the **dissolution** of a limited partnership can vary according to the specific agreement of the partnership, but other restrictions apply independently of those terms. While in general partnerships (i.e. non-limited partnerships), any partner can give a notice to the other partners of his intent to dissolve the partnership, it is not the same with limited partnerships. Only general partners can issue such notice; limited partners are not able to do so. Moreover, unlike general partnerships, limited partnerships are not ended simply by a limited partner's death, retirement, or bankruptcy. The fundamental detail to know is that limited partners have lesser abilities to dissolve the partnership than partners do in general partnerships.

REAL-ESTATE PARTNERSHIPS

Real-estate partnerships, or *real-estate DPPs*, can invest in a number of different real estate assets, and thus these partnerships can be classified in various ways:

- *Public housing partnerships* invest in the construction of low-income and retirement housing. Since these housing programs are government-assisted (e.g. missing rent payments are covered by the U.S. Department of Housing and Urban Development), they are considered the safest form of real-estate partnership.
- *Existing properties partnerships* invest in properties that are already constructed, with the purpose of gaining rental income.
- *New construction partnerships* invest in properties to be built, aiming to make a profit in selling the building.
- *Raw land partnerships* invest in mere land, not purchasing buildings or intending to build on the land. Their aim is to make money on capital gains as the value of the land increases. These are the riskiest form of real-estate DPP.

EQUIPMENT LEASING PARTNERSHIPS

Equipment leasing partnerships seek to make a profit by purchasing and leasing various assets, such as computers, trucks, or machinery. There are two main types of leases for equipment leasing DPPs:

- *Full payout leases* rent out equipment for long periods of time (often the equipment's useful life), so that the first lease is sufficient to cover the cost of the equipment.
- *Operating leases* rent out equipment for rather short periods, or at least for periods where the total rental payments do not cover the cost of the equipment by themselves. In operating leases, the same equipment will be leased out several times. Because of this, they can be riskier than full payout leases.

OIL AND GAS PARTNERSHIPS

Oil and gas partnerships aim to make a profit through various investments involving the extraction of oil and gas:

- *Exploratory oil and gas DPPs* search new areas to find new oil and drill for it. This is the riskiest oil and gas DPP, and its activity is also called "wildcatting."
- *Developmental oil and gas DPPs* search for new reserves in areas near wells that are already extracting oil or gas.
- *Income oil and gas DPPs* purchase wells that already exist.
- *Combination oil and gas DPPs* involve any assortment of the previous three.

DEDUCTIBLE EXPENSES FOR OIL AND GAS PARTNERSHIPS

Oil and gas partnerships are eligible for a number of tax benefits:

- *Tangible drilling costs (TDCs)* are any costs for items used in extracting oil or gas that have a salvage value upon disposal (e.g. storage tanks, drills)—basically, the equipment used in drilling. These costs can be deducted as the equipment is depreciated, with the deduction equaling the depreciation expense for that year. They can be depreciated either on a straight-line basis (the same amount every year of their use) or on an accelerated basis (more depreciation earlier and less later).
- *Intangible drilling costs (IDCs)* are costs of extraction that don't involve objects with salvage value (whether or not the costs are "intangible" in the sense of being nonphysical). These costs include wages, fuel, costs for repairs and maintenance, and other things. Unlike TDCs, IDCs are fully deductible in the year the expenses are incurred. However, IDCs can only be deducted for costs related to the drilling and preparation of well; once it is producing oil or gas, IDCs cannot be deducted.
- *Depletion cost* is a tax deduction for the amount of natural resources depleted in a reserve. This is deducted according to the oil or gas sold, not how much of a resource is actually extracted or stored.

CERTIFICATE OF LIMITED PARTNERSHIP, PARTNERSHIP AGREEMENT, AND SUBSCRIPTION AGREEMENT

These three documents are involved with the formation of partnerships and introduction of new partners:

- The **certificate of limited partnership** must be sent to the secretary of state for the state where the partnership does business, allowing the partnership to be legally recognized.
- The **partnership agreement** is the contract between the partners to form the partnership, outlining the nature of the business, the capital contributions of each partner, the entitlements to profit and liabilities to loss (e.g. 50-50), and other rights and duties.
- The **subscription agreement** is an application for a new investor to join a partnership as a limited partner.

FORMATION OF LIMITED PARTNERSHIPS

Limited partnerships can be sold either through **private placement** or by **public offering**. When DPPs are privately placed, they do not need to be registered with the SEC, and a few wealthy investors each contribute sizable investments. When done by way of public offering, large numbers of investors put in a small amount of money. A syndicator takes care of selling the limited partnership to investors and receives a fee for those services. Each limited partnership requires three documents: the *certificate of limited partnership*, the *partnership agreement*, and the *subscription agreement*.

EVALUATION OF LIMITED PARTNERSHIPS

Besides determining whether an investor should invest in limited partnerships generally—i.e. whether the general risks of limited partnerships, in comparison to other investments, fits the investor—the registered representative also ought to evaluate the merits and risks of particular DPPs. This evaluation involves four main considerations:

- the program's economic soundness
- the general partner's talent, knowledge, and expertise
- the program's basic objectives
- the DPP's start-up costs

Options

LISTED OPTIONS

Listed options are options traded on an exchange, and thus are also called *exchange-traded options*. Consequently, listed options are required to follow exchange rules. **Listed options** can be classified as either *American style* or *European style* options, with European style options (the less common style) having a smaller timeframe in which they can be exercised.

EQUITY, INDEX, AND YIELD-BASED OPTIONS

Equity options are contracts that provide the right to buy or sell an equity security, such as a stock, at a given price (the strike price), independent of the actual market price for the stock at that time. **Index options** are options whose underlying instrument is a set of stocks linked to an index, such as the S&P 500. **Yield-based options** are options whose underlying instrument is a bond. The profit or loss on these options is the difference between the strike price and the yield of the bond.

PUBLICATION OF OPTION INFORMATION

Tables displaying options for sale list not only the security, date, type of option (call or put), strike price, bid price, and ask price, but also have a number of other factors which are meant to be useful to investors in evaluating options. These factors include extrinsic bid/ask price, which measures the time premium value of the option, the implied volatility of the option, and a number of Greek factors: Delta, Gamma, Vega, and Theta.

CALL OPTIONS, PUT OPTIONS, SPREADS, AND "IN THE MONEY"

An option with the right to buy is a **call option**, and an option with a right to sell is a **put option**. The **spread** for a stock option is the difference between the strike price (that is, the price at which one can exercise the right to engage in the transaction) and the current market value of the stock. "**In the money**" means that the strike price and market value of the stock are such that exercising the option would be a gain for the investor. For instance, if a trader has a call option and the strike price is less than the market value, then he is in the money. The same goes for a trader with a put option, if the strike price is greater than the stocks' market value. Keep in mind, however, that an option can be "in the money" without necessarily being profitable, because the gain on the closing transaction also needs to make up for the cost of the option itself.

UNDERLYING INSTRUMENT, EXERCISE PRICE, AND EXPIRATION DATE

The **underlying instrument** for an option is the entity which the buyer of the option contract has the right either to buy (for call options) or to sell (for put options). If an investor purchases a call option to buy shares of ABC stock for $15/share before February 1, then the ABC stock is the underlying instrument of the option contract. The **exercise price** is the price at which the holder of the option can buy or sell the underlying instrument, regardless of the market price. (The gain or loss by the investor depends upon the difference between the exercise price and the actual price.) In the above example, $15/share is the exercise price. The **expiration date** is the final date at which the holder of an option can exercise the right to buy or sell the underlying instrument. After the date, the option expires, and he can only buy or sell the instrument at the actual market price. In the example above, February 1 is the expiration date.

LEAPS

Long-term equity anticipation securities (LEAPS) are simply long-term options; the expiration date is a great deal in the future from the time the contract is formed, sometimes up to three years.

115

LEAPS allow investors to avoid stringing together several short-term options, and they also allow investors to potentially profit from long-term price changes without needing to invest in the asset itself for that entire period, which would be less affordable.

LONG AND SHORT POSITIONS FOR OPTIONS

There are different "positions" which investors enter into when they buy or sell option contracts. A **long position** is a position where the trader wants the price to increase, and a **short position** is a position where the trader wants the price to decrease. Naturally, then, every single option contract involves one person in the long position and another in the short; someone will profit from the price growing and the other from the price dropping. For instance, if a trader buys a call option, then he is in a long position with respect to the underlying asset: he wants its actual price to go up, so that when he buys it, he can then sell it for the higher price at a profit. But the seller will be in a short position. And if a trader buys a put option, he is in a short position with respect to the underlying asset, since he wants the actual price to go down, so that he can sell high and buy low. Note: for put options, the buyer will be in a short position with respect to the underlying asset, but in a long position with respect to the option contract itself. The value of a put option increases as the price of the underlying asset decreases. The key thing to remember is that long position = wants price to increase, and short position = wants price to decrease.

OPENING AND CLOSING TRANSACTIONS FOR OPTIONS

Traders enter into options contract either by **buying** them (purchasing a right to buy or sell something in the future) or **writing/selling** them (being paid to have an obligation to buy or sell something in the future). Since entering into an option contract involves "opening a position," whether the position is long or short, any opening transaction for an option contract is either *buy-to-open* (if you're buying the contract) or *sell-to-open* (if you're writing/selling the contract). Likewise, since the termination of the contract, whether by exercising the option or by expiration, involves closing the long and short positions of the traders, then the trader needs to submit a closing order—either a *buy-to-close order* (if it is a call option) or a *sell-to-close order* (if it is a put option).

OPTION ASSIGNMENTS

Option assignments are notices received by the writers (i.e. sellers) of options, informing the writer that the buyer has now exercised the option. Thus, if the option is a put option, then an assignment means that the writer is at that point obligated to buy shares from the option-holder at the strike price. And if the option is a call option, then the writer is obligated to sell shares to the option-holder. (If the writer of a call option already owns the shares he is obligated to sell, then he is said to be *covered*; otherwise he is said to be *naked*, and must buy the shares on the market in order to sell them to the option-holder.) The exercise date is different from the **settlement date** for options, which is the date by which the actual transaction needs to be made. For options, the settlement date is one business day after the date when the option is exercised.

AMERICAN-STYLE EXERCISING AND EUROPEAN-STYLE EXERCISING FOR OPTIONS

Exercising an option is activating the right contained in the option contract. If a trader exercises a call option, he is at that point entitled to the underlying securities at the strike price. There are different rules governing the exercising of options:

- *American-style exercising* means that, at any time before the option has reached its expiration date, the option-holder is able to exercise it. There are not restrictions on when he can exercise it besides the expiration date.
- *European-style exercising* means that the *only* time when the option-holder may exercise the option is at the expiration date. Option-holders are prohibited from exercising these options prior to the expiration date.

As you can imagine, since American-style options give the option-holder a much higher chance of profit, they also command a higher price than European-style options, all other things being equal.

OPTION PREMIUMS

Premiums are the prices paid to purchase an option contract, or in other words, they are the profits made by writers of option contracts. There are two main components to it: the *intrinsic value*, which is the value inherent to the right embedded in the option, and the *time value*, which is the value of owning the option for a particular duration of time. As the expiration date nears, the time value of the option diminishes, in which case the premium, if it would be traded to a different person (i.e. if the trader currently holding the option traded it to someone else), would more closely reflect the intrinsic value of the option.

VOLUME AND OPEN INTEREST FOR OPTIONS

Volume is the number of option contracts that have been traded in a certain time period. It helps to show how meaningful price differences are. **Open interest** is the number of option contracts that are still open, i.e. not yet closed, for a certain time period. This number is very closely related to volume, but still different. Suppose X purchased an option from Z, who wrote the option. This transaction would increase volume by 1 and open interest by 1, since a transaction occurred and the option is not yet closed (since it was just bought). But suppose that X then sold the same to Y, so that Y was the option-holder in relation to the writer, Z. In this case, volume would have increased by 1 again, but open interest would not change.

POSITION LIMITS AND EXERCISE LIMITS FOR OPTIONS

Position limits are restrictions placed upon the number of options contracts an investor can hold with respect to a particular security. It is possible for investors to hold a long position on one option contract, and then, with respect to the same asset, hold a short position on a different option contract. To limit the ways these can be exploited, position limits exist. **Exercise limits** are restrictions placed upon the number of option contracts an investor can exercise for a given security in a given time period. For instance, an investor (probably an institutional one) might be forbidden from exercising 6,000 option contracts on a particular share of stock in the span of five days. Note, however, that the investor is not limited on the *total* options he can exercise—only on the total number he can exercise *for a particular security*.

OCC

The **Options Clearing Corporation (OCC)** is an organization under the authority of the SEC and the Commodities Futures Trading Commission (CFTC), and its purpose is as the issuer and guarantor of all listed options (i.e. all options listed on public exchanges). The OCC is authoritative over which options trade and the strike price at which they trade. Moreover, when investors decide to exercise their options, the OCC determines (randomly) which firm on the other end is obligated to close the option with the holder.

STOCK DIVIDENDS

The issuance of **stock dividends** by a company requires the strike price and shares per option contract to change, although the number of option contracts stays the same. Stock dividends increase the number of shares that an outstanding option contract can buy and then lowers the strike price accordingly.

- For instance, suppose a call option permitted the holder to purchase 100 shares of company X at $30 per share, and company X then issued 5% stock dividends. This call option would now permit the holder to purchase 105 shares according to the contract, a 5% increase from 100 shares. Yet, the price per share would decrease to $28.57 ($30/share x 100 shares / 105 shares).
- If a company issues cash dividends, no changes are made to the terms of the option contract. *Cash dividends* affect the stock price (e.g. the stock price decreases by the dividend amount on the ex-dividend date), but not the contract itself.

STOCK SPLITS

Since **stock splits** involve multiplying the quantity of stocks and dividing their value (whether twofold, threefold, or whatever), this could potentially wreak havoc on options contracts. Imagine an investor who had an option to buy various stocks which suddenly were halved, even though the value of the company did not meaningfully change; he would experience unnecessary and great losses. Because of this, the *Options Clearing Corporation (OCC)* ensures that options contracts are adjusted when stock splits occur, so that the value of the adjusted contract is equivalent to the pre-split value. Moreover, the actual number of contracts are multiplied, so that option holders are entitled to purchase the same amount of ownership as they could before the split.

OPTIONS MARGIN

Options margin refers to the minimum amount of cash required to be deposited in an options trading broker account for the trader to begin trading options. Since brokerage firms are liable to cover any traders who are unable to pay their options contracts (as ensured by the OCC), they wish to lower their risk by requiring specific amounts of cash in option traders' accounts. Different brokers have varying *margin requirements*.

COVERED CALL

If an investor believes the price of a stock will go down in the future, the investor can write a call on the stock, giving the call buyer the right to purchase the stock from the investor in the future at a specific price. If the stock falls in price or stays even, the call writer makes money on the option premium. However, if the stock rises and the call becomes "in the money," the call writer will have to deliver the stock to the call owner. A call is **covered** if the call writer actually owns the stock he is writing a call on. If the investor does not own the stock, but would have to purchase it to honor the call, it is said to be **uncovered**. If the investor purchases the stock at the same time he writes the call option, then he is engaging in a "buy-write" strategy.

CURRENCY OPTIONS AND YIELD-BASED OPTIONS

Currency options are options that give the trader the right to purchase (or sell) some currency at a specified exchange rate. This allows investors to profit, or especially to avoid losses, from changes in exchange rate, and is especially utilized by corporations to hedge the value of receivables or payables denominated in a foreign currency. **Yield-based options** are options that give the trader

118

the right to purchase (or sell) a bond whose value derives from its yield. The value of the option thus depends on any difference between the option's strike price and the bond's yield.

HEDGING FOR EQUITY

Suppose an investor has a number of stocks which have done well over the previous few years, increasing by 30% or so in value. If he is concerned about the price peaking and dropping, he can purchase a put option to ensure that he will not experience losses in selling those stocks should the price drop. This is called **hedging for equity**. Yet, because determining and acquiring proper put options for each stock can be difficult or otherwise time-consuming, a good idea for the investor would be to purchase a put option on an **index**, so that the option varies with the value of a number of major companies comprising the index (and assuming his investments are in these kinds of companies).

BULLISH INVESTOR

A **bullish investor** thinks a stock will go up, and will therefore be long on the stock. But to protect against risk, there are some things a long investor can do to minimize the risk in case the investor is wrong. For *short-term protection*, the investor can write a call on the stock, giving someone else the right to purchase it for lower than the market price. This limits their upside potential, and is only advisable for stock with low volatility. For *long-term protection*, the investor can buy a put on the same stock, giving the investor the right to sell the stock at a certain price.

BEARISH INVESTOR

A **bearish investor** thinks stock will decline in price and might therefore be a short seller, borrowing shares he doesn't own and hoping to replace them with stocks bought at a lower price down the road. To protect against the risk of loss, a short seller can use options. For partial protection, the short seller can sell a put against the same stock. For full protection, the short seller can buy a call on the same stock. Each approach has its advantages and disadvantages, but both offer some protection against the risks of short selling.

SPREAD

A **spread** is a pair of options transactions an investor makes at the same time and on the same security. Investors use **straddles** to protect their positions and to take advantage of discrepancies in options pricing. A *call spread* is when the investor buys a call and sells a call on the same stock, and a *put spread* is when the investor buys a put and sells a put on the same stock.

DEBIT AND CREDIT SPREAD

A **debit spread** is a spread used by an investor who's bearish, purchasing a higher-priced option and selling a lower-priced option. An investor who's bullish uses a **credit spread**, which involves selling the higher-priced option and purchasing the lower one. In any spread, the person who sells the lower strike price and buys the higher strike price is bearish, and the investor who sells the higher strike price and buys the lower strike price is bullish.

STRADDLES AND COMBINATIONS

Straddles are a kind of spread where the investor either purchases a call and a put or sells a call and a put, with both having the same expiration date and strike price. An investor who expects a stock's price to move up or down substantially, but isn't sure which way it will go, will use a long straddle by buying a call and a put. An investor who doesn't expect much price movement in the stock either way will use a short straddle by selling a call and a put on the stock. **Combinations** are similar to straddles, except that they don't necessarily involve an identical expiration date and strike price. But the strategy is still generally the same: investors expecting volatility in the price will engage in a long combination, buying a call and put on the stock, whereas investors expecting little volatility will engage in a short combination, selling both options contracts.

BREAKEVEN POINTS

Although option traders always concern themselves with the stock's value in relation to the strike price, their profit or loss is not determined solely by it. Rather, the **breakeven point** for the option trader—that is, the price at which an option trader will make no profit or loss—is determined by the strike price and the option premium, or the price paid for the option. For the holder of a call option, the breakeven point is the strike price plus the premium. If I have an option to buy stocks at $40/share and I paid $2/share for the option, then the stocks must rise to $42 for me to break even. I would buy the stocks at the strike price of $40, sell them for $42, and cover my premium of $2. On the other hand, for the holder of a put option, the breakeven point is the strike price minus the premium. If I have an option to sell stocks at $40/share and I paid $2/share for the option, then the stocks must drop to $38 for me to break even. I would sell the stocks at the strike price of $40 and cover my premium of $2.

TAXES FOR OPTIONS

Options are subject to **capital gains taxation**. That is, the underlying asset for options (e.g. stocks) are subject to capital gains and losses, but the option contracts themselves also have value and can be traded, resulting in capital gains or losses. If the holder of an option chooses not to exercise the option, but trades it to someone else before it expires, then any difference in price is a capital gain or loss. If the holder held the option for less than one year, then it is considered short-term; otherwise it is considered long-term. If the holder of an option trades it to someone else, the writer of the option does not experience any capital gain or loss; he is still just as obligated as before to fulfill his end of the contract. However, if the writer buys back the option himself, then he will have a capital gain or loss for the difference. Moreover, if an option-writer buys back the option, it will always be considered a short-term capital gain, even if it occurs over one year after being written.

Retirement Plans

Individual Retirement Accounts

IRAs

Individual Retirement Accounts (IRAs) were created in the early 1980s so that people could supplement whatever retirement plans and Social Security they had with their own savings and investments. IRAs are given *preferential tax treatment* in order to encourage people to save for their own retirement. Unlike many retirement plans, anyone may open an IRA, regardless of whatever other plans they're covered under. For 2020, people with earned income may contribute up to $6,000 per year ($7,000 if the person is age 50 or older), or up to $12,000 per year if the person has a spouse that doesn't work ($14,000 if both are age 50 or older). Any contributions in excess of the maximum amount are subject to a tax on 6% of the excess per year until the excess (and any gains it has produced) is removed from the IRA.

IRA Distributions

Anyone who owns an IRA may begin taking money out of it without suffering a penalty after reaching the age of $59\frac{1}{2}$ years. **Withdrawals** before the required age are subject to a 10% penalty in addition to any income tax on the money withdrawn. There are a few exceptions in which money may be withdrawn before the age of $59\frac{1}{2}$ years without incurring a penalty: if the person become disabled; if taking out the money to purchase a first home which the person will be using as a residence; to pay education-related expenses for himself, his spouse, or their children or grandchildren; and for certain medical expenses. IRA owners must begin withdrawing the money by the first day of April after reaching the age of 72 years, or they will pay a 50% penalty on their withdrawals.

Traditional and Roth IRAs

The two different types of IRAs vary in terms of their tax benefits. **Traditional IRAs** allow for tax-deductible contributions, and the investments in them grow tax-deferred, but distributions are taxed. In other words, someone placing contributions in his Traditional IRA can deduct that amount from his taxes for that year, and he doesn't have to pay any taxes on capital gains (or dividends, or interest income, or whatever) which his investments earn. However, he does have to pay income tax at the applicable rate whenever he withdraws money. **Roth IRAs** have after-tax contributions, but grow tax-free and have tax-free distributions. After the contributions are made, no taxes ever have to be paid on the account.

SEP IRAs, SIMPLE IRAs, and Keogh Plans

Simplified Employee Pension (SEP) IRAs are designed for owners of small businesses and self-employed persons, as well as their employees. (That is, eligible employers can directly make contributions to their employees' SEP IRAs.) While the tax benefits mirror those of Traditional IRAs, SEP IRAs are noteworthy for their increased contribution limits. For 2020, the maximum contribution limit is 25% of income or $57,000, whichever is less. S**avings Incentive Match Plan for Employees (SIMPLE) IRAs** are similar to SEP IRAs, in that they have the tax benefits of a Traditional IRA and are designed for small business owners and self-employed persons. Their main difference is that they permit employees to make contributions to the plan themselves. Moreover, employers are required to contribute a certain amount, either a match or a percentage of income. SIMPLE IRAs also have higher contribution limits. **Keogh plans** are similar in some ways to IRAs.

They are for self-employed persons and professionals, such as doctors and lawyers. The maximum contribution to a Keogh by the owner is the same as for SEP IRAs—for 2020, the lesser of 25% income or $57,000. However, if a person establishes a Keogh plan for his own benefit, that person is legally obligated to cover any employees who work for him, but at a lesser amount. This makes Keoghs a very unattractive option for anyone with more than a handful of employees.

APPROVED INVESTMENTS FOR IRAS

Because of the nature of an Individual Retirement Account (IRA), the government encourages fairly **conservative investment strategies** by IRA owners and discourages speculative and highly risky investments. Most stocks and corporate bonds are approved for IRA purchases, as are federal government securities, mutual funds, and annuities. But municipal bonds are forbidden, as are collectibles (except U.S.-issued gold and silver coins). Options are forbidden, except for covered calls. Short selling and buying on margin are also forbidden.

TRANSFERS AND ROLLOVERS

Transfers and rollovers are different way of moving funds from one account to another. The movement can be between different IRA accounts (e.g. to switch from Traditional to Roth, or because the IRA holder is dissatisfied with the investment-management in a particular account), or between employer plans, or between IRAs and employer plans. The terms are not synonymous. **Transfers** are direct movements of funds without the individual possessing the assets for any period. **Rollovers** involve a temporary period when the individual can hold the assets without any early withdrawal penalties or taxes. There are rules restricting rollovers, however. As one example, an individual cannot roll over funds between IRAs more than once within a twelve-month period.

RMDS

In order to maintain the tax advantages for an IRA without penalty, the individual must make certain **required minimum distributions (RMDs)** on the account, though there is no maximum limit. The RMD is determined by the value of the account and the age of the IRA holder. The IRS has a table listing factors for RMDs, so that, for any given year, the RMD equals the value of the total IRA divided by that year's factor. The factors decrease as the individual's age increases, so that the fraction of the IRA which must be distributed increases from year to year. The first RMD must be paid by April 1 after the individual turns 72, and then they are required to be distributed annually by December 31 of subsequent years. (If the first RMD is due on April 1 in the year after the IRA holder turns 72—e.g. if the individual turns 72 in May and then has the first RMD by next April— then the next RMD will be due on December 31 of that same year.)

Other Retirement Plans

QUALIFIED AND NON-QUALIFIED RETIREMENT PLANS

There are all sorts of retirement plans, and they all have unique features. But one key feature that sets many of them apart from others is the fact that contributions to them are tax-deductible. Plans that feature tax-deductible contributions are known as **qualified plans**; the ones that don't are known as **nonqualified plans**. Two of the best-known nonqualified plans are *payroll deduction plans* and *deferred compensation plans*. Nonqualified plans still benefit from tax-deferred growth. For qualified plans, distributions are taxed entirely as income, but for nonqualified plans, since the original contributions were from after-tax dollars, only the distributions in excess of the original contributions are taxed as income.

PAYROLL DEDUCTION RETIREMENT PLANS

Under a **payroll deduction retirement plan**, an employee allows the employer to take out a certain amount or percentage of the employee's wages and invest that money. The money comes out of the employee's net pay after taxes have been paid. Payroll deduction plans are often confused with 401(k) plans, but they are not the same, though they share similarities. Payroll deduction plans are considered nonqualified retirement plans. 401(k) plans, on the other hand, are classified as qualified plans, because they are considered to be salary reduction plans, not payroll deduction plans.

DEFERRED COMPENSATION RETIREMENT PLANS

In a **deferred compensation retirement plan**, an employee agrees to forego some present income on the condition that his employer pay that portion after the employee retires from the company. The advantage of this plan is that most employees who take advantage of it will likely be in a lower tax bracket after retirement, and will therefore be able to pay lower taxes on the income than if they received it when they earned it. One risk of a deferred compensation plan is that the company might go out of business before the employee retires, or the employee could leave the firm before becoming vested. In either case, the employee could wind up with little or nothing.

CORPORATE PENSION PLANS

There are two types of private, corporate pension plans. The first is the **defined benefit plan**, in which the corporation promises to pay the employee a certain amount of money after the employee retires. The defined benefit plan was once quite common, but is now becoming increasingly scarce. This is due to the fact that many corporations have found themselves with massive unfunded pension liabilities, because they didn't set aside enough money to fulfill all the promises they made. In recent years, corporations have been less willing to promise specific amounts of money, and have switched to **defined contribution plans** (sometimes called *money-purchase pension plans*), in which the corporation agrees to contribute a certain amount of money, but makes no promises of what the investments will be worth when the employee retires.

ERISA

The **Employee Retirement Income Security Act (ERISA)** was passed in 1974 with the purpose of protecting the retirement assets of American employees in qualified retirement plans. Since employees invest assets for retirement in a fund of plan assets, the growth of that investment is very important. ERISA requires plans to inform employees about these investment strategies and makes fiduciaries in charge of those plan assets accountable to the employees for any asset mismanagement.

401(k) Plans, 403(b) Plans, and 457 Plans

Most corporations now use 401(k) plans to fund their employee retirement pensions. With a **401(k)**, employees contribute a portion of their wages or salary, which are not counted as part of their gross income. Their contributions and the earnings on the contributions are tax deferred until withdrawal. In addition, the corporation may choose to match part of the employee's contribution. Most companies will have a variety of investment vehicles that an employee can choose to contribute to; the employee may put all his money in one or spread the money out among several. **403(b)** plans are also called *tax-sheltered annuity (TSA) plans*. They are only available to people who work in educational institutions, including college, universities, elementary schools, middle schools, high schools, religious institutions, private hospitals, and institutions with an educational purpose, such as zoos and museums. In addition, the employees must be at least 21 years old, and must have at least one year of service before being eligible for coverage. The benefits of 403(b) plans are very similar to 401(k)s. **457 plans** are nonqualified plans available to government employers (as well as certain non-government employers), similar in structure to 401(k)s and 403(b)s. They are deferred-compensation plans, and unlike 401(k)s and 403(b)s, they have no penalty on early distributions, even though distributions are taxed as income.

Custodial, Educational, and Health Savings Accounts

UGMA AND UTMA ACCOUNTS

UGMA stands for the **Uniform Gift to Minors Act**, which governs fiduciary accounts set up for minors (that is, accounts handled by a custodian for the sake of the minor). Anyone may donate either cash or securities to a UGMA account. Once they have, the gift may not be revoked or returned. The account administrator, or custodian, trades on behalf of the minor, and may use proceeds of the account to pay for the minor's living expenses, education, etc., when appropriate. The minor has no control whatsoever of the funds until reaching adulthood, at which point the account becomes his to manage. Only one minor and one custodian can be on each account, although a minor can be the beneficial owner of more than one account, and a custodian can manage more than one account. **UTMA** stands for the **Uniform Transfer to Minors Act**. UTMA accounts are very similar to UGMA accounts, the main difference being that they permit gifts besides cash and securities, e.g. land, intangible assets (like patents), art, etc.

RESPONSIBILITIES OF A UGMA OR UTMA FIDUCIARY

Margin activity is prohibited to UGMA and UTMA accounts; they must be **cash accounts** only. The custodian is not allowed to use the assets of the account as collateral on a loan. Any cash coming into the account, along with interest and dividends, must be put to use by investing it within a reasonable time period. Except for covered calls, where the underlying stock is already owned, options trading and commodities trading are off limits to UGMA accounts. The custodian is not allowed to borrow money from the account, although the custodian can make loans to the account. All investments are expected to be prudent and have the minor's best interests at heart.

CESAs

Coverdell Education Savings Accounts (CESAs), formerly known as Coverdell IRAs, were created by Congress to enable parents to help fund their children's future college education. For 2020, the maximum contribution per year is $2,000, and anyone is allowed to contribute (i.e. not just the parents), so long as the sum total of all contributions for one child is no more than $2,000. Contributions must cease once the child turns 18, but the earnings are not taxed if directly applied to the beneficiary's educational expenses. However, for 2020, anyone making over $95,000 per year ($190,000 for couples) can't give the full $2,000, and anyone making over $110,000 per year ($220,000 for couples) is not allowed to participate.

529 COLLEGE SAVINGS PLAN ACCOUNTS

529 plans, named after section 529 of the Internal Revenue Service code, are another way, besides Coverdell Educational Savings Accounts, for parents to pre-fund their child's college education. Taxes are deferred on the money invested in **529 plans**, the money is generally not taxed in most states, and it isn't taxed by the federal government when withdrawn if applied directly to legitimate college educational expenses of the named beneficiary. There are two kinds of 529 plans. One is a *pre-paid tuition plan*, which allows a parent to purchase a certain number of units of tuition, "locking in" the units, which will be used in the future, at today's rates, thereby protecting against rises in tuition over the years. The other kind of 529 is a *savings plan*. Plans vary greatly state by state, but one thing they have in common is that, because contributions to 529 plans are gifts, there are certain restrictions on contributions. However, these are much more lenient than for Coverdell accounts. 529 plans generally have lifetime contribution limits rather than annual limits.

HSAs

Health savings accounts (HSAs) are accounts designed for people with *high-deductible health plans (HDHPs).* These accounts allow tax-deductible contributions which are then used to pay for qualified medical expenses not covered by the health plans. Moreover, any investment in the account grows tax-free, and there are no taxes on distributions, so long as they are used for qualified medical expenses.

Rules and Regulations

CONTINUING EDUCATION REQUIREMENTS

FINRA Rule 1250 establishes the need for **continuing education** for a FINRA licensed broker. Unless otherwise instructed, individuals must complete their continuing education requirements within 120 days of the second anniversary of holding their license. Failure to complete the continuing education requirements results in having one's license put into inactive status until brought up to date. The continuing education may be provided by the firm that the broker works for, provided that certain elements are in place. This includes the following:

1. The firm has a designated principal or officer in charge
2. The delivery takes place at a site under the control of the firm
3. The continuing education is supervised by a proctor
4. The sites are made available to FINRA for examination

A letter of attestation is sent to the designated examining authority (DEA) detailing items 1-4 above

REPORTING REQUIREMENTS

Under FINRA Rule 4530, FINRA member firms should report **violations** within 30 calendar days of their occurrence. Part B of Rule 4530 allows the member time to determine that an actual violation has occurred and specifies the firm "to report to FINRA within 30 calendar days after the firm has concluded, or reasonably should have concluded, on its own that the firm or an associated person of the firm has violated any securities, insurance, commodities, financial or investment-related laws, rules, regulations or standards of conduct of any domestic or foreign regulatory body or self-regulatory organization." Rule 4530 further goes on to state that customer "statistical and summary information" regarding **customer complaints** should be filed each quarter by the 15th calendar day following the end of the quarter.

Some FINRA members create their own reporting guidelines, but these guidelines must always be at least as frequent as those outlined in Rule 4530. Many members set up stricter reporting guidelines. Following stricter reporting dates will help prevent the registered person from violating FINRA rules.

REGISTRATION REQUIREMENTS

Registration requirements (NASD Rule 1031) - any person engaged as a representative in the investment banking or securities business of a member must be registered. In order to be registered, he must pass a *Qualification Examination* according to their category of registration. A representative is defined as a person associated with a member including assistant officers other than principals, involved in the investment banking or securities business including functions such as supervision, solicitation, and training. If a person's registration has lapsed for two or more years, the person is required to retake a Qualification Examination for Representatives corresponding to his registration.

CATEGORIES OF REPRESENTATIVE REGISTRATION
GENERAL SECURITIES REPRESENTATIVE

General Securities Representative - any representative associated with a member is required to register as a General Securities Representative, unless his activities are limited enough to qualify him for one of the limited categories of representation.

LIMITED REPRESENTATIVE

Limited Representative - Investment Company and Variable Contracts Products - a representative associated with a member may register as a Limited Representative - Investment Company and Variable Contracts Products if his activities are limited to the solicitation, purchase, or sale of certain investment companies' redeemable securities, certain closed-end investment companies' securities, and certain exempt variable contracts and insurance premium funding programs, and the person passes a corresponding Qualification Examination.

Limited Representative - Direct Participation Program - a representative associated with a member may register as a Limited Representative - Direct Participation Program if his activities are limited to the equity interests in or the debt of direct participation programs, and the person passes a corresponding Qualification Examination. A person seeking this registration must already have been registered as a Limited Representative - Corporate Securities or Limited Representative - Government Securities.

Limited Representative - Options and Security Futures - a representative associated with a member may register as a Limited Representative - Direct Participation Program if his activities involve solicitation or sale of option or security futures contracts, and the person passes a corresponding Qualification Examination.

Limited Representative - Corporate Securities - a representative associated with a member may register as a Limited Representative - Corporate Securities if he has passed a corresponding Qualification Examination and his activities involve the solicitation, purchase, or sale of securities other than municipal securities, option securities, redeemable securities, variable contracts of certain insurance companies, and direct participation programs.

Limited Representative - Equity Trader - every representative associated with a member must register as a Limited Representative - Equity Trader if in regards to equity securities he engages in proprietary trading, transacting on an agency basis, or supervises such activities. A person seeking this registration must have already been registered as a General Securities Representative or a Limited Representative - Corporate Securities and the person must pass a corresponding Qualification Examination.

Limited Representative - Government Securities - a representative associated with a member may register as a Limited Representative - Government Securities if the person's activities involve the solicitation, purchase, or sale of government securities and the person passes a corresponding Qualification Examination.

Limited Representative - Private Securities Offerings - a representative associated with a member may register as a Limited Representative - Private Securities Offerings if his activities involve effecting sales as part of certain primary non-public offerings but not the sales of municipal, government, or equity interest or debt of direct participation programs. Such person also must pass a corresponding Qualification Examination.

Limited Representative - Investment Banking - a representative associated with a member must register as a Limited Representative - Investment Banking if his activities involve advising on debt or equity securities or advising on or facilitating mergers and acquisitions, tender offers, financial restructurings, asset sales, divestitures or other corporate reorganizations, unless such person's activities are limited to advising on the placement of direct participation program securities, private securities offerings, or retail or institutional sales activities. He also must pass a corresponding Qualification Examination.

REGISTRATION OF RESEARCH ANALYST

Registration of research analysts (NASD Rule 1050) - all research analysts associated with a member are to be registered. The analysts must first be registered as a General Securities Representative and have passed a Qualification Examination.

Persons exempt from registration (NASD Rule 1060) - certain persons associated with a member are exempt from registration including: clerical or ministerial persons; persons not actively engaged in investment banking or securities business; persons that are nominal officers or capital participants; certain persons registered on the floor of a national securities exchange; and persons engaged in only municipal securities, commodities, or security futures. Compensation can be given to certain non-registered foreign-associated persons.

COMMUNICATIONS WITH THE PUBLIC

Communications with the public (FINRA Rule 2210) - a qualified registered principal must approve all retail communication before its use or filing with FINRA, unless another member has already filed it and it has been approved and the member has not altered it. For institutional communications, members are to establish written procedures for review by a qualified registered principal of institutional communications. The procedures are to be designed to ensure that institutional communications company with the standards. All communications, retail and institutional, are to be retained according to requirements, and must include:

1. a copy of the communication;
2. the name of any registered principal approving of the communication;
3. if not approved by a registered principal prior to first use, the name of the person who prepared it;
4. information about the source of information used in graphic illustrations; and
5. if approval is not required for retail communication, the name of the member that filed it with FINRA, as well as the letter from FINRA.

RULE 472

Rule 472 sets general standards that apply to all communications with the public published by a member firm. **Rule 472** states that a member firm may not publish any communication which contains:

- An untrue statement or omission of a material fact that is false or misleading.
- The promise of a specific result or return.
- An exaggerated or unwarranted claim.
- An opinion that does not have a reasonable basis.
- A projection or forecast that is not clearly labeled as a forecast.

Rule 472 also sets specific standards that apply to recommendations, records of past performance, projections and predictions, comparisons, dating reports, identification of sources and testimonials.

RULE 2220

Rule 2220 defines three types of options communications with the public:

- *Advertisements* are directed at a mass audience using a public media such as newspaper, magazine, radio, television, film, video and billboard. Advertisements are not required to be accompanied or preceded by an option disclosure statement.

- *Educational material* is provided to customers or the public. The purpose of educational material is to explain the nature of standardized options markets or options strategies.
- *Sales literature* is a written communication distributed to customers or the public. Sales literature contains analysis, performance reports, projections or recommendations regarding options. Information communicated during seminars and lectures that pertains to options is also considered sales literature.

COMPLAINTS RELATED TO OPTIONS TRANSACTIONS

FINRA Rule 2360 requires members to keep a central file at their principal place of business to log *complaints*. The central file should make it easy to identify and retrieve information concerning complaints. This central file should at least include the identity of the complainant, the date that the firm received the complaint, the registered person servicing the account, a description of the complaint, and a record of the action taken by the member to resolve the complaint. The rule further goes on to require that the firm retain the options trading agreement at both the servicing branch and the OSJ branch. Additionally, statements must be maintained at both locations for at least six months, unless easily accessible (i.e., electronically stored), in which case statements need only be stored in one location.

COMMUNICATIONS TO CUSTOMERS

According to **Rule 791**, member firms, allied members and employees of member firms shall not distribute any advertisement, educational material, sales literature or other communication to a customer or the public that contains the following:

- An untrue statement or omission of material fact that is false or misleading.
- A promise of specific results, unwarranted claims, opinions that do not have a reasonable basis or forecasts of future events that are unwarranted.
- A hedge clause or disclaimer which is not legible, which disclaims responsibility for the content of the communication or is inconsistent with the communication
- Would constitute a prospectus as defined under the Securities Act of 1933

EDUCATIONAL MATERIAL

Educational materials are exempt from disclosure if the material complies with *SEC Rule 134A*. In order to comply, the **educational material** must meet the following guidelines:

- The risks involved in options trading and the strategies addressed in the material must be explained.
- Performance figures and annualized rates of returns cannot be used in the material.
- There is no recommendation to purchase or sell an option contract.
- The only securities identified are those that are exempt from registration, index options and foreign currency options.
- The name and address where an options disclosure document can be obtained must be listed in the material.

MSRB SUPERVISION

Rule G-27 of the Municipal Securities Rulemaking Board (MSRB) states that all municipal securities firms are required to employ a principal to oversee the company's representatives, and to write and maintain a written manual of supervisory procedures. Further among the responsibilities of the *financial and operations principal*, or *FinOp*, are to approve or reject (in writing) the opening of new accounts, approve or reject in writing all municipal securities transactions, approve or reject in writing steps taken to resolve client complaints, and approve or reject in writing correspondence pertaining to the trading of municipal securities. All broker/dealers (not including bank dealers) must employ FinOps to keep financial records and books.

FINRA 2330 MEMBERS' RESPONSIBILITIES REGARDING DEFERRED VARIABLE ANNUITIES

Application - this rule applies to recommended purchases and exchanges of **deferred variable annuities** and **recommended initial subaccount allocations**. The Rule states that documents can be created, stored, and transmitted in electronic or paper form, and electronic signatures are acceptable as well as written form.

Principal review and approval - before submitting a customer's application to an insurance company for processing, a member must have the application package approved by a registered principal.

Supervisory procedures - a member must implement procedures for surveillance to determine if associated persons have rates of effecting deferred variable annuity exchanges that raise for review, whether such rates are consistent with FINRA or SEC rules. A member must also have policies and procedures designed to implement corrective measures addressing inappropriate exchanges.

Training - a member must develop and document training policies or programs designed to ensure that associated persons who effect and registered persons who review transactions of deferred variable annuities are compliant.

A member is not to recommend to a customer, a deferred variable annuity unless the member believes that the customer has been **informed of the features** of deferred variable annuities, the customer would benefit from such features, and the specific annuity is suitable for the customer. The same standard applies to the exchange of a deferred variable annuity, but the member must also take into account any surrender charge, product enhancements, and other deferred variable annuities the customer may have had in the last 36 months. Prior to recommending, a member must make a reasonable effort to get important information from the customer material to investment decisions, such as age, income, financial situation, investment objectives, risk tolerance, etc. After receiving all information necessary to complete an application for a deferred variable annuity, it must be sent to an *office of supervisory jurisdiction*.

COMMUNICATIONS WITH THE PUBLIC ABOUT VARIABLE LIFE INSURANCE AND VARIABLE ANNUITIES

Communications with the public about variable life insurance and variable annuities - in addition to the standards in FINRA Rule 2210, additional guidelines must be met regarding communications with the public about variable life insurance and variable annuities. All communications must clearly describe the product as a variable annuity or life insurance policy. There is to be no representation that the investments are short term, and all references to liquidity must include clear language that describes the negative aspects of early redemption. The relative safety of guarantee must not be overemphasized, and there can be no representation that a guarantee applies to the investment return or value of the account.

INVESTMENT COMPANY SALES LITERATURE

Pursuant to **Rule 156 of the Securities Act of 1933**, there are 2 requirements related to material facts. The first requirement is that investment company sales literature *may not contain an untrue statement* of material fact. Additionally, investment company sales literature *may not omit to state a material fact* that is necessary in order to make a statement made not misleading. Each circumstance is considered within the context in which the statement is made, and will be evaluated in conjunction with other statements made in connection with the sale of the same security and the absence of other explanations or qualifications that are necessary to make a statement not misleading, among others. Potential investors need to be made aware of all materials facts related to an investment company security to allow them to make an informed investment decision.

ADVERTISEMENT BY AN INVESTMENT COMPANY

In order to comply with **Rule 482 of the Securities Act of 1933**, any advertisement of an investment company must include a statement that advises an investor to consider the investment objectives, risks, and charges and expenses of the investment company carefully before investing; explains that the prospectus and, if available, the summary prospectus contain this and other information about the investment company; identifies a source from which an investor may obtain a prospectus and, if available, a summary prospectus; and states that the prospectus and, if available, the summary prospectus should be read carefully before investing. This *disclosure* is important because it ensures that each piece of investment company advertising will remind investors to carefully consider their investments and points them in the right direction to obtain additional information that is necessary to make an informed decision.

RESEARCH ANALYST AND RESEARCH REPORT

Rule 2711 places the following restrictions on research analyst *compensation*:

- Research analysts cannot receive any bonus, salary or other compensation based on a specific investment banking service.
- A committee must review and approve the compensation paid to a research analyst. This review must be performed annually and reported to the member's board of directors.
- Investment banking may not be represented on the compensation review committee.
- The committee must consider the research analyst's performance, the correlation between recommendations and investment performance and recommendations from the member's clients and employees.
- The compensation review cannot take into account the research analyst's contribution to the investment banking business.
- The basis for the research analyst's compensation must be documented.
- The committee must make an annual attestation of the review.

Rule 2711 places the following restriction on research analysts when *publishing research reports* and *making public appearances* on behalf of a subject company:

- An underwriter of a new issue cannot publish a research report or make a public appearance for 40 days after the offering date.
- An underwriter of offering is prohibited from publishing a research report or making a public appearance for 10 days after the offering date.
- An underwriting group member cannot publish a research report or make a public appearance for 25 days after the offering date.
- A party to a lock-up agreement is prohibited from publishing a research report or making a public appearance for the 15 days prior to and after the expiration, waiver or termination of the lock-up agreement.
- Notice must be given before research coverage of a subject company is terminated. A final research report must be published that is comparable in scope to previous research reports and that contains a final recommendation.

ANALYST CERTIFICATION

Securities & Exchange Commission (SEC) Regulation Analyst Certification (AC) requires investment analysts to attest to the fact that their research reports are truthful and accurate and the views they express in their public appearances are honest and complete. In addition, under SEC Regulation AC, analysts must disclose what compensation they have received that is related to their opinions and views.

FAIR DISCLOSURE

Adopted on August 15, 2000, **Regulation FD (Fair Disclosure)** is a set of rules with the purpose of addressing three insider trading issues: selective disclosure, insider trading liability, and family member or non-business relationship trades. *Selective disclosure* refers to when a securities issuer releases material nonpublic information, usually to certain industry professionals. The Regulation prohibits this without public disclosure of the information. The Regulation also states that *insider trading liability* (Rule 10b5-1) arises when an individual trades a security while aware of material nonpublic information. It provides for some exception when the individual can prove that the information was not a factor in the decision to trade. The Regulation also defines (Rule 10b5-2) how a *family member* - or an individual of another non-business relationship - can be liable for insider trading.

TELEMARKETING

FINRA Rule 3230, which sets forth guidance on telemarketing activities, states that no member or person associated with a member shall initiate any outbound telephone call to:

1. Any person's residence before 8 a.m. or after 9 p.m., unless:
    a. The member has an established business relationship with the person,
    b. The member has received that person's prior express invitation or permission, or
    c. The person called is a broker or dealer.
2. Any person that previously has stated that he or she does not wish to receive an outbound telephone call made by or on behalf of the member, or
3. Any person who has registered his or her telephone number on the Federal Trade Commission's national do-not-call registry.

TELEPHONE CONSUMER PROTECTION ACT OF 1991

Registered representatives who desire to prospect for clients through telemarketing must follow regulations set forth by the **Telephone Consumer Protection Act of 1991**, or *TCPA*. These guidelines are as follows: calling individuals with whom the individual does not have a business relationship must be confined to the hours between 8 a.m. and 9 p.m. local time for the recipient of the call; the individual placing the call must identify himself and his firm and how he may be contacted and identify the purpose of the call; and, if the call recipient requests to be placed on a do-not-call list, the caller must comply. The do-not-call status must be maintained for five years. The TCPA applies to phone calls, fax machines and email, and these regulations must be applied to each method of communication.

INFLUENCING OR REWARDING EMPLOYEES OF OTHERS

Influencing or rewarding employees of others (FINRA Rule 3220) - a member is not to give anything of value in excess of $100 per individual per person per year in relation to the business of the employer.

Arbitration disclosure to associated persons signing or acknowledging Form U4 (FINRA Rule 2263) - a member is to provide an associated person with a specific written statement at any time the person is asked to sign or initial a Form U4. This statement ensures the person understands predispute arbitration.

POLITICAL CONTRIBUTIONS AND PROHIBITIONS ON MUNICIPAL SECURITIES BUSINESS

The Municipal Securities Rulemaking Board (MSRB) established **Rule G-37** to prevent underwriters trying to win the business of municipal securities issuers from effectively buying their business through political contributions. *Political contributions* are not an issue when the underwriting firm is decided through a competitive bid. In that case, the issuer simply selects the underwriter that will charge the firm the least of all the bidders. Rule G-37 takes effect through negotiated underwritings. In negotiated underwritings, a municipal securities issuer will select an underwriter and negotiate costs. Rule G-37 prevents underwriters from making political contributions to politicians who may be associated with municipal securities issuers because the politicians may direct business only to firms that make contributions to their campaign.

CODE OF PROCEDURE

Purpose and application- the **Code of Procedure** outlines the proceedings for disciplining a member or person associated; proceedings for regulating the activities of a member with financial or operational difficulties; proceedings for suspension, cancellation, bars, prohibitions, or limitations; and proceedings for obtaining relief from FINRA eligibility requirements.

Definitions (Rule 9120)

1. *Adjudicator* - a person or group that presides over a proceeding and renders a decision or recommendation.
2. *Chief Hearing Officer* - designated by the CEO of FINRA to manage the Office of Hearing Officers.
3. *Counsel to the National Adjudicatory Council* - an attorney of the Office of the General Counsel of FINRA responsible for advising the National Adjudicatory Council.
4. *Extended Hearing Panel* - an adjudicator that conducts an extended hearing.
5. *Extended Proceeding Committee* - an appellate adjudicator that participates in the National Adjudicatory Council's consideration of an extended proceeding.

General Counsel — the Chief Legal Officer of FINRA.

Head of Enforcement — the individual designated by the FINRA CEO to manage the Department of Enforcement.

Hearing Officer — an attorney employed by FINRA that acts in an adjudicative role regarding disciplinary proceedings.

Hearing Panel — an adjudicator that conducts a disciplinary proceeding.

Market Regulation Committee — a FINRA committee designated to consider federal securities laws and FINRA rules in relation to securities quotes, transaction execution and reporting, and trading practices.

Panelist — a member of an FINRA panel that is not a Hearing Officer.

Primary District Committee — the District Committee designated to provide a panelist for a disciplinary proceeding.

Statutory Disqualification Committee — a subcommittee of the National Adjudicatory Council that makes a recommended decision to grant or deny an application for relief from FINRA eligibility requirements.

THE EMPLOYEE RETIREMENT INCOME SECURITY ACT (ERISA)

The **Employee Retirement Income Security Act (ERISA)** was passed in 1974 with the purpose of protecting the retirement assets of American employees in *qualified retirement plans*. Since employees invest assets for retirement in a fund of plan assets, the growth of that investment is very important. ERISA requires plans to inform employees about these investment strategies and makes fiduciaries in charge of those plan assets accountable to the employees for any asset mismanagement.

REGULATION T

Creditor - broker/dealers that extend credit.

Customer - a person to whom a creditor extends credit.

OTC margin stock - any equity security traded over-the-counter that meets certain qualifications to be able to be treated as if it were traded on a national exchange.

Margin security - any security traded on a national securities exchange; any security traded on the NASDAQ; any non-equity security; any security issued by certain investment companies; any foreign margin stock; and any debt security convertible into a margin security.

Exempted securities mutual fund - a security issued by certain investment companies provided that the company has 95% of its assets in exempted securities.

Non-equity security - a security that is not an equity security.

Separation of accounts - requirements of an account may not be met by considering items in another account. If cash or securities are being withdrawn from one account to be used for another account to meet requirements, and it is permitted by Regulation T, written entries need to be made.
Maintenance of credit - credit once extended must be maintained, regardless of:

1. reductions in customer's equity from changing market prices
2. a security ceasing to be a margin or exempted security
3. a change in margin requirements

Guarantee of accounts - a customer's account cannot be guaranteed.

Receipt of funds or securities - a creditor can accept as immediate payment cash, checks, or securities. If a payment has been sent by another creditor, the funds can be considered received upon written notification from the creditor that it has been sent.

Arranging for loans by others - a creditor can arrange for credit to be extended to customers from another creditor.

APPROVAL PROCEDURES FOR DAY-TRADING ACCOUNTS

Approval procedures for day-trading accounts (FINRA Rule 2130) - a day-trading member may not open an account for a non-institutional customer without furnishing to the customer a risk disclosure statement and without having approved the customer's account for day trading according to certain criteria. In lieu of approving the customer's account, the member can obtain a written agreement from the customer stating the customer does not intend the account to use for day-trading activities.

DISCLOSURE OF FINANCIAL CONDITION

Disclosure of financial condition (FINRA Rule 2261) - a member is required to furnish recent financial statements to other members upon request when the member is party to an open transaction or has on deposit cash or securities of another member.

MARGIN DISCLOSURE STATEMENT

All FINRA members must provide to any non-institutional customers opening a margin account, a **margin disclosure statement** in written or electronic form before or at the time of opening the account. The disclosure is also required to be delivered to each margin customer annually. If customers are able to open an account on the internet, the disclosure statement is to be posted on the website in a clear a conspicuous manner. The statement is provided in *FINRA Rule 2264* and makes various statements warning customers of risk.

DAY-TRADING RISK DISCLOSURE STATEMENT

Day Trading Risk Disclosure Statement (FINRA Rule 2270) - in addition to providing the customer with the risk disclosure statement, the member must post the same disclosure on the member's website. The risks disclosures include: day trading is extremely risky; be cautious of claims of large profits from day trading; day trading requires knowledge of securities markets; day trading requires knowledge of a firm's operations; day trading will generate substantial commissions, even if the per trade cost is low; day trading on margin or short selling may result in losses beyond your initial investment; and potential registration requirements.

NETWORKING ARRANGEMENTS BETWEEN MEMBERS AND FINANCIAL INSTITUTIONS

Networking arrangements between members and financial institutions (FINRA Rule 3160) - a member that is a part of a networking agreement under which it conducts broker-dealer services on or off the premises of a financial institution is subject to the Rule.

Setting - the member is to be clearly identified and have its services distinguished from the services of the financial institution, have its name displayed where it conducts business, and maintain its services physically separate from that of the financial institution if at all possible

MARGIN REQUIREMENTS

When a customer chooses to purchase securities on margin in an account, there are **minimum initial margin amounts** that must be met. In general, this amount is $2,000 of equity, with the exception of pattern day traders, who are required to have an initial margin of $25,000 of equity.

Many customers are required to hold much more than this amount. Specifically, broker-dealers can calculate the **margin requirements** using the following calculations:

1. 25 percent of the current market value of all long positions
2. The greater of $2.50 per share or 100 percent of the current market value for any short equity positions with a price per share under $5.00
3. The greater of $5.00 per share or 30 percent of the current market value for any short equity positions with a price per share over $5.00
4. The greater of 5 percent of the principal amount or 30 percent of the current market value for any short bond positions

5. 20 percent of the current market value for any short or long futures contract
6. 100 percent of the current market value for any positions that are not margin eligible

CUSTOMER ACCOUNT INFORMATION

Financial Industry Regulatory Authority (FINRA) Rules 4512 and *4515* describe the exact information that a broker-dealer is required to have on file prior to opening an account for a new customer. The information includes the following:

1. Name
2. Address
3. If the customer is of legal age
4. Name of any other individuals that will be responsible for the account
5. Signature of the partner, officer, or manager indicating that the account is good standing
6. The names of anyone who is authorized to make trades in the account
7. Tax ID or Social Security number
8. Occupation of the customer, including the name and address of the employer

DISCRETIONARY ACCOUNTS

Excessive transactions - when a member has discretionary powers over the account of a customer, the member may not transact purchases or sales that are in excessive size or frequency in comparison to the size and character of the account.

Authorization and acceptance of account - a member may not exercise its own discretion in a customer's account unless they have received written authorization from the customer.

Approval and review of transactions - a member shall quickly and in writing approve all discretionary transactions and regularly review all discretionary accounts to prevent any excessive transactions.

Exceptions - the Rule does not apply to the time and price that an order received from the customer is executed at, though such orders are only valid through the end of the business day. It also does not apply to certain bulk exchanges of net asset value of money market mutual funds.

TRANSACTIONS FOR OR BY ASSOCIATED PERSONS

NASD Rule 3050 imposes certain obligations on associated persons who work with accounts that are owned by investment advisers, banks, or other financial institutions. Prior to opening the account or placing trades for one of the above customers, associated persons must notify their employer in writing of either the intent to execute the transactions or the intent to open the account. Additionally, the associated person must provide the customer with duplicate copies of confirmations, statements, or other information about the account or order upon the written request of either the customer or the associated person's member firm. Finally, if the customer's account was opened prior to the associated person's association with the member firm, then the associated person must comply with this rule on an ongoing basis immediately upon their association.

DILIGENCE AS TO ACCOUNTS

In order to ensure that investment advisors are acting in the best interest of their customers when making recommendations, the NYSE created **Rule 405**. Rule 405, also endorsed by FINRA, requires that a representative gather enough information from the customer to make appropriate and suitable investment recommendations. The advisor must review a customer's income level, financial and investment objectives, tax bracket, retirement needs, current holdings, college expenses and general attitude about investing. The advisor should frequently review this type of information with the customer and make any changes necessary. Advisors should also know if the customer is married, has children and is employed. The rule operates on the basis that the more information an advisor has about a customer, the better and more suitable their recommendations will be.

SUITABILITY OF RECOMMENDATIONS AND TRANSACTIONS

MSRB Rule G-19 requires that, prior to trading in a retail customer's account, the registered individual must collect suitability information regarding the customer's financial status, tax status, investment objective concerning the municipal security being traded, and any other information that might be required to ensure that the transaction meets the customer's suitability needs. The claim that the security is a suitable investment must be supported by complete and accurate information obtained from the customer for that purpose, and information provided by the issuer. MSRB G-19 also addresses suitability issues concerning discretionary accounts, and requires that the investment be suitable in such accounts. Finally, G-19 expressly forbids churning in accounts through multiple transactions, or unreasonably large transactions to provide larger commissions to the registered person.

SUPERVISION

Rule G-27 of the Municipal Securities Rulemaking Board (MSRB) states that all municipal securities firms are required to employ a principal to oversee the company's representatives, and to write and maintain a written manual of supervisory procedures. Further among the responsibilities of the **financial and operations principal**, or *FinOp*, are to approve or reject (in writing) the opening of new accounts, approve or reject in writing all municipal securities transactions, approve or reject in writing steps taken to resolve client complaints, and approve or reject in writing correspondence pertaining to the trading of municipal securities. All broker/dealers (not including bank dealers) must employ FinOps to keep financial records and books.

SEC RULE 17A-3

Memorandum of each brokerage order given or received for the purchase or sale of securities (for customer and firm accounts) - whether executed or unexecuted. The memorandum is to show the terms and conditions; the account for which entered; the time the order was received; the time of entry; the price it was executed; the identity of any associated persons responsible for the account; the identity of the person who entered or accepted the order; and the time of execution or cancellation.

Memorandum of each purchase and sale for the account of the firm - including the price, the time of execution, and if the transaction was with a customer other than a broker or dealer, a memorandum of each order received showing the time of receipt, the terms and conditions; the identity of each associated person responsible for the account; and the identity of the person who entered or accepted the order.

Blotters or other records of original entry - are to contain an itemized daily record of all purchases and sales of securities, all receipts and deliveries of securities, all receipts and disbursements of cash, as well as all other debits and credits.

Copies of customer confirmations - and copies of notices of all other debits and credits for accounts of customers.

Identification data on beneficial owners of all accounts - all cash and margin accounts are to have identification data including the name and address of the beneficial owner of the account.

Ledgers or other records reflecting all assets and liabilities - including income and expense and capital accounts.

RECORDS TO BE PRESERVED BY CERTAIN EXCHANGE MEMBERS

Records to be preserved by certain exchange members, brokers and dealers (Rule 17a-4) - every broker and dealer is to keep general records for six years. For the first two years of record retention, the records are to be kept in an easily accessible place. Records of associated persons are to be kept until three years after the person's employment has terminated. Records can be produced or reproduced on micrographic media. If records are to be maintained by an outside service bureau, such bureau is to file with the Commission.

COD ORDERS

FINRA Rule 11860 prohibits *cash on delivery transactions* for securities unless the transaction adheres to a strict set of rules. Before the transaction is entered into, the FINRA member must be aware that the transaction will be cash on delivery, the transaction should be marked as such, and the customer must receive a confirmation of the transaction by the end of the next business day. The FINRA member must receive a signed agreement from the customer stating that the "customer will furnish his agent instructions with respect to the receipt or delivery of the securities involved in the transaction promptly upon receipt by the customer of each confirmation, or the relevant data as to each execution" to help ensure that good and prompt delivery is made.

CUSTOMER ACCOUNT TRANSFER CONTRACTS

Customers who wish to transfer securities from one FINRA member to another may submit an **automated customer account transfer form**, or *ACAT*. Per *FINRA Rule 11870*, each FINRA member must "expedite and coordinate activities" to comply with the customer's request. Rule 11870 also provides for non-ACAT transfers via non-ACAT forms. ACAT forms will vary from member to member, but will generally contain the same information. The member that receives the instructions must validate (declare valid) the request or claim that the request is not valid (take issue) within one business day. After that, they must act in a reasonably speedy manner to facilitate the request. If the ACAT requests that the securities be liquidated first, it will generally take longer to process.

RULE 4210 – MARGIN REQUIREMENTS

TERMS

Basket: a group of stocks eligible to be executed in a single trade.

Designated account: an account of certain banks, investment companies, insurance companies, state or political subdivisions, or pension plans.

Margin: the necessary amount of equity to be maintained for a security position in an account.

Major foreign sovereign debt: a debt security issued by a foreign entity that has debt securities that are subordinated in relation and the security has been ranked in the top rating category by a nationally recognized rating organization.

Exempt account: any member or registered broker-dealer, or certain persons with a net worth of $45 million or more.

Other marginable non-equity securities: includes certain debt securities that are not traded on a national exchange and certain private pass-through securities.

Pattern day trader: a customer who executes four or more trades within five business days, unless those trades represent 6% or less of the customer's total trades.

Day-trading buying power: the equity the day-trading customer has in their account less any maintenance margin, multiplied by four (for equity securities).

Special requirements for pattern day traders: the special requirements for pattern day traders include:

1. a minimum equity requirement of $25,000
2. they cannot trade in excess of their day-trading buying power
3. if a pattern day trader fails to meet maintenance margin calls as required, they will be permitted only to trade on a cash available basis for 90 days or until the margin call is met
4. minimum equity funds deposited cannot be withdrawn for a minimum of two business days after deposit

INITIAL AND MAINTENANCE

Initial margin - the required opening deposit in a margin account.

Maintenance margin - the required margin which must be maintained in an account, calculated as:

1. 25% of the current market value of securities
2. the greater of $2.50 per share or 100% or the current market value for any stock short positions of stock trading at less than $5 per share
3. the greater of $5 per share or 100% or the current market value for any stock short positions of stock trading at more than $5 per share
4. the greater of $5 per share or 30% of the current market value for each bond short position; E. 20% of the current market value for any security futures contracts
5. 100% of the current market value for non-margin eligible securities held "long"

ADDITIONAL

Additional margin - a procedure must be in place for members to review type and limit of credit extended, to formulate their own margin requirements, and to review the need for instituting higher margin requirements.

Exceptions to rule for offsetting long and short positions - if a security in "long" position is exchangeable or convertible into a security in "short" position, the margin required is 10% of current market value of the "long" security. If the "long" and "short" are for the same security, the margin required is 5%.

EXEMPTIONS

Exempted securities - net "long" and "short" positions in obligations that are guaranteed by the United States or that are highly rated foreign sovereign debt securities are exempted and given their own margin requirements. "Long" and "short" positions in exempted securities other than United States obligations shall maintain a margin of 7% of the current market value.

Non-equity securities - "long" and "short" positions in non-equity securities are to maintain a margin of 10% of the current market value for investment grade securities, and the greater of 20% of the current market value or 7% of the principal for other non-equity securities.

Baskets - a member can make basket transactions for a registered market maker based on a margin determined to be adequate by the concerned parties.

Specialists' and market makers' accounts - a member can have a margin account for an approved market maker based on a margin determined to be adequate by the concerned parties.

Broker-dealer accounts - a member can have a proprietary margin account for another broker-dealer based on a margin determined to be adequate by the concerned parties.

Shelf-registered and other control and restricted securities - securities that are part of a continuous or delayed offering (shelf-registered securities) are subject to the same maintenance requirements as other securities. For other control and restricted securities, the margin to be maintained is 40% of the current market value for "long" securities.

KNOW YOUR CUSTOMER

Know your customer (FINRA Rule 2090) - members of FINRA are to use reasonable diligence when opening and maintaining accounts for customers, and to get to know essential facts about the customer and concerning the authority of each person acting on behalf of a customer.

Suitability (FINRA Rule 2111) - a member must have a reasonable basis to believe that an investment or strategy is suitable for the customer based on the information the member has gained, according to the "know your customer" rule. Pertinent information includes the customer's age, other investments, financial situation, tax status, objectives, experience, investment time horizon, liquidity needs, and risk tolerance. For an institutional customer, the member is to have reasonable belief the customer is capable of evaluating risks and has indicated that it is exercising independent judgment.

SUITABILITY ISSUES

FINRA Rule 2111 states that advisers must "have a reasonable basis to believe that a recommended transaction or investment strategy involving a security or securities is suitable for the customer, based on the information obtained through the reasonable diligence of the [firm] or associated person to ascertain the customer's investment profile." Thus, Rule 2111 reinforces the need for the registered person to gather complete and accurate suitability information regarding time horizon, liquidity needs, and risk tolerance. The advisor's diligence should include a mutually exclusive analysis of time horizon and liquidity needs as well. While those with a long-time horizon may be well positioned to accept the risks associated with liquidity, their goals and desires may require that they have liquidity to invest in other securities.

RECOMMENDATIONS TO CUSTOMERS IN OTC EQUITY SECURITIES

No member is to recommend a customer purchase or sell short any OTC equity security, unless the member has reviewed the current financial statements and material business information of the issuer and determined that the information provides a reasonable basis. The registered person designated to make this review is to be a **General Securities Principal** or **General Securities Sales Supervisor** with appropriate skills, background, and knowledge. If the issue has not met any of its necessary filing requirements, the review is to include inquiry about the circumstances of the failure to file, and any subsequent recommendation to a customer is to be in writing.

STANDARDS OF COMMERCIAL HONOR AND PRINCIPALS OF TRADE

FINRA Rule 2010—Standards of Commercial Honor and Principles of Trade states that "a member, in the conduct of its business, shall observe high standards of commercial honor and just and equitable principles of trade." Broadly speaking, this rule encourages members to be just and equitable in their dealings, although no real specific guidance is provided. One example of a violation of this rule would be a member who treats different customers differently based upon their gender, ethnicity, religion, or other personal attributes. This biased approach to customers violates the just and equitable charge of Rule 2010, as well as a number of other FINRA rules, and would result in significant repercussions for the member. A member must treat each customer equitably, considering each customer's individual circumstances and investment objectives.

NET TRANSACTIONS WITH CUSTOMERS

Net transactions with customers (FINRA Rule 2124) - a member executing a net transaction with a customer must first disclose it and obtain consent from the customer. A net transaction is a when a member, after receiving an order from a customer, purchases the security at a different price and subsequently sells it to the customer to fulfill the original order, keeping the proceeds that make up the difference in price.

MEMBERS' RESPONSIBILITIES REGARDING DEFERRED VARIABLE ANNUITIES

Application - this rule applies to recommended purchases and exchanges of **deferred variable annuities** and **recommended initial subaccount allocations**. The Rule states that documents can be created, stored, and transmitted in electronic or paper form, and electronic signatures are acceptable as well as written form.

Principal review and approval - before submitting a customer's application to an insurance company for processing, a member must have the application package approved by a registered principal.

Supervisory procedures - a member must implement procedures for surveillance to determine if associated persons have rates of effecting deferred variable annuity exchanges that raise for review, whether such rates are consistent with FINRA or SEC rules. A member must also have policies and procedures designed to implement corrective measures addressing inappropriate exchanges.

Training - a member must develop and document training policies or programs designed to ensure that associated persons who effect and registered persons who review transactions of deferred variable annuities are compliant.

COMMUNICATIONS WITH THE PUBLIC ABOUT VARIABLE LIFE INSURANCE AND VARIABLE ANNUITIES

Communications with the public about variable life insurance and variable annuities - in addition to the standards in FINRA Rule 2210, additional guidelines must be met regarding communications with the public about variable life insurance and variable annuities. All communications must clearly describe the product as a variable annuity or life insurance policy. There is to be no representation that the investments are short term, and all references to liquidity must include clear language that describes the negative aspects of early redemption. The relative safety of guarantee must not be overemphasized, and there can be no representation that a guarantee applies to the investment return or value of the account.

BREAKPOINT SALES

Breakpoint sales (FINRA Rule 2342) - a member is not to sell investment company shares at a price below the point that the sales charge is reduced on quantity transactions in order to gain the applicable higher sales charges.

Prompt payment for investment company shares (NASD Rule 2830) - a member engaging in retail transactions for investment company shares are to transmit payments from customers for the shares to the payees by the later of either the end of the 3rd business day after the order to purchase, or the end of one business day after receipt of the payment from the customer.

USE OF MANIPULATIVE, DECEPTIVE OR OTHER FRAUDULENT DEVICES

FINRA Rule 2020—Use of Manipulative, Deceptive or Other Fraudulent Devices states: "No member shall effect any transaction in, or induce the purchase or sale of, any security by means of any manipulative, deceptive, or other fraudulent device or contrivance." The importance of this rule is in ensuring the integrity of the capital markets and the confidence of retail investors that the markets are not "rigged" for the larger, institutional investors or those with critical inside information. A member would be in violation of Rule 2020 if he used falsified, enhanced financial reports to entice an investor to purchase a certain security. In addition to being dishonest and illegal, such activities have significantly negative repercussions for the markets as they reduce market efficiency and drastically reduce market participation among smaller investors if discovered.

PROHIBITION AGAINST TRADING AHEAD OF CUSTOMER ORDERS

Prohibition against trading ahead of customer orders (FINRA Rule 5320) - a member that accepts an order from a customer and does not immediately execute it is prohibited from trading that same security on the same side of the market for its own account at a price that would satisfy the customer's order unless the member immediately after executes the customer order at the same or better price.

PAYMENTS FOR MARKET MAKING

Payments for market making (FINRA Rule 5250) - a member may not receive payment from an issuer of a security in exchange for publishing a quote or acting as a market maker in a security. *Quote and order access requirements (FINRA Rule 6250)* - an ADF trading center, for each security displays a bid and/or offer, must provide other ADF trading centers direct electronic access. This access is to include access for broker-dealers that are not ADF trading centers. The ADF trading center is required to keep certain information for each order they receive to include a unique order identifier; order entry firm; order side; order quantity; issue identifier; order price; order negotiable flag; time in force; order date; order time; minimal acceptable quantity; market making firm; and trade-or-move flag

FRONT RUNNING

Front-running is the practice of a registered individual benefitting from the knowledge of a customer or multiple customers' placing a block order that may affect the price of the security in question by placing trades on the underlying security in their own accounts. This is unethical in every situation, and bears more than a passing resemblance to insider trading. **Front-running** is closely regulated by *FINRA Rule 5270*, and should be monitored closely by all registered principals who are responsible for approving trades. Front-running should be easily identifiable to diligent principals (via automatically generated reports that search for such activity), and appropriate disciplinary action should be taken concerning the individual that committed front-running.

TRADING AHEAD OF RESEARCH REPORTS

Trading ahead of research reports occurs when a person expects a security to be affected by the release of a research report. The reasons for the trade determine the **ethicality** of the trade. If a trade desk is placing the trade based on public knowledge and they only expect a change, then the trades placed are legal and ethical under FINRA Rule 5280. However, if the trade desk is privy to material non-public information concerning the security, whether or not they have non-public access to the research report, a trade would be illegal and unethical according to *FINRA Rule 5280*. A firm that trades ahead of a research report should document their reasons well, and have proof that the reasons are public knowledge.

143

PROHIBITIONS WITH RESPECT TO SECURITIES EXEMPTED FROM REGISTRATION

Prohibitions with respect to securities exempted from registration (Rule 10b-1) - it is prohibited to use any manipulative or deceptive device in connection with securities exempt from registration pursuant to the SEA.

Duties of trust or confidence in misappropriation insider trading cases (Rule 10b5-2) - a duty of trust and confidence exists:

1. when a person agrees to maintain information in confidence
2. when the persons involved in communicating the material nonpublic information have a history or practice of sharing confidences to the extent that the communicator trusts the information will remain confidential
3. or when a person receives information from a spouse, parent, child, or sibling

EMPLOYMENT OF MANIPULATIVE AND DECEPTIVE DEVICES BY BROKERS OR DEALERS

Employment of manipulative and deceptive devices by brokers or dealers (Rule 10b-3) - it is prohibited for a broker or dealer to purchase or sell a security otherwise than on a national exchange with an act that is manipulative, deceptive, or fraudulent. The same is also prohibited for municipal securities dealers and municipal securities.

Employment of manipulative and deceptive devices (Rule 10b-5) - it is prohibited for any person to employ and device, scheme, or artifice to defraud; to make any untrue statements of material fact; or to engage in any act, practice, or course of business that would be a fraud or deceit upon any person in connections with the purchase or sale of any security.

FRAUD AND MISREPRESENTATION

Fraud and misrepresentation (Rule 15c1-2) - it is prohibited to make untrue statements of material fact, or to omit to state a material fact with knowledge or reasonable grounds to believe that the statement is such.

Misrepresentation by brokers and dealers as to registration (Rule 15c1-3) - it is prohibited for a broker or dealer to represent that his registration is approval of the SEC of the financial standing or conduct of the business.

Use of pro forma balance sheets (Rule 15c1-9) - it is prohibited to use financial statements that project the receipt and application of proceeds from the sale or exchange of securities unless the assumptions upon which the statement is made are included in the caption in type that is at least as large as the font in the body of the statement.

EMPLOYMENT OF MANIPULATIVE AND DECEPTIVE DEVICES

Employment of manipulative and deceptive devices by brokers or dealers (Rule 10b-3) - it is prohibited for a broker or dealer to purchase or sell a security otherwise than on a national exchange with an act that is manipulative, deceptive, or fraudulent. The same is also prohibited for municipal securities dealers and municipal securities.

Employment of manipulative and deceptive devices (Rule 10b-5) - it is prohibited for any person to employ and device, scheme, or artifice to defraud; to make any untrue statements of material fact; or to engage in any act, practice, or course of business that would be a fraud or deceit upon any person in connections with the purchase or sale of any security.

Trading "On the Basis Of" Material Nonpublic Information in Insider Trading

Trading "on the basis of" material nonpublic information in insider trading (SEA Rule 10b5-1) - a person is deemed to be trading on the basis of material nonpublic information if the person was aware of the information at the time of the transaction unless:

1. he became aware of the information after entering into an agreement to transact
2. he instructed another to transact prior to becoming aware of the information
3. he adopted a written plan for trading securities before becoming aware of the information

The Securities Investor Protection Act of 1970

The *Securities Investor Protection Act of 1970* is federal legislation that established the **Securities Investor Protection Corporation (SIPC)**.

The SIPC is a federally mandated insurance company that serves to insure securities investors in the event the investor's broker-dealer defaults for one reason or another. The SIPC protects investors in the event of a broker-dealer bankruptcy as well as in instances of broker-dealer fraud by providing coverage to investors for up to five hundred thousand dollars. Broker-dealers are members of the SIPC and provide the funding for its operation.

The SIPC is a non-profit corporation. It should be noted that although the SIPC provides nationwide protection to the clients of broker-dealers, the SIPC is not a federal regulatory body or an agency of the federal government.

Publication of Transactions and Quotations

Publication of transactions and quotations (Rule 5210) - no member shall publish communication about a purchase, sale, or quote unless the member believes it was bona fide.

Offers at stated prices (Rule 5220) - a member may not make an offer unless they are prepared to transact at that price. Though sometimes "backing-away" is constituted, regularly "backing-away" puts into question the validity of the dealers quotes and disrupts the course of regular business.

Order entry and execution practices (Rule 5290) - an order cannot be split up into smaller orders simply for the purpose of increasing commissions or payments.

Adjustment of Orders

Adjustment of orders (FINRA Rule 5330) - When a member holds an order from another broker-dealer, the member is to adjust the price and/or number of shares to compensate for any dividend, payment, or distribution on the day of the quote for the security, according to guidelines outlined in the Rule.

Short-interest reporting (FINRA Rule 4560) - members are to maintain records of all of the short equity positions in all accounts and report regularly to FINRA such information.

Best Execution and Interpositioning

Best execution and interpositioning (Rule 5310) - a member must use due diligence in ensuring that the transaction is made on the market best for the security so the price to the customer is favorable. Additionally, a member cannot put a 3rd party between himself and the best market, unless there is an acceptable circumstance.

Displaying priced quotations in multiple quotation mediums (Rule 6438) - if a member displays quotes on multiple real-time quotation mediums, the same priced quotes for a security are to be displayed in each medium.

Recording of quotation information (Rule 6430) - any OTC market maker that displays real-time quotes must keep record of certain information including the submitting firm, inter-dealer quotation system, trade date, time quote displayed, security name and symbol, bid and bid quote size, offer and offer quote size, prevailing inside bid, and prevailing inside offer.

DESIGNATED SECURITIES

Designated securities — NMS stocks defined in Rule 600(b)(47).

Normal market hours — 9:30 AM Eastern Time to 4:00 PM Eastern Time.

Normal unit of trading — 100 shares, unless otherwise determined.

Otherwise than on an exchange — a transaction that takes place somewhere else than on a national exchange.

Round lot holder — any holder of a normal unit of trading.

Stop stock price — the price at which a stop stock transaction will be executed.

Stop stock transaction — a transaction that executes at a stop stock price or better.

Terms defined here are to have the same meaning as in FINRA by-laws and rules; Rule 600 of Regulation NMS; and the Joint Self-Regulatory Organization Plan Governing the Collection, Consolidation, and Dissemination of Quotation and Transaction Information for NASDAQ-Listed Securities Traded on Exchanges on an Unlisted Trading Privilege Basis, unless otherwise defined.

SHORT SALE DELIVERY REQUIREMENTS

Short sale delivery requirements (FINRA Rule 4320) - if a participant in a registered clearing agency has failed to deliver a security to fulfill a short sale for 13 consecutive days, he is to close out the position and purchase a security of like kind and quality. Until the participant closes out this position and purchases a security of like kind and quality, he is not to accept any additional short sale orders for the security. If the participant in a registered clearing agency reasonably allocates a portion of the failure to deliver to a broker-dealer for whom he clears transactions, then the rule is applied to the broker-dealer, not the participant. The participant is not exempted as stated if he has entered into an agreement to purchase securities for a person that he knows will not deliver during settlement.

REGULATION SHO

Regulation SHO, effective as of September 7, 2004, was created to establish a standard for dealing with the short sale of securities. **Regulation SHO** accomplished three specific goals. First, it created *uniformity among delivery requirements*. This helped to reduce the occurrences of delivery failure and naked short selling. Second, Regulation SHO created *uniform marking requirements* for all equity securities. Finally, Regulation SHO created a *standard procedure* for the removal of short sale price tests and restrictions when these provisions become unnecessary. Regulation SHO established a requirement that broker dealers who trade equity securities must locate available securities before conducting any short sales. Requiring broker dealers to locate securities prior to conducting a short sale is an effort to reduce the occurrence delivery failures.

CUSTOMER ACCOUNT STATEMENTS

NASD Rule 2340 - Customer account statements - members are to send an account statement at least once a quarter to customers that contains a description of any positions, money balances, or account activity, unless there has been none in the quarter. The account statement is to include a statement advising customers to promptly report any inaccuracies in the account statement.

DPP/REIT Securities - a member may provide an estimated per share value to the customer for direct participation programs (DPPs) or real estate investment trusts (REITs).

CONFIRMATION OF TRANSACTIONS

Confirmation of transactions (SEC Rule 10b-10) - broker/dealers must disclose certain information to the customer in writing at or before the completion of a transaction. This disclosure must contain specific information including the date and time of the transaction; the identity, price, and number of shares; agency disclosure of the broker/dealer; disclosure of any odd-lot differential fee paid for by the customer; and certain other disclosures for debt securities. There are some exceptions to the Rule such as certain transactions that are part of an investment company plan.

Customer confirmations (FINRA Rule 2232) - a member is to send to the customer a written notification at or before the completion of a transaction.

SETTLEMENT CYCLE

Settlement cycle (SEC Rule 15c6-1) - a broker or dealer is not to enter into a transaction calling for settlement beyond the 3rd business day after execution unless both parties expressly agree to it. This rule does not apply to certain contracts for purchase or sale of limited partnership interests not listed on an exchange or for purchase or sale of securities the SEC exempts from the Rule. The Rule also does not apply in certain situations where the pricing of the security happens after 4:30 PM Eastern Time and sold by an issuer to an underwriter.

FINRA rules regarding clearance and settlement (FINRA Rules 6274 and 6350) - members must clear and settle transactions with a clearing agency that uses a continuous net settlement system.

REPORTS OF SALES OR PURCHASES

Brokers, dealers, and municipal securities dealers are required to report to the board information about each purchase and sale of municipal securities to the **Real-Time Transaction Reporting System (RTRS)**. The information collected under this rule is used to make public reports about market activity, prices charged, and transaction fees assessed. It allows the board to ensure that the board rules are being followed and identify and be in contact with members who are not in full compliance. There are a few securities that are not subject to the reporting requirements including those that do not have assigned Committee on Uniform Securities Identification Procedures (CUSIP) numbers, municipal funds, and those interdealer transactions (i.e., the movement of the securities are not eligible for comparison in a clearing agency).

UNLAWFUL REPRESENTATIONS AND NAMES

Section 35 of the Investment Company Act of 1940 states the following: "It shall be unlawful for any person, issuing or selling any security of which a registered investment company is the issuer, to represent or imply in any manner whatsoever that such security or company—(A) has been guaranteed, sponsored, recommended, or approved by the United States, or any agency, instrumentality, or officer of the United States, (B) has been insured by the Federal Deposit Insurance Corporation, or (C) is guaranteed by or is otherwise an obligation of any bank or insured depository institution. The decision as to whether or not a name is misleading is ultimately made by the Commission.

BORROWING FROM OR LENDING TO CUSTOMERS

As stated in **FINRA Rule 3240**, borrowing from or lending to customers is prohibited unless:

1. The member maintains written procedures for such transactions
2. The borrowing or lending arrangement is with a customer who is immediate family or with a customer who is a financial institution in the business of providing credit or loans
3. The customer is a registered person with the same member firm
4. The lending arrangement is based on a personal relationship with the customer
5. The lending arrangement is based on a business relationship outside of the broker-customer relationship

These guidelines are meant to protect the broker-customer relationship and to ensure that all transactions between the two parties fit within the scope of appropriate transactions that are covered within the regulatory guidelines.

OUTSIDE BUSINESS ACTIVITIES OF A REGISTERED PERSON

FINRA established **Rule 3270** to prevent employees of FINRA members from being subject to **conflicts of interest** that may arise from dual employment. For example, a registered representative (RR) of a well-regarded FINRA member may present an investment not actually associated with their FINRA member employer, and the buyer may associate the stability of the investment with the FINRA member's reputation. To prevent situations like this, FINRA Rule 3270 requires that before member employees accept outside employment, they must first receive permission from their employer, and disclose in a timely fashion any changes or additional employment taken. FINRA Rule 3270 does not apply to passive income because the employee cannot affect truly passive income activities. Before the activity is approved, it is the job of the registered principal to determine if it will "interfere with or otherwise compromise the registered person's responsibilities to the member and/or the member's customers or be viewed by customers or the public as part of the member's business based upon, among other factors, the nature of the proposed activity and the manner in which it will be offered."

PRIVATE SECURITIES TRANSACTIONS

According to **NASD Rule 3040**, which governs the private securities transactions of an **associated person**, an associated person must provide written notice detailing the proposed private securities transaction prior to participating in any private securities transaction. Additionally, the written notice must describe the associated person's role in the transaction and disclose whether or not any selling compensation may be received as a result of the proposed transaction. If the transactions may result in selling compensation, the member firm must either approve or disapprove the person's participation and, if approved, the transaction will be recorded on the books of the member firm and the member shall supervise the person's activities as if the transaction were executed on behalf of the member. If the member disapproves the transaction, then the person may not participate, directly or indirectly, in the transaction.

DISCLOSURE OF CONTROL RELATIONSHIP WITH ISSUER

Rule 2262 states that if common control exists between a member firm and the issuer of a security, the firm must disclose the relationship in writing to any customer wanting to buy or sell said security. For example, if Firm A is selling an equity security in Company B to a customer and Firm A and Company B have a common majority owner, this relationship has to be disclosed to the customer.

Rule 2269 states that if a firm is participating in or has a financial interest in any security either in primary or secondary distribution, this has to be disclosed in writing to the customer. For example, if a firm will receive a financial gain from a specific equity security, this must be disclosed to the customer before selling this same equity to a customer.

UNDERWRITING COMPENSATION AND ARRANGEMENTS

Underwriting compensation and arrangements - all underwriting terms and agreements have to be fair and reasonable. All compensation in relation to underwriting a security has to be fair and reasonable.

Items included in compensation - all items of value received or that will be received by an underwriter in connection with a distribution starting from 180 days before the filing date are considered to be compensation and have to be disclosed in the prospectus.

Valuation of non-cash compensation - a security cannot be received by an underwriter as compensation in connection with a public offering unless the security is identical to the security issued to the public or the security can be accurately valued. Calculated compensation value is usually in some way based on, or derived from, the market price or public offering price.

Non-cash compensation - is restricted, and includes small gifts, occasional meals, and entertainment events.

PUBLIC OFFERINGS OF SECURITIES WITH CONFLICTS OF INTEREST

Public offerings of securities with conflicts of interest (FINRA Rule 5121) - no member with a conflict of interest can participate in certain public offerings unless the conflict is properly disclosed, a qualified independent underwriter has prepared it, the security is investment grade, and there is a bona fide public market.

Offerings resulting in affiliation or public ownership of member - when comprising more than 5% of the offering, it creates a conflict of interest.

Escrow of proceeds - any member offering securities under the Rule must place all proceeds in an escrow account where they must stay until the member is able to prove that they meet the net capital requirement, which requires the member to have enough funds to pay off certain obligations such as non-subordinated debt.

Discretionary accounts - no member with a conflict of interest may sell to a discretionary account.

RESTRICTIONS ON THE PURCHASE AND SALE OF INITIAL EQUITY PUBLIC OFFERINGS

FINRA Rule 5130 was established to ensure that **initial public offerings (IPO)** are executed on a fair and unbiased basis. Rule 5130 applies to new issues, and its goals are to ensure that members do not keep a portion of the IPO for themselves or others that might entice them to and to prevent insiders from taking advantage of a new issue that retail investors may not have the same insight into. FINRA Rule 5130 established a list of persons prohibited from buying new issues. This list includes members of FINRA and their employees, representatives of the underwriters that underwrote the new issue, a shareholder that owns more the 10 percent of a FINRA member firm, portfolio managers, and immediate family members of the preceding. Rule 5130 also prohibits "spinning," or the act of sending an unfair proportion of the IPO to a person that may be able to send business back.

SALE OF SECURITIES IN A FIXED PRICE OFFERING

FINRA Rule 5141 states that those affiliated with a selling syndicate, a syndicate group, or an underwriter for a fixed price offering may not sell or offer that security for less than the stated public price. This rule will remain in place until the public offering is complete or until the member firm is unable to continue selling the offering at the stated public price.

DISCLOSURE OF PRICE AND CONCESSIONS IN SELLING AGREEMENTS

Each underwriter member of a syndicate can either sell the securities, or enlist the aid of agents to sell the securities. These agents along with the underwriter that enlisted them are considered a **selling group**. The agents receive compensation from the underwriter member that enlisted them in the form of a concession. The group is managed by the managing underwriter.

Selling agreement - each selling group is governed by a selling group agreement. FINRA Rule 5160 states that selling group agreements have to include the price at which the securities are sold to the public and what concessions if any are allowed to be given.

Liability - there are two different agreements among underwriters that divide the liability of any unsold portion of the issue differently:

1. *Undivided (Eastern)* - each syndicate member is responsible for all of the unsold securities in an issue, according to their percentage of participation.
2. *Divided (Western)* - each syndicate member is responsible for the unsold securities of only their portion of the issue.

NOTIFICATION REQUIREMENTS OF OFFERING PARTICIPANTS

FINRA Rule 5190 outlines the required notifications for new public offerings. It provides requirements for securities subject to a restricted period under SEC Regulation M as well as actively traded securities:

1. *Securities subject to a restricted period* - a written notice must be submitted relaying to FINRA information regarding whether a one-day or five-day restricted period applies (according to Rule 101 of SEC Regulation M), the name and symbol of the security, the type of security, identification of participants and purchasers, the pricing, and the number of shares offered, among other things.
2. *Actively traded securities* - a written notice must be submitted relaying to FINRA information regarding the fact that no restrictive period applies, the name and symbol of the security, the type of security, identification of participants and purchasers, the pricing, and the number of shares offered, among other things.

FINRA Rule 5190 outlines the required notifications for **penalty bids** and **syndicate covering transactions**. When a member is imposing a penalty bid or is conducting a syndicate covering transaction, a written notice must be submitted relaying to FINRA information regarding the intent to carry out the activity and identification of the security and symbol, before imposing the bid or conducting the transaction. A confirmation is to be submitted to FINRA within one business day of the completion of the activity, including identification of the security and symbol, the total number of shares, and the date of the activity.

NET PRICES TO PERSONS NOT IN INVESTMENT BANKING OR SECURITIES BUSINESS

Net prices to persons not in investment banking or securities business (NASD Rule 2410) - no member is to offer a security or to confirm a purchase or sale of a security from any person not involved in investment banking or securities business using a price that has a concession, discount or allowance. All such transactions are to be in a **net dollar** or **basis price**.

DEALING WITH NON-MEMBERS

NASD Rule 2420 states that members shall deal with non-members at the same prices, fees, and terms and commissions as in their dealings with the general public. Additionally, the rule states that no member shall:

1. In any transaction with any non-member broker or dealer, allow or grant to such non-member broker or dealer any selling concession, discount, or other allowance allowed by such member to a member of a registered securities association and not allowed to a member of the general public;
2. Join with any non-member broker or dealer in any syndicate or group contemplating the distribution to the public of any issue of securities or any part thereof; or
3. Sell any security to or buy any security from any non-member broker or dealer except at the same price at which at the time of such transaction such member would buy or sell such security, as the case may be, from or to a person who is a member of the general public not engaged in the investment banking or securities business.

POST-FILING FREE WRITING PROSPECTUSES IN CONNECTION WITH CERTAIN REGISTERED OFFERINGS

Rule 164 - provides for some leniency in the free writing prospectus requirements for certain offerings.

Conditions for WKSIs - A WKSI can use a free writing prospectus as long as a registration statement has been filed that includes a prospectus.

Conditions for non-reporting and unseasoned issuers - if the issuer is to give compensation for the dissemination of the free writing prospectus, a registration statement has to have been previous filed that includes a prospectus. The free writing prospectus has to be accompanied by the original prospectus.

DEFINITION OF TERMS

Affiliate: a person who directly or indirectly controls or is under common control with the specified person.

Amount: for debt, it means the principal; for shares it means the number of shares; and it means the number of units if relating to any other security.

Associate: in reference to an organization, it is a person who is an officer, partner, or the beneficial owner of at least 10% or more of any class of securities. In reference to a trust or estate, it is anyone who is a trustee or has any interest in it. Relatives are also associates.

Automatic shelf registration statement: a shelf registration filed by a WKSI (well-known seasoned issuer).

Business combination related shell company: a company formed to combine multiple other businesses, or to change the corporate domicile of an existing company.

Dividend or interest investment plan: a plan that allows current security holders to reinvest dividends or interest.

Electronic filer: a person or entity that submits filings according to Rule 100 and 101.

Electronic filing: document submitted to the SEC in electronic format.

Employee: does not include director, trustee, or officer.

Employee benefit plan: a written purchase, saving, option, bonus, appreciation, profit sharing, thrift, incentive, pension, or similar plan available to employees.

Equity security: any stock, certificate of interest, transferable shares, limited partnership interest, joint venture interest, and certificate of interest. Any security entitling a person to interest in equity.

Executive officer: any president, vice president, or other policy making officer.

Fiscal year: either calendar year or other annual accounting period.

Foreign government: government of foreign country.

Foreign issuer: a foreign government, foreign person, or organization formed under the laws of a foreign government.

Foreign private issuer: certain foreign issuers other than foreign governments.

Free writing prospectus: a written communication that is an offer to transact a security meeting certain requirements.

Graphic communication: all forms of electronic media that are not being communicated in real-time (live).

Ineligible issuer: an issuer who has not met certain filing requirements put forth by the Securities Exchange Act of 1934 or violated other SEC rules and regulations.

Majority-owned subsidiary: a subsidiary of which the securities with voting rights are more than 50% owned by one parent.

Material: describes a fact to which a reasonable person would likely attach importance.

Officer: president, vice president, secretary, treasurer, principal financial officer and accounting officer, or any person performing these same functions, in an organization.

Parent: of a person is an affiliate that controls it either directly or indirectly.

Predecessor: a person that previously owned the majority portion of a business and assets before an acquisition.

Principal underwriter: the underwriter in privity of contract with the issuer.

Promoter: any person that takes initiative to found and organize an issue, or any person with a connection to the founding and organizing of an issue that receives more than 10% of the proceeds of the issue.

Prospectus: a prospectus that meets the requirements in section 10(a) of the Securities Act of 1933.

Registrant: issuer of securities that has filed for registration.

Share: a share of corporate stock or unit of interest in other types of organizations.

Shell company: a registrant other than an asset-backed issuer that has little-to-no operations and little-to-no assets.

Significant subsidiary: a subsidiary of a registrant that comprises more than 10% of the registrant's total assets.

Smaller reporting company: certain issuers that are not investment companies or asset-backed issuers and that have less than $75 million in public float.

Subsidiary: an affiliate control directly or indirectly by a specific person.

Succession: direct acquisition of assets by merger, consolidation, purchase, or other direct transfer.

Totally held subsidiary: a subsidiary that is owned 100% by its parent or its parents' other subsidiaries and is not significantly indebted to any other person.

Voting securities: securities that provide the owners with the right to vote on election of directors.

Well-known seasoned issuer: a status given by the SEC to certain well-known issuers that have a market value of $700 million or more.

Wholly owned subsidiary: a subsidiary, the outstanding voting securities of which are owned 100% by a parent or a parent's other wholly owned subsidiaries.

Written communication: any communication via written, printed, radio, television, or graphic media.

PROSPECTUS

Prospectus for use prior to effective date (Rule 430) - prospectus can be used prior to effective date so long as all requirements are met.

Prospectus in a registration statement at time of effectiveness (Rule 430A)- a prospectus submitted as part of a registration statement can omit certain details so long as certain requirements are met, such as the securities only being offered for cash.

Prospectus in a registration statement after effective date (Rule 430B) - a prospectus filed with a registration statement can omit certain unknown or unavailable information.

REGULATION M

Regulation M is composed of rules 100 to 105. **Regulation M** deals with the several areas of activity involved in a security offering. It regulates the activities of distribution participants, activities of issuers, activities of passive market makers, advanced short selling and stabilization techniques. The regulation replaced rules 10b-6, 10b-6A, 10b-7, 10b-8 and 10b-21 under the Securities Exchange Act of 1934. The regulation created a de minimis exception as well as more thoroughly defined the person to whom the rule must apply. Additionally, the rule defines covered securities and affiliated purchasers, as well as clearly establishes restricted time periods.

DISCLOSURES IN CONNECTION WITH NEW ISSUES

Under **Rule G-32**, underwriters of a primary offering of municipal securities are required to send an official statement to *Electronic Municipal Market Access (EMMA)* within 1 business day after receipt of the statement from the issuer. If the official statement is not submitted by the underwriter by the closing date, the underwriter must submit to EMMA the following information:

1. The date that the official statement will be available and a commitment to send it when available
2. The preliminary official statement and a commitment to send the official statement when available
3. The fact that no official statement has been prepared because it is an exempt offering

DEFINITION OF "EQUITY SECURITY"

Equity security (Rule 3a11-1) - any stock or similar security, certificate of interest or participation in any profit sharing agreement, preorganization certificate or subscription, transferable share, voting trust certificate or certificate of deposit for an equity security, limited partnership interest, interest in a joint venture, or certificate of interest in a business trust; any security future on any such security; or any security convertible, with or without consideration into such a security, or carrying any warrant or right to subscribe to or purchase such a security; or any such warrant or right; or any put, call, straddle, or other option or privilege of buying such a security from or selling such a security to another without being bound to do so.

SEA RULE 10B-18

Rule 10b-18 was put in place to list the criteria that an issuer must follow in order to repurchase company common stock without violating the *Securities Exchange Act*, ensuring that the issuer is not able to influence the price of outstanding shares in an unfair manner. The rule initially only applied to common stock and did not apply to other situations such as a merger or acquisition. But under recent amendments, mergers and acquisitions have been added to the definition, since companies have a vested interest in boosting the trading value of their shares between the date a merger is announced and the date it is complete.

NYSE RULE 13 – TYPES OF ORDERS

Auto ex order - initiates an automatic execution when entered into the system. Includes market orders, limit orders, cancel orders, among others.

Closing offset (CO) order - an order for execution at the close of trading, assuming there is an imbalance at that time.

Day order - expires at end of trading (4 PM Eastern Time).

Do not reduce (DNR) order - the price is not to be reduced according to the amount of the ordinary cash dividend on dividend date.

Do not ship (DNS) order - an order that is not to be shipped to another market. If in standard process the security should be shipped to another market, it will be cancelled.

Do not increase (DNI) order - the price is not to be increased according to the amount of the cash dividend on dividend date.

Limit "at-the-close" order - a limit order set for potential execution at the close of the market day.

Market order - an order to purchase a security at the most advantageous price.

Market "at-the-close" (MOC) orders - a market order set for execution at the close of the market day.

Market "on-the-open" (MOO) orders - a market order set for execution at the opening of the market day.

TRADING HALTS

According to **NYSE Rule 80B**, trades will be stopped if the DJIA drops 10%, 20% or 30% in one day. Each percentage drop is accompanied by a specific length of time for which trades must be halted. If the DJIA drops 30% in one day, all trading is stopped for the remainder of the day. Trading will stop for the remainder of the day if the DJIA drops by 20% at 2:00 PM or later. Trades are stopped for only one hour in two circumstances: the DJIA drops 10% before 2:00 PM or it drops 10% between 1:00 and 2:00 PM. If the DJIA drops 20% prior to 1:00 PM, trades are halted for two hours. Trading will only be halted for thirty minutes if a 10% drop occurs between 2:00 and 2:30 PM.

DESIGNATED MARKET MAKERS

NYSE Rule 123D - Designated market makers (DMMs) are to ensure that registered securities open as close to the opening bell as possible. In the event that this is not possible, there are specific rules to follow. The NYSE has established processes for certain trading halts including equipment changeover, investment company units or index-linked securities, and dissemination of net asset value.

1. *Equipment changeover* - applicable when trading in a certain security is inhibited due to systems or equipment concerns.
2. *Investment company units or index-linked securities* - applicable in regards to investment company units or index-linked securities to allow for "closing the room."
3. *Dissemination of net asset value* - applicable when the NYSE sees that net asset value information is not being disseminated to all market participants at the same time.

PROHIBITION ON TRANSACTIONS, PUBLICATION OF QUOTATIONS, OR PUBLICATION OF INDICATIONS OF INTEREST DURING TRADING HALTS

Prohibition on transactions, publication of quotations, or publication of indications of interest during trading halts (FINRA Rule 5260) - if trading is halted for a specific security, no trading activities can be made on the security.

Trading halts (FINRA Rule 6120) - FINRA will halt the trading of a security otherwise than on an exchange in certain situations when the market in power calls for a trading halt, or to permit dissemination of material news, obtain material information, obtain material information in the public interest. Other reasons include when extraordinary market activity is occurring.

Trading halts due to extraordinary market volatility (FINRA Rule 6121) - FINRA will halt all trading activity otherwise than on an exchange in any stock if other major securities markets have done the same in response to extraordinary market volatility, or if directed by the SEC.

TRANSACTIONS HALTED ON INITIAL PUBLIC OFFERINGS

Transactions related to initial public offerings (FINRA Rule 6130) - a member is not to execute a transaction outside of an exchange in an initial public offering security until the security has been opened for trading on a national securities exchange.

Obligation of lead underwriter - it is the obligation of the lead underwriter to notify NASDAQ the IPO has been released by the SEC.

IDENTIFICATION OF QUOTATIONS

Identification of quotations (Rule 15c2-7) - when a quote is submitted, the inter-dealer quotation system must be informed and must disclose each published quotation. If two broker-dealers enter into an arrangement to each enter certain quotations for a security, it must be disclosed to all broker-dealers with similar quotations.

Initiation or resumption of quotations with specified information (Rule 15c2-11) - in order to publish a quote, a broker-dealer must have certain documents or information regarding the security. These documents or information can include a copy of the prospectus, a copy of the offering circular, or a copy of the issuer's most recent annual report.

DEFINITION OF PENNY STOCK

Definition of penny stock (SEC Rule 3a51-1) - Rule 3a51-1 defines penny stock by describing what a penny stock is not. The definition includes any equity security that:

1. is not a security continuously registered on a national securities exchange
2. is not a registered security on a national securities exchange that meets certain criteria
3. is not issued by an investment company registered by the Investment Company Act of 1940
4. is not a put or call option from an Options Clearing Corporation
5. does not have a price of $5 or more

EXEMPTIONS FOR CERTAIN TRANSACTIONS

Exemptions for certain transactions (SEC Rule 15g-1) - the following transactions are exempt from Rules 15g-2, 15g-3, 15g-4, 15g-5, and 15g-6:

1. Transactions by a broker/dealer whose commissions from penny stock transactions do not exceed 5% of total commissions and who has not been a market maker in a penny stock.
2. Transactions with an institutional investor as the customer.
3. Transactions that meet the requirements in Regulation D.
4. Transactions with the issuer, director, or other person who owns more than 5% of the issuers stock as the customer.
5. Transactions that are not recommended by the broker/dealer.
6. Other transactions exempted by the SEC.

RISK DISCLOSURE DOCUMENT RELATING TO THE PENNY STOCK MARKET

Risk disclosure document relating to the penny stock market (SEC Rule 15g-2) - a broker/dealer must have the customer sign a Schedule 15G document before transacting in penny stocks in the customer's account. The broker/dealer cannot transact in penny stocks on behalf of the customer within two days of sending such document, and must keep a copy of this document in records.

Broker or dealer disclosure of quotations and other information relating to the penny stock market (SEC Rule 15g-3) - a broker/dealer must disclose to the customer the inside bid/offer quotes and the number of shares applicable before transacting in penny stock on behalf of the customer.

DISCLOSURE OF COMPENSATION TO BROKERS OR DEALERS

Disclosure of compensation to brokers or dealers (SEC Rule 15g-4) - a broker/dealer must disclose to the customer the total compensation received in connection with transaction before transacting in penny stock on behalf of the customer.

Disclosure of compensation of associated persons in connection with penny stock transactions (SEC Rule 15g-5) - a broker/dealer must disclose to the customer the total compensation received by any associated person of the broker/dealer in connection with the transaction before transacting in penny stock on behalf of the customer.

ACCOUNT STATEMENTS FOR PENNY STOCK CUSTOMERS

Account statements for penny stock customers (SEC Rule 15g-6) - a broker/dealer must send a monthly account statement to customers within ten days following the end of the month during which they have transacted in penny stocks.

Sales practice requirements for certain low-priced securities (SEC Rule 15g-9) - a broker/dealer must approve a customer's account for trading in penny stocks using specific criteria. The broker/dealer must receive an agreement from the customer to a specific transaction in penny stocks, and cannot make the transaction until after two days from sending such document to the customer.

Series 7 Practice Test

1. A customer purchased 100 shares of SHC stock at $30 and simultaneously writes 1 SHC Oct 40 call at $2. If the customer closes both positions three months later when SHC is trading at $35 and Oct 40 calls are at $3, what is the realized gain or loss?

    a. $600
    b. $900
    c. $400
    d. $1100

2. Frank Samuelson is the CEO of Mega Corporation, a large multi-national conglomerate that has recently negotiated the acquisition of Accretive Corp. The deal will be announced in a week, but Frank is so excited that he tells his friend Bill, over lunch in a popular restaurant. Their conversation is overheard by the waiter, John, who later phones his uncle Mike to share the news. Bill, John, and Mike all buy shares of Accretive the day after the lunch. The following persons have violated the insider trading rules:

    I. Frank
    II. Bill
    III. John
    IV. Mike

    a. I only
    b. II and III only
    c. I, II, III, and IV
    d. I and II only

3. Each of the following statements is TRUE with regard to the U.S. balance of payments EXCEPT:

    a. When U.S. investors purchase Japanese securities, the U.S. balance of payments decreases.
    b. When U.S. investors purchase UK securities, the U.S. balance of payments increases.
    c. The greater the amount of foreign oil that the U.S. imports, the greater is the amount of money flowing out of the country.
    d. The greater the amount of U.S. goods that are sold overseas, the greater is the amount of money flowing into the country.

4. A customer has a margin account which contains securities having a market value of $40,000 and a debit balance of $15,000. Assuming that current SEC regulations apply, how much buying power does the customer have to purchase additional securities?

    a. $15,000
    b. $5,000
    c. $10,000
    d. $20,000

5. When performing strategic asset allocation for a 60-year-old customer, each of the following is TRUE EXCEPT:

    a. The customer's retirement plans should be considered.

    b. A general rule of thumb is to invest 100 minus the customer's age in stocks (40% here) and the rest in bonds and cash.

    c. A large percentage of the customer's portfolio should be in cash if the equity markets have been particularly weak during the previous 12 months.

    d. Portfolio rebalancing should be performed regularly when needed.

6. A stock's support level is which of the following?

    a. The average trading price of the security.

    b. The lower price of the security's recent trading range.

    c. The upper price of the security's trading range.

    d. The price at which fairly priced call options will be profitable.

7. You determine with your customer Renee Retired, a 65-year-old retiree, that she should have a "defensive" investment strategy. Each of the following would be suitable investments for Renee's account, EXCEPT:

    a. High-yield bonds

    b. Treasury bonds

    c. Blue chip stocks

    d. Money market funds

8. Which of the following would be of least interest to a fundamental analyst?

    a. The P/E ratio

    b. Working capital

    c. Statement of cash flows

    d. Historical prices

9. ABC broker-dealer is a member of a syndicate that is offering new shares of XYZ Corp common stock to the public. The size of the total offering is 10,000,000 shares, with ABC's allocation being 1,000,000. After selling its entire allotment, 1,000,000 shares remain unsold by other members of the syndicate. How many of the remaining shares is ABC responsible for?

    I. 0 shares if the offering was on an Eastern account basis.

    II. 0 shares if the offering was on a Western account basis.

    III. 100,000 shares if the offering was on an Eastern account basis.

    IV. 100,000 shares if the offering was on a Western account basis.

    a. II and III only.

    b. I and III only.

    c. II and IV only.

    d. I and IV only.

10. UGMA stands for _____.

    a. Uniform Grant to Minors Act

    b. Uniform Grant to Minorities Act

    c. Uniform Gift to Minors Act

    d. Uniform Gift to Minorities Act

11. An investor has the following investment results for the current year:

- Capital gains: $20,000
- Capital losses: $45,000

What is the tax status for this investor?

    a. $3,000 loss for the current year, $22,000 carried over to the following year
    b. $25,000 loss for the current year
    c. $5,000 loss for the current year, $20,000 carried over to the following year
    d. $3,000 loss for the current year, $3,000 carried over to the following year

12. All of the following statements are FALSE regarding callable municipal revenue bonds, EXCEPT:

    a. Callable bonds increase in price faster than non-callable bonds in a rising interest rate environment.
    b. Callable bonds usually have lower yields than non-callable bonds.
    c. The issuer will typically call their bonds in a decreasing interest rate environment.
    d. When bonds are called, the call premium is set to offset the missed interest payments the investor would have received had the bond not been called.

13. A customer is interested in purchasing equity securities with the objective of receiving dividends. Which of the following is LEAST likely to be a suitable investment recommendation?

    a. ABC common stock
    b. DEF warrants
    c. QRS preferred stock
    d. XYZ convertible preferred stock

14. Each of the following is a type of municipal note EXCEPT:

    a. AONs
    b. BANs
    c. PNs
    d. RANs

15. Each of the following is TRUE of discretionary accounts, EXCEPT:

    a. All discretionary account must be approved by a principal
    b. Discretionary accounts must be regularly reviewed by a principal
    c. Discretionary account cannot trade on margin
    d. Each order for a discretionary account must be marked as such

16. ABC common shares are offered in new issue with a public offering price of $30. After trading commences, the shares begin to drop in price. The XYZ syndicate responsible for the offering may place any of the following stabilizing bids EXCEPT:

    a. $30.25
    b. $30.00
    c. $29.75
    d. $29.50

17. A client writes a June 40 put for 5 and is exercised before expiration. A month later, the client sells the underlying stock in the market for 44. Assuming no commission, the result of these transactions is:

    a. A profit of $100

    b. A loss of $100

    c. A profit of $900

    d. A loss of $900

18. John Tradesalot is an active trader, placing at least 10 trades a week for the last several months. How often must he be sent account statements?

    a. Daily

    b. Monthly

    c. Quarterly

    d. Annually

19. With regard to a customer account, a registered representative with limited trading authorization may:

    a. Automatically collect a monthly fee for handling the account

    b. Buy and sell investment securities for the account

    c. Transfer securities in and out of the client's account

    d. Direct funds to third parties

20. If ABC Corp. declares a 3-2 stock split, how many additional shares would be received by an investor who initially held 600 shares?

    a. 200

    b. 300

    c. 500

    d. 900

21. Sally Shortseller has a short margin account with short market value (SMV) of $5000 and a credit balance (CR) of $8000. How much excess equity (SMA) does Sally have in her account?

    a. $3000

    b. None, the account is restricted.

    c. $1000

    d. $500

22. Which of the following statements are true regarding individual retirement accounts (IRAs):

    I. Contributions to an IRA are made from pre-tax dollars

    II. Contributions to an IRA are made from post-tax dollars

    III. Contributions to a Roth IRA are made from pre-tax dollars

    IV. Contributions to a Roth IRA are made from post-tax dollars

    a. I and III only

    b. II and IV only

    c. II and III only

    d. I and IV only

23. If each of the following bonds were all issued by the same corporation, each bond is callable, and the Federal Reserve has recently raised interest rates by 0.25%, which bond is most likely to be called?

    a. 7% bond maturing 12/31/18

    b. 4.5% bond maturing 12/31/18

    c. 7% bond maturing 12/31/12

    d. 4.5% bond maturing 12/31/12

24. Victor Vance maintains an unrestricted long margin account at BD Securities. After a significant move in the S&P 500, his SMA has risen by $12,000. Given this move, how much did the value of the stocks held in his account move (his equity)?

    a. $12,000

    b. $18,000

    c. $24,000

    d. There is not sufficient information provided

25. A double-barreled municipal bond is

    a. backed by income streams from two different municipal projects

    b. pays twice as often as a regular municipal bond

    c. is backed by the full faith and credit of the issuer if the revenues obtained from the backing project are insufficient

    d. is automatically exempt from all federal, state, and local taxes

26. Under which of the following circumstances may it be possible to receive a reduction in the maximum sales charge when purchasing the shares of an investment company?

    I. Shares are purchased by the trustee of a company pension plan.

    II. The purchase represents a significant dollar investment amount in the shares.

    III. The investor elects to have all dividend income reinvested.

    IV. A unit investment trust purchases the shares as one of many investments for the underlying plan.

    a. I only

    b. I and II

    c. I, II, and III

    d. I, II, III, and IV

27. Fiscal policy for the United States is determined by which of the following branches or departments of government?

    a. Federal Reserve Board

    b. U.S. Treasury

    c. Office of Management and Budget (OMB)

    d. U.S. Congress

28. XYZ Corp. is offering 8,000,000 new shares to the public. The price to the syndicate is $28 and the public offering price will be $29.25. The takedown and concession for each share sold is $0.75 and $0.30 respectively; the managing underwriter will earn $0.25 as an override on all shares. The selling group is allotted 1,000,000 shares and sells them all. How much does the selling group make in profits?

   a. $250,000
   b. $300,000
   c. $850,000
   d. $2,500,000

29. When investing in variable annuities, an investor may select the following:

   I. Periodic payment immediate annuity
   II. Periodic payment deferred annuity
   III. Single payment immediate annuity
   IV. Single payment deferred annuity

   a. I and II only
   b. I, II, and IV
   c. II and IV only
   d. II, III, and IV

30. Which of the following investment strategies is a long straddle?

   a. Buy 1 ABC Oct 60 call; sell 1 ABC Oct 50 put
   b. Buy 1 ABC Oct 60 call; buy 1 ABC Oct 50 put
   c. Sell 1 ABC Oct 60 call; sell 1 ABC Oct 60 put
   d. Buy 1 ABC Oct 60 call; buy 1 ABC Oct 60 put

31. In a margin account, each of the following transactions will cover a put writer EXCEPT:

   a. A cash deposit equal to the exercise price of the put.
   b. A purchase of shares of the underlying stock.
   c. A short sale of shares of the underlying stock.
   d. The purchase of a put option with the same exercise price and expiration.

32. Which of the following investments is a violation of the wash sale rule:

   I. 25 days after selling Xenon Corp common at a loss, the customer buys Xenon put options
   II. 30 days after selling Xenon Corp common at a loss, the customer buys Xenon call options
   III. 35 days after selling Xenon Corp common at a loss, the customer buys Xenon warrants
   IV. 20 days after selling Xenon Corp common at a loss, the customer buys Xenon convertible bonds

   a. I and III only
   b. II and IV only
   c. I, II, and III
   d. I, II and IV

33. All of the following are possible reasons that a broker-dealer may be allowed to deviate from the NASD 5% rule EXCEPT:

    a. The trade involves an illiquid security

    b. The trade is very small on an absolute dollar basis

    c. The broker's cost basis is more than 5% above the security's current market value

    d. The trade involves an odd lot

34. A principal must review (and in some cases approve) each of the following activities or occurrences EXCEPT:

    a. Letters recommending securities to clients

    b. Forms establishing discretionary authority by a registered rep

    c. Written complaints received by customers

    d. Internal communications between registered reps

35. A customer has a short margin account with ABC Brokers. The account currently has a short market value of $52,000, a credit balance of $104,000 and SMA of $3000. What is the minimum NYSE equity maintenance on this account?

    a. $15,600

    b. $19,900

    c. $30,800

    d. $31,200

36. If there is no trade activity in a customer's account, but the account contains a positive balance, how often must an account statement be sent to the customer?

    a. Monthly

    b. Quarterly

    c. Semi-annually

    d. Annually

37. An investor purchases an ABC Jul 45 call for 4 each while ABC trades at 47. If ABC increases to 50, which of the following statements is TRUE?

    a. The investor has a cost basis of 49 if the options are exercised

    b. The investor will realize a $450 profit if she exercises the option and sells the stock

    c. The investor has purchased a long strangle

    d. The investor may benefit from offsetting the position with a put

38. When a municipality chooses an underwriter to complete the issuance of a new issue, the offering is considered to have taken place

    a. On a negotiated basis

    b. Privately

    c. On a competitive basis

    d. All of the above

39. The par value of a corporation's stock

    a. Is directly related to the market value of the stock

    b. Is inversely related to the market value of the stock

    c. Is the liquidation value of the stock that shareholders would receive in bankruptcy

    d. Is an arbitrarily determined placeholder on the company's balance sheet

40. Peter Farnsworth wishes to invest $25,000 into the XYZ Technology Fund, which has a current NAV of $9.00 and a POP of $9.89. The sales charges and breakpoints are listed in Exhibit 1. How many shares can Peter buy?

Exhibit 1

Breakpoint	Sales Charge %
$0 - $9,999	9%
$10,000 - $24,999	7.75%
$25,000 - $49,999	6.5%
$50,000 and up	5%

    a. 2527 shares
    b. 2561 shares
    c. 2596 shares
    d. 2639 shares

41. Each of the following instruments trade in the "money market" EXCEPT:

    a. CDs
    b. CDSs
    c. Repos
    d. T-bills

42. Assume that Fran Cassada has the following holdings in her account with XYZ Brokers:

- $150,000 in cash
- $75,000 in common stock
- $75,000 in preferred stock
- $150,000 in corporate bonds

If XYZ goes bankrupt, for how much is Fran covered?

    a. $150,000
    b. $300,000
    c. $450,000
    d. $500,000

43. Which of the following types of bonds are required in the creation of a sinking fund?

    a. Balloon bonds
    b. Series bonds
    c. Serial bonds
    d. Term bonds

44. Joan Dwindle is long 1 ABC Oct 60 put at $8 and is short 1 ABC Oct 50 put at $2.50. Each of the following is a TRUE statement about Joan's net position EXCEPT:

    a. Joan will profit if the difference in the premiums widens
    b. Joan has a debit spread in ABC options
    c. Joan will profit only if the options are both exercised
    d. Joan needs at least one of the options to be in-the-money to profit

45. Peter Piper has made several very successful options trades over the course of the past six months and would like to use these successes as a basis to attract more customers. If he intends to include these picks in his advertisements, he must also include:

    a. All of the options trades made by his firm for the last year
    b. All of the options trades made by Peter for the last six months
    c. All of the securities recommendations made by his firm for the past year
    d. A disclaimer that the advertised trades are just a few of those recommended by the firm

46. A customer purchases a new issue of ABC automotive bonds, anticipating that the government will back the car-maker if times get tough. The confirmation that is sent to the customer must include:

    I. The customer's name
    II. The settlement date
    III. The current yield at the time of the sale
    IV. The nominal yield

    a. I only
    b. I, II, and III
    c. II, and III only
    d. I, II, and IV

47. The Federal Reserve Board administers monetary policy by controlling the money supply with each of the following tools EXCEPT:

    a. Changing the reserve requirements
    b. Changing the discount rate
    c. Changing the prime rate
    d. Participating in open market operations

48. At a shareholder's meeting, Bill Francis intends to vote for the three open slots on the Board of Directors. If he owns 1000 shares of the corporation's stock and voting is conducted on a cumulative basis, each of the following is an acceptable way for Bill to vote EXCEPT:

    a. 1000 votes for each of the three candidates
    b. 3000 votes for each of the three candidates
    c. 1000 votes for one candidate
    d. 3000 votes for one candidate

49. An investor with the following two option positions has created a:

    • Short 1 XYZ Jul 60 call at 4
    • Write 1 XYZ Jul 55 put a 6

    a. Short straddle
    b. Credit spread
    c. Debit spread
    d. Short combination

50. Each of the following occurrences will cause an increase in the deficit of the U.S. balance of payments EXCEPT:

   a. An increase in the discount rate
   b. U.S. Investors buying ADRs
   c. Foreigners investing in U.S. businesses
   d. Tightening of the U.S. dollar

51. What organization is both the issuer and the guarantor of all listed options?

   a. The SEC
   b. The CBOE
   c. The OCC
   d. The OAA

52. Sally Peterson wants to open a new account at Speedy X Brokers. According to the "know your customer" rule, Michael Hunt, the registered representative at Speedy's should obtain which of the following information:

   I. Sally's investment objectives
   II. Sally's birth date
   III. Sally's level of risk tolerance

   a. I and II only
   b. II and III only
   c. I and III only
   d. I, II, and III

53. What regulatory body is responsible for determining which OTC securities may be purchased on margin?

   a. The FRB
   b. The NASD
   c. The SEC
   d. The exchange upon which the stock is listed

54. Each of the following must be registered at either the individual state level or with the SEC EXCEPT:

   a. Variable annuities
   b. Private placements
   c. Interstate offerings
   d. Intrastate offerings

55. None of the following are considered owners of a corporation EXCEPT:

   a. Zero coupon bondholders
   b. Convertible debenture holders
   c. Call option holders
   d. Common stock holders

56. Sara Sweet owns 10 of Mega Corporation's convertible bonds at 110, which may be converted at $22. The 8% coupon bonds have 23 years to maturity and form a majority of Sara's non-stock holdings. What is the current yield of the bonds?

- a. 7.3%
- b. 6.9%
- c. 8.5%
- d. 8%

57. Of the following options investors, which one(s) would receive a dividend payment if the option were to be exercised prior to the ex-dividend date?

- a. The seller of a call option
- b. The writer of a call option
- c. The buyer of a call option
- d. The holder of a put option

58. 65 shares of ABC common trade at $256 per share in the OTC market. Which of the following holdings is considered to have traded for reporting purposes?

- a. 65 round lots
- b. 1 round lot
- c. 65 odd lots
- d. 1 odd lot

59. Which of the following BEST describes dollar cost averaging:

- a. Purchasing a fixed number of shares at regular intervals
- b. Negotiating a reduced per share cost
- c. Purchasing a fixed dollar amount at regular intervals
- d. Buying when the price of the investment declines

60. Each of the following statements about variable annuities are false EXCEPT:

- a. The payouts to investors are dependent on the performance of the separate account
- b. "Life with period certain" results in the highest payouts
- c. If investors deposit money into the annuity account by April 15 of the following year, they may claim deductions in the current year
- d. The interest rate is assumed to be the rate required to beat one or more broad equity market indexes

61. Sam Steiner purchases an 8% coupon Billing Corporation Bond with basis of 8%. The bond may be called in 8 more years, with a yield to call of 8.75%. Billings recently received an upgrade from Moody's, but not S&P. How much did Sam pay for the Bond?

- a. $975
- b. $1000
- c. $1075
- d. $1235

Use the following to answer questions 62 - 63

Specialist's Book: Mega Corporation		
BID	**PRICE**	**ASK**
15 DLJ	35.	
8 Bear Stearns (GTC)	.10	
19 Morgan	.20	9 UBS (stop)
	.30	
	.40	
23 Goldie (stop)	.50	
	.60	9 Merrill
	.70	12 Salamon

62. Given the information in the exhibit, which of the following prices would be an example of an acceptable quote for the specialist to enter for his own inventory?

   a. $35.30
   b. $35.10
   c. $35.65
   d. $35.95

63. Given the information in the exhibit, what is the range that defines the inside market?

   a. 35.00 - 35.70
   b. 35.10 – 35.60
   c. 35.20 – 35.60
   d. 35.50 – 35.60

64. Each of the following is TRUE of open-end investment companies EXCEPT:

   a. New shares are constantly being issued
   b. Only common stock may be issued
   c. Investors may redeem their shares
   d. Investors purchase shares at the NAV plus a commission

65. If XYZ Corporation is trading at $45, which of the following options is in-the-money?

   a. XYZ Jul 40 calls
   b. XYZ Jul 45 calls
   c. XYZ Jul 40 puts
   d. XYZ Jul 35 puts

66. Franche Enterprises deals in widgets in both the U.S. and in Europe. The company accepts most payments within 30 days of billing and wants to take a hedge position to protect itself from moves in the currency markets. Which of the following would accomplish this goal on a bill to an Italian customer?

   a. Buy Euro puts
   b. Sell Euro calls
   c. Buy Euro call
   d. None of the above

67. Which of the following is not a part of the cooling off period?

a. A due diligence meeting
b. Blue-skying the issue
c. Issuance of a preliminary prospectus
d. Placement of a stabilizing bid

68. Which of the following securities are exempt from state income taxes in all states?

    I. GNMAs
    II. Puerto Rican Commonwealth bonds
    III. Treasury Bonds
    IV. Revenue bonds issued to improve public schools

a. I only
b. I, II, and IV
c. II and III only
d. I, II, III, and IV

69. If a registered representative wishes to purchase shares of a risky private equity fund for a customer, according to FINRA, the due diligence process should require

a. No special actions by the registered rep
b. Written notice to FINRA of the trade
c. Written consent from the customer prior to the trade
d. That the trade be disallowed

70. When is the latest time that an investor may exercise a listed option?

a. 5:30 p.m. EST on the third Friday of the expiration month
b. 4:00 p.m. EST on the third Friday of the expiration month
c. 8:30 p.m. EST on the Saturday after the third Friday of the expiration month
d. 11:59 p.m. EST on the Saturday after the third Friday of the expiration month

71. Barry Bonds purchases an ABC 8 % corporate bond at 80. How much does Barry have to claim on his taxes each year, if the bond matures in ten years and he holds it to maturity?

a. $120
b. $100
c. $80
d. $60

72. If a technical analyst identifies a "head and shoulders topping formation," this indicates which type of condition?

a. Bullish
b. Bearish
c. Reversal of a bullish trend
d. Reversal of a bearish trend

73. When applying the NASD 5% rule, each of the following is FALSE EXCEPT:

a. The 5% rule is a guideline for the sales of open-ended investment companies
b. Securities sold through a prospectus are exempt from the rule
c. The security type or class is not a consideration
d. Riskless arbitrage transactions are exempt from the rule

74. If an investor buys an ABC corporate bond with an 8% coupon and 10 years until maturity for 80, and then sells it 5 years later for 89, what gain or loss is realized by the investor?

a. A gain of $70
b. A loss of $70
c. A gain of $10
d. A loss of $10

75. Which of the following MUST be a closed-end fund?

a. POP - $15, NAV - $13.90
b. POP - $21, NAV - $19.10
c. POP - $8, NAV - $7.35
d. POP - $11, NAV - $10.25

76. Each of the following is a FALSE statement about an ADR, EXCEPT:

a. The actual shares are not held in a custodian bank
b. The investor cannot receive dividends in cash
c. ADRs represent shares of U.S. securities trading in foreign markets
d. The investor does not receive the actual certificate

77. Determine the purchase price of a 6% corporate bond that carries a 6.5% yield-to-call after five years and a 6% basis.

a. Above $1000
b. $1000
c. Below $1000
d. Not enough information provided

78. Unless specifically stated to the contrary, a CMO has an S&P rating of

a. AAA
b. AA
c. A
d. BBB

79. Dewey, Cheetum & Howe Brokerage acquires a large block of ABC Corp for $39 per share. Two weeks later, shares of ABC are quoted in the market at 34 – 34.15. Which of the following prices must the firm use as its basis when selling shares to its customers?

a. $39.00
b. $34.00
c. $34.15
d. $36.50

80. A request to extend credit to a customer that originates with a non-clearing broker should be made through

a. The broker's clearing agent
b. The broker can make this request
c. The broker's designated examining authority (DEA)
d. The broker's controlling self-regulatory authority (SRO)

81. If the Fed announces that it is easing rates by adjusting the discount rate, which two of the following effects would be most likely to occur?

    I. U.S. exports will be more competitive
    II. U.S. imports of foreign goods will be more competitive
    III. Bonds prices will rise
    IV. Bonds prices will fall

  a. I and III
  b. I and IV
  c. II and III
  d. II and IV

82. Sam Specs purchases 1000 shares of Mega Corp at $30 in his margin account. If this initial transaction is at the outer bounds allowed under Reg T, what is the "loan amount" given to Sam by his broker?

  a. $10,000
  b. $12,000
  c. $14,000
  d. $15,000

83. Jon Bondman purchases a callable municipal revenue bond trading at a current market price of 97.2. The bond may be called after 5 years with a half percent call premium, has a coupon of 6%, and is triple tax-free to Jon. What is the current yield?

  a. 6%
  b. 6.08%
  c. 6.17%
  d. 6.67%

84. Which of the following is a coincident indicator?

  a. M1
  b. ISM industrial production
  c. Unemployment
  d. New housing starts

85. None of the following are covered by the Trust Indenture Act of 1939 EXCEPT:

  a. Debentures
  b. Treasuries
  c. Agencies
  d. GO bonds

86. If a corporation raises $10,000,000 by issuing preferred stock with a par value of $100, which of the following will increase:

    I. Net worth
    II. Current assets
    III. Total liabilities
    IV. Quick assets

  a. I and II only
  b. I and III only
  c. I, II, and IV
  d. II, III, and IV

87. An investor would NOT pursue a covered call writing program to

a. Increase the yield of a portfolio
b. Hedge a long stock position
c. Reduce the size of a concentrated long position over time.
d. Generate profits when the underlying stock is expected to drop significantly

88. Rule G-39, which addresses cold-calling standards, states

    I. Calls must be made after 8:00 a.m. or before 9:00 p.m. local time of the customer
    II. Calls must be made after 8:00 a.m. or before 9:00 p.m. local time of the caller
    III. The caller must indicate that the call is a sales call
    IV. The caller must give contact information for both himself and the firm

a. I and IV only
b. I, II, and III
c. I, III, and IV
d. II, III and IV

89. Vicky Feather enters an order to buy 200 shares of ABC at 25 stop limit. If the ticker following the order is 24.95, 25, 25.05, SLD 25, 24.98, 25, then the order was triggered and executed at which prices?

a. Triggered 24.95, executed 25.05
b. Triggered 25.00, executed 24.98
c. Triggered 25.00, executed 25.05
d. Triggered 24.95, executed 25.00

90. Which of the following is the BEST representation of a net revenue pledge for a municipal bond?

a. (Gross revenues – operating costs) / debt service
b. (Net revenues – operating costs) / debt service
c. (Principal balance – interest payments) / years-to-maturity
d. (Interest payments + principal balance) / operating costs

91. A registered representative can remain unaffiliated with a broker-dealer for how many years without having to retake all of his or her licensing exams?

a. 1 year
b. 2 years
c. 3 years
d. 5 years

92. Joe Jacobs buys an ABC convertible bond at $85 with a conversion price of $25. If Joe converts the bonds six months later and sells the stock for $23, the whole trade results in a

a. $50 loss
b. $50 gain
c. $70 loss
d. $70 gain

93. The following financial instruments DO NOT trade in the secondary market:

    I. Repos
    II. Fed Funds
    III. ADRs
    IV. Private Placements

    a. I, and II
    b. II, III, and IV
    c. I, II, and IV
    d. II and IV

94. Each of the following occurrences would change the strike price of a listed option EXCEPT:

    a. A 2-for-1 stock split
    b. A 2-for-3 stock split
    c. A $0.15 dividend
    d. A 4% stock dividend

95. Which of the following may NOT be deducted by a limited partnership for tax purposes?

    a. Depletion
    b. Principal expenses
    c. Interest expenses
    d. Depreciation

96. Which of the following statements is TRUE when using the "portfolio margining" method to calculate the margin in a customer's account?

    a. Any customer may request use of this method
    b. Margin requirements are determined based on the net risk of the entire portfolio
    c. Margin requirements are based on the weighted average of each position
    d. The "portfolio margining" method is always used for accounts with more than 20 positions

97. If XYZ has a EPS of $4 and a market price of $64 prior to a straight 2-for-1 stock split, after the split

    a. The EPS will be $4, and the market price will be $32
    b. The EPS will be $2, and the market price will be $64
    c. The EPS will be $8, and the market price will be $32
    d. The EPS will be $2, and the market price will be $32

98. Sara Ross holds a portfolio of stocks and bonds and prefers dividend paying stocks. If she is in the 28% tax bracket and holds a GO bond at 94 with a basis of 7% and a nominal yield of 5.5%, what is the tax equivalent yield Sara receives on this bond?

    a. 9.2%
    b. 9.7%
    c. 7.9%
    d. 6.8%

99. In order for an investor to transfer a securities account from one broker to another, each of the following must occur EXCEPT:

a. The investor must fill out a transfer form from the new broker
b. The original broker must cancel any open orders
c. The investor must allow the original broker ten business days to implement the transfer
d. The original broker must validate the investor's account transfer form

100. Holding a put option, as opposed to selling short, has each of the following advantages:

I. No dividend payments will be required
II. There is limited downside on the position
III. There is no loss of time value
IV. A smaller amount of capital provides the same level of exposure

a. I and II only
b. I and III only
c. I, II, and IV
d. II, III, and IV

101. If the Fed raises the reserve requirements, holding all of factors equal, which of the following is LEAST likely to occur?

a. The money supply will increase
b. Interest rates will increase
c. Bond prices will fall
d. Fed funds borrowing will increase

102. XYZ Company is selling additional shares of common stock to existing shareholders through a rights offering. Those shareholders who want to subscribe and receive additional shares must send the rights certificate and the purchase cost to

a. The company
b. The trustee
c. The registrar
d. The rights agent

103. Which of the following statements are FALSE with regard to Treasury STRIPS?

I. Principal is paid at maturity, and interest is paid semi-annually
II. Principal and interest are paid at maturity
III. Investors pay taxes annually
IV. Investors pay taxes on maturity

a. I and IV
b. I and III
c. II and IV
d. II and III

104. An investor opens a long margin account by purchasing $300,000 in securities. She signs a hypothecation agreement, a loan consent agreement, and a credit agreement. Each of the following are TRUE EXCEPT

a. The securities may be used as collateral for a loan
b. If the market value of the securities declines, the debit balance will increase
c. The securities will be held in street name
d. Interest will be due on the debit balance

105. Which of the following documents officially triggers the acceptance by a general partner of a new limited partner?

   a. Certificate of limited partnership
   b. Agreement of limited partnership
   c. Subscription agreement
   d. New account form

106. Corporations may issue which of the following debt securities?

     I. Mortgage bonds
     II. Income bonds
     III. Moral obligation bonds
     IV. Double barreled bonds

   a. I and II
   b. I and III
   c. I, II, and IV
   d. II and IV

107. Which of the following is a lagging economic indicator?

   a. The unemployment rate
   b. Industrial production
   c. Weekly hours worked in manufacturing
   d. The federal funds rate

108. Which of the following statements is FALSE regarding IDR bonds?

   a. The bonds are issued and backed by a municipality
   b. They are also known as a special tax bond
   c. They are issued to construct a non-revenue-producing facility
   d. The money raised is used to construct a facility for a private corporation

109. Which of the following information is found in the official notice of sale in relation to the competitive offering of a municipal bond?

     I. The priority of execution of orders when released to the public
     II. The allotment to each syndicate member
     III. The method of interest-cost calculation used to determine the winner
     IV. The reoffering yields of the bonds with different maturities

   a. III only
   b. I and II
   c. I, II, and IV
   d. III and IV

110. Which of the following includes a zero-plus tick?

   a. 37.25, 37.20, 37.20, 37.28, 27.15
   b. 8.55, 8.60, 8.60, 8.65, 8.70
   c. 10.00, 10.05, 10.00, 10.00, 9.55
   d. 17.84, 17.80, 17.83, 17.81, 17.78

111. Betty Brown would like to open a cash trading account at XYZ brokerage and give trading authority to her son Jon. Which of the following forms are needed to open the account?

> I. A joint account agreement
> II. A new account form
> III. A limited power of attorney
> IV. A hypothecation agreement

   a. I and III
   b. II and III
   c. I, II, and III
   d. I, II, III, and IV

112. What is the appropriate action for ABC Brokers to take if they receive one signed and one unsigned stock certificate from their customer Agnes?

   a. Return only the unsigned certificate
   b. Return both certificates
   c. Retain both certificates and send a stock power and instructions
   d. Retain both certificates because one signature is sufficient

113. Which TWO of the following investors would benefit if the strike price of an option and the market price of the underlying stock remained the same?

> I. The buyer of a straddle
> II. Seller of a straddle
> III. Buyer of an at-the-money put
> IV. Seller of an at-the-money put

   a. I and II
   b. I and III
   c. II and III
   d. II and IV

114. Which term best defines a general decrease in prices?

   a. Depression
   b. Recession
   c. Deflation
   d. Fluctuation

115. Registered Representatives are not allowed to give gifts to customers or other individuals related to the securities business if the value of such gifts exceeds:

   a. $500
   b. $250
   c. $200
   d. $100

116. An investor owns 100 shares of XYZ at $36. She wants to limit her loss per share to $4 or less and will accept a longer time for the order to be executed in order to make sure the loss does not exceed $4. Which of the following orders would be the best recommendation?

a. Sell limit order
b. Sell stop-limit order
c. Sell stop order
d. Buy stop order

117. Which of the following government securities has the shortest initial maturity?

a. Treasury bills
b. Treasury notes
c. Treasury bonds
d. Treasury STRIPs

118. Michael Hunt wants to sell some of the restricted ABC shares he has been holding for the past 18 months. There are 5 million outstanding shares of ABC common and the total trading for the past two, four, and six weeks respectively is 100,000, 240,000, and 500,000. What is the maximum number of shares that Mike can sell under rule 144?

a. 50,000
b. 60,000
c. 75,000
d. 83,334

119. Which of the following is true regarding bonds purchased at a premium?

a. Yield to maturity is greater than the coupon rate
b. Yield to maturity is lower than the coupon rate
c. Yield to maturity is equal to the coupon rate
d. None of the above

120. An investor places an order of 10,000 shares. He tells a representative that he wants as much as possible very quickly and to cancel the rest. The representative should designate this order as:

a. Fill or kill
b. All or none
c. Firm commitment
d. Immediate or cancel

121. Shareholder approval is required for a corporation to:

    I. Declare a cash dividend
    II. Declare a stock dividend
    III. Split the stock
    IV. Reverse split the stock

a. II only
b. I and II
c. II, III, and IV
d. III and IV

122. A registered representative is out of the office. The representative's assistant receives a call from a customer. The assistant is not a Series 7 registered representative. The customer tells the assistant to buy 100 shares of XYZ at the market and to have the registered representative call him back when he returns. Which of the following is true?

 a. The assistant can tell the trader to buy the stock, but cannot write the actual ticket
 b. The assistant can write the order ticket with approval from a principal
 c. The assistant can write the order ticket but must wait for the broker before it is placed with the trader
 d. The assistant cannot accept this order

123. An investor purchases 3 XYZ Jul 40 puts for 3.50 each and purchases 300 shares of common at $45. Three months later XYZ is trading at $46. At what market price for XYZ does the investor break even?

 a. 41.50
 b. 45
 c. 48.50
 d. It is impossible to tell

124. A corporation wishing to open a new margin account would need to provide the firm their:

 I. Corporate resolution
 II. Corporate charter
 III. Income statement
 IV. List of issued securities

 a. I and II
 b. I and IV
 c. I, II and III
 d. I, II, III and IV

125. A customer sells a 7% corporate bond on October 4th for regular way settlement. The bond pays interest on January 1st and July 1st. How many days of accrued interest is this customer owed?

 a. 98
 b. 96
 c. 92
 d. 88

126. A customer should purchase long term bonds when she believes that:

 a. Long term interest rates are going to decrease
 b. Short term interest rates are going to decrease
 c. Long term interest rates are going to increase
 d. Short term interest rates are going to increase

127. Sam Spade is considering investing in mutual funds. He has selected Mighty Sure investments to be his broker. Mighty Sure should tell Sam that which of the following is the most important consideration when deciding how to invest his money?

    a. Front loaded versus back loaded
    b. Sales charges
    c. Investment objectives
    d. Management fees

128. Which NASDAQ level is known as the "Inside market"?

    a. Level I
    b. Level II
    c. Level III
    d. Level IV

129. Growth stocks would normally have:

    I. Low dividend payouts
    II. High dividend payouts
    III. Low beta ratings
    IV. High beta ratings

    a. I and III
    b. I and IV
    c. II and III
    d. II and IV

130. A customer buying 10 corporate bonds with a 6% coupon rate, a conversion feature at $25 into common, and a call provision after a five-year holding period will receive semiannual payments of:

    a. $30
    b. $60
    c. $300
    d. $600

131. Each of the following are FALSE when using the "portfolio margining" method to calculate the margin in a customer's account EXCEPT:

    a. Only customers meeting specific criteria may request use of this method
    b. Any customer may request this method be used in their account
    c. Margin requirements are based on the weighted average of each position
    d. This method is always used for accounts with more than 20 positions

132. Diane Doughmestic has a margin account that holds securities with a current market value of $35,000 and a debit balance of $18,000. All of the following are TRUE EXCEPT:

    a. The account is currently restricted
    b. The account has a SMA of $0
    c. Diane will receive a margin call for $500
    d. Diane will receive a maintenance call if the market value drops below $24,000

133. A customer owns 200 shares of GHY at $90, and wishes to hedge the position while generating income. What is the best recommendation?

   a. Sell calls
   b. Sell puts
   c. Buy calls
   d. Buy puts

134. Increased money wiring activity to and from a customer's account could indicate which of the following activities?

   a. Interpositioning
   b. Churning
   c. Crossing
   d. Money laundering

135. An investor has just opened an options account and enters an order to buy 1 XYZ Jul 50 Call for $300. What is the maximum potential gain?

   a. $300
   b. $4700
   c. $5000
   d. Unlimited

136. The holding period requirements of Rule 144 apply to which of the following?

   a. A nonaffiliated person who has held control stock for 6 months
   b. A nonaffiliated person who has held restricted stock for 3 months
   c. A corporate insider who has held restricted stock for 2 years
   d. A nonaffiliated person who has held registered stock for 3 years

137. A workable indication is a(n)

   a. firm quote
   b. unqualified quote
   c. likely bid price
   d. likely ask price

138. An investor wishes to purchase shares at $6.50 per share. If the shares are outside the risk profile of the investor, and the investor insists on making the investment over the advice of the registered representative, the registered representative should

   a. enter the order but mark it "unsolicited"
   b. give the order to one of the other brokers that you don't like
   c. refuse the order
   d. require the investor to amend his investment objectives before accepting the order

139. A registered representative requires a written power of attorney to execute which of the following discretionary orders?

I. A market order that specifies which securities to sell
II. An order that leaves the execution time and price up to the registered rep
III. A limit order that specifies the price and quantity of the security to be purchased

a. I and II
b. II and III
c. I and III
d. I, II, and III

140. Which of the following BEST describes a trade in the third-market?

a. A listed security trading on an exchange
b. A listed security trading OTC
c. An OTC security trading OTC
d. Two institutional trading desks trading directly

141. An investor sells XYZ Corp. stock at a loss and buys XYZ call options within 30 days. Which of the following is TRUE?

a. The loss deduction will be allowed for tax purposes
b. The loss deduction will be disallowed for tax purposes
c. The loss deduction can be used to offset capital gains
d. The loss can be used if the holding period would have led to a short-term loss

142. Place the economic cycle in order:

I. Expansion
II. Trough
III. Peak
IV. Contraction

a. I, II, III, IV
b. I, IV, II, III
c. II, IV, I, III
d. I, III, IV, II

143. A customer sells 100 shares of ABC short at $43 and buys 1 ABC Oct 45 Call @3. What is the customer's maximum loss?

a. $500
b. $100
c. Unlimited
d. $4300

144. Which of the following is TRUE regarding a Regulation D offering?

a. It is an offering of securities worth $5,000,000 or less in a one-year period
b. It is an offering of securities only within the issuer's home state
c. It is an offering of securities to no more than 35 unaccredited investors in a one-year period
d. It is an offering of a large block of previously outstanding securities

145. Which of the following documents outlines the allocation of orders?

a. Syndicate agreement
b. Indenture
c. Notice of sale
d. Official statement

146. When an investor buys common stock that increases in value, how is the result to be categorized for tax purposes?

a. Capital gain
b. Ordinary income
c. Appreciation
d. Passive income

147. A company previously issued 6 percent $100 par cumulative preferred stock. During the following two years, the company pays $6 and $4 in dividends respectively. If the company announces a common dividend in year 3, how much does it owe preferred stockholders?

a. $2
b. $8
c. $11
d. $16

148. The indenture of a corporate bond includes all of the following EXCEPT:

a. the nominal yield
b. collateral backing the bond (if any)
c. the rating
d. the maturity date

149. Matty Perry is a 64-year old investor who determines that he should have a defensive investment strategy. Which of the following types of investments would MOST likely meet Matty's needs?

 I. Municipal bond fund
 II. High yield bonds
 III. Global fixed income fund
 IV. Exotic options strategies

a. I and III
b. II only
c. I, II, and IV
d. II, and IV

150. When an investor in a JTWROS account dies, his portion of the account is

a. transferred to the remaining survivor(s) on the account
b. transferred to the investor's estate
c. frozen
d. transferred to the investor's spouse

151. The debt-to-equity ratio of a corporation measures

    a. liquidity
    b. leverage
    c. profitability
    d. none of the above

152. A Rule 147 offering is

    a. an offering of securities worth $5,000,000 or less in a 12-month period
    b. an offering of securities only within the issuer's home state
    c. an offering of securities to no more than 35 unaccredited investors in a 12-month period
    d. an offering of a large block of previously outstanding securities

153. All of the following are TRUE regarding the buyer of a put option EXCEPT:

    a. The maximum gain per share is equal to the strike price minus the premium
    b. The maximum loss is equal to the premium
    c. This position is used as a hedge on a short position
    d. The Options Clearing Corporation (OCC) guarantees the exercise of the option.

154. Alan Capone wants to open an account at Chi-town Brokerage, but does not want his name to appear on the account. How should Chi-town respond to this request?

    a. Chi-town should open a numbered account for Alan
    b. Chi-town should set up an AKA account and give Alan a fictitious name
    c. Chi-town should inform Alan that any account must be in his name
    d. Chi-town should set up a street-named account only if Alan is an accredited investor.

155. Which of the following are characteristics of corporate debt securities?

    I. They are senior securities
    II. They represent ownership of the issuing corporation
    III. They are issued to raise working capital
    IV. They represent a loan to the issuing corporation

    a. I and II
    b. I, II, and III
    c. I, III, and IV
    d. IV only

156. William Torry has a short margin account with a short market value of $40,000, a credit balance of $80,000 and SMA of $2000. What is the NYSE minimum equity maintenance on this account?

    a. $2,000
    b. $10,000
    c. $12,000
    d. $24,000

157. When a variable annuity is "annuitized," the owner of the contract will receive which of the following number of annuity units?

    a. a fixed number based on the value of the accumulation units
    b. a fixed number based on the number of accumulation units
    c. an adjustable number based on the number of accumulation units
    d. an adjustable number based on the value of the accumulation units

158. Which of the following is an advantage of a variable rate municipal bond over a bond with a fixed coupon rate?

    a.   a variable rate bond's price remains relatively stable
    b.   a variable rate bond is non-callable
    c.   a variable rate bond is always issued with a higher coupon rate
    d.   a variable rate bond is more likely to increase in value

159. An investor who wishes to add liquidity to her portfolio could add any of the following EXCEPT

    a.   a money market fund
    b.   private equity limited partnership
    c.   blue chip stocks
    d.   T-bills

160. A customer is long 100 shares of ABC at $65 and sells 1 ABC Oct 80 call at 2. Six months later, ABC is trading at $70 per share and the call is trading at 4. If the customer closes both positions, what is the resulting gain or loss?

    a. $300
    b. $500
    c. $700
    d. $1100

161. If an investor exercises an index call option, the assigned seller may deliver which of the following?

    a.   100 shares of the underlying index
    b.   Cash equal to the current market value of 100 shares of the index
    c.   Cash equal to the intrinsic value of the option times 100 shares at the end of the exercise day
    d.   Cash equal to the margin requirement for 100 shares of the underlying index

162. Term bonds are quoted

    a.   according to a percentage of dollar price
    b.   on a yield-to-maturity basis
    c.   on a current yield basis
    d.   on a nominal yield basis

163. Form 144 is waived for affiliates selling restricted shares when

    I. The net amount of the sale is below $100,000
    II. The net amount of the sale is below $50,000
    III. The sale does not exceed 10,000 shares
    IV. The sale does not exceed 5,000 shares

    a.   I and II
    b.   I and IV
    c.   II and IV
    d.   II and III

164. Which of the following are TRUE of defined contribution plans?

    I. Employers are required to match employee deposits
    II. Annual contribution amounts are generally fixed
    III. Employer contributions may be discontinued based on company performance
    IV. Benefits increase proportionally with term of service

    a. I and II
    b. I and IV
    c. II and IV
    d. II and III

165. According to NASD rules, service charges (not including commissions) on customer accounts must be

    a. no more than 2% per year
    b. 5% per year
    c. fair and reasonable and not discriminatory
    d. adjusted according to account size

166. A floor broker asks a specialist to stop stock. Which of the following is/are TRUE about stopping stock?

    I. The specialist is guaranteeing a price.
    II. The specialist needs permission from an exchange official prior to stopping stock.
    III. This may only be done for public orders

    a. I only
    b. I and II
    c. II and III
    d. I and III

167. If a GTC order remains unexecuted, it will be automatically cancelled:

    a. A year after the order was placed
    b. At the end of the fiscal quarter
    c. At the end of the month
    d. The last business day of April or October

168. If an investor wants to limit his loss on the stock to a specific price using options to protect against a sharp decline in the stock, a reasonable recommendation would be to:

    a. Buy a call option
    b. Sell a call option
    c. Buy a put option
    d. Sell a put option

169. The _____ requires that any recommendations made to a customer by a municipal bond broker or dealer be appropriate for that customer.

    a. Municipal Securities Ruling Bond
    b. Options Trading Board
    c. Options and Securities Rulemaking Board
    d. Municipal Securities Rulemaking Board

170. If the Fed increases the discount rate, all of the following would likely occur EXCEPT:

    a. inflation increases
    b. bond yields increase
    c. the prime rate increases
    d. loan frequency decreases

171. ABC Corp. shares are trading at $45 per share when the company declares a 5 percent stock dividend. After the dividend is paid, an investor who owned 1,000 shares now owns:

    a. 1,000 shares valued at $47.25 per share
    b. 1,005 shares valued at $45 per share
    c. 1,050 shares valued at $45 per share
    d. 1,050 shares valued at $42.86 per share

172. Which of the following is TRUE with regards to bonds sold out of a firm's inventory?

    a. The total amount of the sale should be considered when determining the markup charged
    b. The sale would be subject to the NASD 5% policy
    c. The rating of the bonds is disclosed on the confirmation sent to the customer
    d. The commission amount is disclosed on the confirmation sent to the customer

173. The NASDAQ short sale rule applies to which of the following?

    a. NNM securities
    b. All OTC securities
    c. Penny stocks
    d. Bulletin board stocks

174. Place the following compensations paid out from a new issue in order from largest to smallest:

    I. Concession
    II. Reallowance
    III. Takedown
    IV. Manager's fee

    a. I, II, III, IV
    b. III, I, II , IV
    c. IV, II , I, III
    d. II, IV, I, III

175. What is the time value of a XYZ Oct 60 call trading for a premium of 7 if XYZ trades at 62.50?

    a. 3
    b. 4.5
    c. 5.75
    d. 7

176. Which of the following documents or rules govern the investments which may be purchased for a UGMA account?

    I. The legal list
    II. The prudent man rule
    III. The NASD list of approved investments
    IV. The NYSE list of approved investments

    a. I, II, and III
    b. I and II
    c. I, II, and IV
    d. II and IV

177. All of the following are TRUE of stock index options EXCEPT:

    a. When exercised, the seller delivers cash
    b. When exercised, the seller delivers shares
    c. When exercised, the buyer may owe the seller money
    d. The writer received a premium for selling the option

178. The S&P 500 and housing starts have each been climbing. Which of the following is MOST LIKELY to be falling?

    a. Gold
    b. Employment
    c. Consumer sales
    d. Industrial production

179. An investor purchases 10,000 ABC at $30. After ABC increases to $40, the investor wants to protect his profit. A registered representative could recommend which of the following orders?

    a. Sell limit at $45
    b. Sell limit at $35
    c. Sell stop at $40.25
    d. Sell stop at $39.75

180. A Regulation A offering is

    a. an offering of securities worth $5,000,000 or less in a 12-month period
    b. an offering of securities only within the issuer's home state
    c. an offering of securities to no more than 35 unaccredited investors in a 12-month period
    d. an offering of a large block of previously outstanding securities

181. Which of the following pieces of legislation was enacted to address standards for publicly traded companies, their boards of directors, and the accounting firms employed by them?

    a. Securities Investor Protection Act of 1970
    b. Securities Exchange Act of 1933
    c. Sarbanes-Oxley Act of 2002
    d. 1940 Investment Protection Act

182. All of the following transactions settle on the third business day after the trade date EXCEPT:

    a. A T-bill
    b. 100 shares of common stock
    c. A municipal bond
    d. A convertible corporate bond

183. Which of the following can be inferred from a tight money yield curve?

    I. Short maturity bonds are yielding less than long maturity bonds
    II. Short maturity bonds are yielding more than long maturity bonds
    III. Interest rates are rising
    IV. Interest rates are falling

    a. I and III
    b. II and III
    c. I and IV
    d. II and IV

184. John MacNamara is a registered rep, working for Speedy Brokers. He wants to earn a little extra money on the weekends by finding a job selling cars. If John wants to accept an additional position, he needs to inform:

    a. His employer
    b. His employer and the NASD
    c. The NASD
    d. The NASD and NYSE

185. Which of the following parties prepares the legal opinion prior to the issuance of a municipal bond?

    a. The trustee
    b. The issuer
    c. The syndicate manager
    d. The bond counsel

186. Which of the following is not used by the Federal Reserve to control the money supply of the United States?

    a. The discount rate
    b. The fed funds rate
    c. Open market activities
    d. Reserve requirements

187. A customer in the 28% tax bracket holds a GO bond at 94 with a basis of 7% and a nominal yield of 5.5%. What is the tax equivalent yield on this bond?

    a. 9.3%
    b. 9.7%
    c. 7.9%
    d. 10.1%

188. While the U.S. government is thought to "stand behind" a variety of securities, it only directly backs which of the following?

   a. GNMA

   b. FNMA

   c. FHLMC

   d. Federal Farm Credits

189. Which of the following is NOT important to the marketability of a specific municipal bond?

   a. The coupon rate

   b. The accrued interest

   c. The dollar price

   d. The name of the issuer

190. Simplified arbitration is used for

   a. member-to-member disputes up to $25,000

   b. member-to-customer disputes up to $25,000

   c. member-to-member disputes over $10,000

   d. member-to-customer disputes over $10,000

191. Which of the following characteristics are features of preferred stock?

     I. A fixed rate of return

     II. Priority to assets over common

     III. Priority to dividends over common

     IV. Fixed date of maturity

   a. I, II, and IV

   b. I and III

   c. II and IV

   d. I, II, and III

192. Frank Furkel buys an ABC convertible bond at $85 with a conversion price of $25. If Frank converts the bonds six months later and sells the stock for $23, the whole trade results in

   a. $50 loss

   b. $50 gain

   c. $70 loss

   d. $70 gain

193. Which of the following investments have tax advantages?

     I. Hedge funds

     II. FNMAs

     III. IRAs

     IV. Municipal bonds

   a. I and II

   b. II and III

   c. III and IV

   d. All of the above

194. When a municipality issues a limited tax bond, which of the following is limited in the debt indenture?

a. The type of taxes that may be used to pay off the debt
b. The number of taxes from which funds may be drawn to pay off the debt
c. The rate of taxes that can be levied to pay off the debt
d. Limited tax bonds may only be paid from real estate taxes

195. Tracy Goepel is expecting a large amount of passive income for the next few years. Which of the following investments has the potential to offset a significant amount of passive income?

a. Oil and gas exploration
b. Junk bonds
c. Corporate bonds
d. Hedge funds

196. Which of the following departments transfers orders to the proper market for execution?

a. Cashiering
b. Margin
c. Purchase and sales
d. Order

197. When a customer fails to pay for a trade and the account is now frozen, when must the customer pay for any subsequent purchase transactions?

a. Within five business days after the trade date
b. Prior to the trade
c. By the settlement date (T+3)
d. Within five business days after the trade date with the firm's permission

198. Michael Gluckman purchases a callable corporate bond trading at a current market price of 98.3. The bond may be called after 6 years with a two percent call premium. The bond has a coupon of 7.8%, and is triple tax-free. What is the current yield?

a. 6.9%
b. 7.58%
c. 7.8%
d. 7.93%

199. Which of the following investment instruments has shares that trade in the secondary market?

a. mutual funds
b. face-amount certificates
c. closed-end funds
d. UITs

200. Which type of oil and gas DPP offers the GREATEST amount of diversification?

a. Exploratory program
b. Developmental program
c. Income program
d. Combination program

201. Which of the following is NOT a prohibited activity for a registered rep?

a. Commingling
b. Interpositioning
c. Hypothecation
d. Backing away

202. Which of the following TWO statements are false regarding indications of interest during the registration period?

I. They are binding on the broker-dealer
II. They are not binding on the broker-dealer
III. They are binding on the customer
IV. They are not binding on the customer

a. I and III
b. I and IV
c. II and III
d. II and IV

203. Each of the following would affect the debit balance in a long margin account EXCEPT:

a. Cash deposit
b. Stock dividends
c. Cash dividends
d. The sale of securities held in the account

204. Which of the following is (are) considered promotional material and thus need approval from a principal?

I. Form letter
II. Market letter
III. Research report
IV. Official statement abstract

a. I and II
b. I, II, and III
c. II, III, and IV
d. I, II, III, and IV

205. If a customer wishes to maximize the allowable margin under Reg T in his purchase of 500 shares of ABC Corp. at $45, what is the minimum he must deposit in the account to make the trade?

a. $11,250
b. $12,250
c. $14,375
d. $15,500

206. After shorting a stock at 75, an investor holds the position as the stock declines to 68. Which of the following strategies could the investor use to protect the gain?

a. Buy stop-limit at 70
b. Write calls
c. Write puts
d. Buy calls

192

207. In a municipal bond underwriting, which group receives the "takedown"?

a. The members of the managing underwriter
b. Syndicate members
c. The selling group
d. Post-underwriting selling groups

208. Each of the following is true of warrants EXCEPT:

a. Warrants are issued to increase the attractiveness of new offerings
b. Warrants have a longer duration than rights
c. Warrants can be separated from the stock or bonds of the issuer
d. Warrants represent a perpetual interest, similar to stocks

209. Which of the following money market instruments pay interest?

    I. Commercial paper
    II. Banker's acceptance
    III. Jumbo CDs
    IV. T-bills

a. I and II
b. III only
c. I, II and IV
d. II and IV

210. Determine the purchase price of a 5.5% corporate bond that carries a 6.15% yield-to-call after ten years and a 5.5% basis.

a. $1075
b. $1000
c. $930
d. $925

211. The NYSE has 2,100 advancing stocks and 1,250 declining stocks at a particular point in the day. What is the advance-decline ratio at that time?

a. 1.68
b. 0.63
c. 0.59
d. 1.74

212. Sue owns 12,000 shares of ABC Financial, which has fallen sharply in the last year. If the company announces a 1-for-4 reverse split, how many shares will Sue own after the split becomes effective?

a. 2,000
b. 3,000
c. 4,000
d. 6,000

213. Which of the following is TRUE of the tax treatment of dividends received from an investment in a foreign corporation?

    a. If taxes were withheld abroad, the investor is not required to pay any taxes in the U.S.
    b. If no taxes were withheld abroad, the investor has no tax responsibility
    c. If taxes were withheld abroad, the investor must match the amount in U.S. taxes
    d. If taxes were withheld abroad, the investor can claim a foreign tax credit

214. Which of the following is a zero-coupon government security?

    a. Treasury bonds
    b. Treasury notes
    c. Treasury receipts
    d. All of the above

215. Your existing customer has just been approved by your firm to trade options. How long does the customer have to return a signed options agreement?

    a. 10 days
    b. 15 days
    c. 30 days
    d. 45 days

216. What is the most common reason for a municipal bond to trade ex-legal?

    a. The bonds are illegal
    b. The legal opinion is in doubt
    c. No legal opinion was obtained
    d. The legal opinion has been withdrawn

217. Which of the following is the most appropriate hedge for a customer expecting a large payment in Japanese yen six months forward?

    a. Buy calls on the U.S. dollar
    b. Buy puts on the U.S. dollar
    c. Buy calls on the Japanese yen
    d. Buy puts on the Japanese yen

218. What gain or loss is realized by the owner of a BBB corporate bond with a 6% coupon and 15 years until maturity when the bond is purchased for 85 and sold 5 years later for 92?

    a. A gain of $80
    b. A loss of $80
    c. A gain of $20
    d. A loss of $20

219. Which of the following is NOT TRUE of treasury stock?

    a. it is part of the outstanding shares
    b. it is issued stock that has been repurchased by the company
    c. it has no voting rights
    d. it has no dividend entitlement

220. Which of the following would BEST meet a customer's goal of current income with only moderate risk?

    a. Hedge Funds
    b. Common stock of a growth company
    c. AA rated corporate bonds
    d. Convertible preferred stock

221. Which of the following order types will be adjusted downward when a stock goes ex-dividend?

    I. Buy stop
    II. Buy limit
    III. Sell stop
    IV. Sell limit

    a. I and II
    b. I, II, and III
    c. II and III
    d. II and IV

222. When a bank and an insurance company trade with each other, the trade takes place on the

    a. First market
    b. Second market
    c. Third market
    d. Fourth market

223. Which of the following factors may cause a customer to change his or her investment objectives?

    I. Age
    II. Investment experience
    III. Marital status
    IV. The inheritance of a large amount of money

    a. I and II
    b. I, II, and III
    c. II, III, and IV
    d. I, II, III, and IV

224. On the maturity date of a corporate bond, the holders of the bonds will

    a. Receive par value from the issuer
    b. Receive the current market value plus accrued interest
    c. Continue to earn interest until they redeem the bonds
    d. Receive the current market value of the bond

225. Municipal bonds settle regular way in

    a. one day
    b. three days
    c. five days
    d. seven days

226. Which of the following federal laws requires the full disclosure of all material information about new security issues?

   a. The Securities Act of 1933
   b. The Glass-Steagall Act
   c. The Securities Exchange Act of 1934
   d. Regulation T

227. Corporate bonds which are secured by securities held by a trustee are called

   a. Guaranteed bonds
   b. Debentures
   c. Collateral trust bonds
   d. Equipment trusts bonds

228. Which of the following statements is TRUE regarding the payouts received from a ten-year certain annuity that has already begun making payments?

   a. If the purchaser dies seven years after payments begin, the annuity will not make any more payments
   b. The annuity will stop making payments after ten years, even if the purchaser is still alive
   c. The annuity will not stop making payments after ten years, if the purchaser is still alive
   d. If the purchaser is still alive after ten years, payments will go to the beneficiary

229. If ABC has 4,000,000 shares currently outstanding, what will the holder of 20,000 shares receive if ABC plans to issue an additional 200,000 shares through a rights offering?

   a. 2,000 rights to buy 1,000 shares
   b. 2,000 rights to buy 400 shares
   c. 20,000 rights to buy 1,000 shares
   d. 20,000 rights to buy 400 shares

230. In technical analysis, a consolidating market has what type of trend line?

   a. Erratic
   b. Sideways
   c. Upwards
   d. Downwards

231. Once shelf registration is obtained, the issuer may delay selling all or part of its stock for up to

   a. 180 days
   b. 270 days
   c. 1 year
   d. 2 years

232. Which of the following is the appropriate response to a customer who has placed a trade but wishes to cancel the trade because of a subsequent negative move in the stock?

   a. The customer owns the stock and must submit payment
   b. The broker-dealer will repurchase the securities
   c. The registered rep will repurchase the securities
   d. The customer should be assured that the stock will recover

233. Which of the following is TRUE with regard to IDRs?

a. The municipality is responsible for payment of the debt
b. They are not subject to the substantial user requirement
c. They have few similarities with private activity bonds
d. They do not need voter approval to be issued

234. What is the ad valorem tax on a property with an assessed value of $550,000, a current market value of $535,000, and a tax rate of 16 mills?

a. $8,800
b. $9,600
c. $10,400
d. $12,800

235. All of the following agencies or departments enforce MSRB rules EXCEPT

a. NASD
b. Comptroller of the Currency
c. Federal Reserve
d. FGIC

236. All of the following are good delivery for a trade of 470 shares of stock EXCEPT

a. forty-seven certificates for 10 shares each
b. eight certificates for 50 shares each, one certificate for 40 shares, and one certificate for 30 shares
c. four 100-share certificates and one 70-share certificate
d. two 100-share certificates and nine 30-share certificates

237. If the Federal Reserve Board increases the reserve requirements, which of the following outcomes is most likely to result?

I. The multiplier effect increases.
II. The multiplier effect decreases.
III. Interest rates increase.
IV. Interest rates decrease.

a. I and III
b. II and III
c. I and IV
d. II and IV

238. In what type of interest rate environment is call protection valuable on a callable bond?

a. table
b. Falling
c. Fluctuating
d. Rising

239. What documentation must a corporation provide to open a cash account with a broker-dealer?

a. Corporate charter
b. Corporate resolution
c. Corporate bylaws
d. Margin agreement

240. When a syndicate member retains shares of a hot issue in hopes of later selling them for a greater profit, the member has violated rules relating to

    a. Withholding
    b. Marking to market
    c. Freeriding
    d. Comingling

241. A trade confirmation must be sent to the customer

    a. on the trade date
    b. on or before the settlement date
    c. before the settlement date
    d. before the trade date

242. When can a registered rep open a joint account with a customer?

    I. Under no circumstances
    II. With approval from a principal
    III. With a signed proportionate sharing agreement from the customer

    a. I and II
    b. II and III
    c. I and III
    d. I, II, and III

243. According to the Investment Advisers Act of 1940, who is required to register?

    a. All registered reps
    b. Individuals who execute trades for customers
    c. Persons who give investment advice for a fee
    d. Publications giving general investment advice

244. A client writes a Jan 65 put for 6, is exercised, and is assigned the stock. A month later the client sells the underlying stock in the market for 69. The result of these transactions, assuming no commission, is:

    a. A profit of $100
    b. A loss of $100
    c. A profit of $1000
    d. A loss of $1000

245. Which of the following is TRUE regarding the official disclosure statement of a revenue bond?

    a. It includes information about the tax base of the municipality
    b. It needs to be filed with the SEC
    c. A final version does not need to be prepared
    d. It must only be sent to certain prospective purchasers

246. Which TWO of the following positions have the same directional bias?

    I. Long calls and short calls
    II. Long calls and short puts
    III. Long puts and short puts
    IV. Long puts and short calls

a. I and III
b. II and III
c. I and IV
d. II and IV

247. When an underwriter agrees to keep whatever shares of the offering are not sold, this is characterized as what type of underwriting?

a. Best efforts
b. All or none
c. Mini max
d. Firm commitment

248. A technical analyst would draw which TWO of the following conclusions with regard to a stock trading at its resistance levels?

    I. The stock is have difficulty going up
    II. The stock is have difficulty going down
    III. The stock is overbought
    IV. The stock is oversold

a. I and III
b. II and III
c. II and IV
d. I and IV

249. If a customer owns a convertible bond at 105, with a 7.5% coupon, what is the current yield of the bond?

a. 7.1%
b. 6.9%
c. 8.7%
d. 8%

250. Each of following statements is TRUE regarding civil penalties for insider trading violations EXCEPT:

a. Civil penalties are only levied against registered persons
b. They may be as large as three times the gain or loss
c. They may be levied for improper supervision of a registered rep
d. They center around the use of material, non-public information

Answer Key and Explanations

1. C: The question requires you to determine the gain or loss on both the stock position and the option position. On the stock position alone, the customer realizes a profit of $500 from the $5 / share increase in the price of the stock (100 * ($35 - $30)). On the option position alone, the customer has lost $100 (this is the cost of his or her hedge on the SHC stock position). The loss on the option is calculated by multiplying the $1 increase by 100; remember that a call writer is short a call, so an increase in price represents a loss when the option is later repurchased to close the position. The net gain on the combined position is $400 ($500 - $100).

2. D: The insider trading rules apply to those individuals who disclose or receive and act upon non-public material information; a pending takeover that has not yet been made public qualifies as both non-public and material, as it is likely to have a significant impact on the price of the stock. The exception to the insider trading rules applies to those individuals who inadvertently receive this type of information and have no reason to know that the information is privileged. Frank and Bill both know that the information is non-public and material. John may realize that the information is valuable, but has no duty to keep it private- neither he nor Mike violates the rules by acting on the information.

3. B: The U.S. balance of payments is a measurement of all capital flowing into the U.S. as compared to the capital flowing out; this measurement includes both capital flows resulting from the export / import of goods as well as those resulting from investment. In "EXCEPT" questions, when two answers seem to give opposite options, one of these choices is usually correct (the detail of Japanese versus UK securities is irrelevant), so choices A and B should be the focus. When U.S. investors purchase foreign securities, this kind of financial activity sends capital out of the country, thereby decreasing, rather than increasing, the U.S. balance of payments. Choice B is the FALSE answer and therefore the correct choice.

4. C: The buying power in an account is measured as the dollar value of securities that the customer can buy on margin with the excess equity (SMA) in the account. The customer has LMV of $40,000 and a debit balance (DR) of $15,000, and thus, she has $25,000 of equity ($40,000 - $15,000 = $25,000). Under Reg T, a customer is required to have no less than 50% of her LMV in a margin account; any amount above this minimum requirement is considered excess equity and thus SMA. In this case, the customer needs a minimum equity amount of $20,000 (50% * $40,000 or Ret T * LMV). The excess equity is, therefore, $5000 ($25,000 - $20,000). The buying power is the dollar value of the securities that can be purchased on margin with the account's SMA (2 * $5000 = $10,000).

5. C: The general rule of thumb is that customers should have 100 minus their age invested in stocks. However, years to retirement, retirement plans, and specific investment objectives should also be taken into account. Furthermore, as the customer ages, appropriate portfolio rebalancing should be conducted as a matter of routine procedure. Answer C is correct for two reasons: first, the question refers to strategic asset allocation, while answer C refers to a decision that would fall into the category of tactical asset allocation. Second, the performance of stocks in the most-recent 12 months is insufficient to guide an advisor with regard to the investment objectives of his or her customers.

6. B: In technical analysis (or charting), a stock's support level refers to the bottom patterning of a stock's recent trading range. Around this price, the stock seems to reverse direction and trade higher, and is said to have "price support." If the stock falls below this bottoming level pattern, and particularly if the stock closes below this level, it is referred to (by technical analysts) as a "breakdown." As a result, the stock price is expected to continue to fall until a new, but lower, trading range is established. The support level is determined by the price action of the stock and has nothing to do with the options.

7. A: As a retiree, Renee selects a defensive strategy because she is likely to prefer to take less risk-preferring capital preservation and current income. Of the listed choices, treasury bonds and money market funds will provide her with current income at a relatively low risk level. Blue chip stocks also present a lower risk profile and may offer additional income through the payment of dividends. High-yield bonds are considered a riskier investment, and thus inappropriate for Renee's account and her goal of defensive investing.

8. D: Fundamental analysis examines the quality of a company's earnings, its growth prospects, and its position within the industry in which it competes; it also tries to identify securities that are mispriced based on the analyst's view of what the company's stock should be worth. Unlike the technical analyst, who examines the price action of the stock, its volume, and its historical behavior, the fundamental analyst is only trying to determine what the "true value" of the stock is so that appropriate trading decisions can be made. D is the correct answer because the fundamental analyst doesn't track the stock's price action in order to assign value to it. The value is set according to "fundamentals."

9. A: There are two types of syndicates that may be set up to offer new shares for sale to the public – those that operate on a Western (or divided) account basis and those that operate on an Eastern (or undivided) account basis. Under the Western basis, each firm is responsible only for those shares which they originally were allotted. Under the Eastern basis, each firm is responsible for any unsold shares on the same percentage basis as in the original allotment. In this case, ABC was originally responsible for 10% of the total shares offered (1,000,000 / 10,000,000). ABC is, therefore, responsible for an additional 100,000 of the unsold shares if the syndicate is operating on an Eastern basis; otherwise, ABC has fulfilled its obligation and is not responsible for any additional shares.

10. C: The Uniform Gifts to Minors Act, commonly known as UGMA, is an act in some states of the United States that allows assets such as securities, where the donor has given up all possession and control, to be held in the custodian's name for the benefit of the minor without an attorney needing to set up a special trust fund.

11. A: An investor may use any capital losses in a given tax year to offset capital gains, and then carry forward any unused losses to use in future years. However, only $3000 of losses per year may be written off against income gains. In this case, the investor has a net capital loss of $25,000 ($45,000 losses - $20,000 gains). The investor may, therefore, write off the maximum allowable $3000 in the current tax year and carry forward the remaining $22,000 into the following year. Next year, any capital gains may be offset against the $22,000, but if additional losses accrue, only another $3000 may be written off.

12. C: The key to the question is in the fact that the bonds are callable; there is no significance to the fact that they are municipal revenue bonds. Callable bonds, like any bonds, decrease in price when interest rates rise, so answer A is false. Callable bonds usually have a higher yield to compensate the bond holder for the risk that the bonds may be called early. Answer D is also false because the call premium (the penalty the issuer is required to pay when the bonds are called) is not tied to the lost coupon payments. If it were, bonds would never be called. Answer C is true, and thus the correct answer, because when rates are falling, issuers will often call outstanding bonds and reissue them at lower rates.

13. B: Common stock, preferred stock, and convertible preferred stock all MAY provide the holder with regular dividends payments – the specific features of each will vary from issue to issue and be dependent on the specific company issuing the security. A warrant gives the holder the right to purchase stock at a specified price for a specified period of time, but is not equivalent to stock. Holders do not receive dividends, so warrants would not be an appropriate investment recommendation for a customer whose goal is to receive dividends.

14. A: All or none (AON) is a type of underwriting or an order qualifier on certain types of securities orders. Bond anticipation notes (BANs), project notes (PNs), and revenue anticipation notes (RANs) are all short-term municipal notes. The trick in this question is somewhat obvious, and is designed to make sure the test-taker is paying attention. AONs are three letters, making PNs the stand-out. This is roughly the depth of understanding that is required about the specific municipal securities that are commonly encountered on the test.

15. C: All discretionary accounts must have a written power of attorney giving the rep the authority to make investment decisions -on behalf of the client. The Power of Attorney can specify any additional rules which must be followed, including whether or not the rep may employ leverage in the account and the degree to which it may be employed. All discretionary accounts must be approved and reviewed by a principal; the principal should pay particular attention to ensuring that excessive trading (called churning) is not taking place to generate unnecessarily high commissions. Additionally, all orders for discretionary accounts must clearly be marked "discretionary." As some discretionary accounts may trade on margin, the correct answer is C.

16. A: A stabilizing bid is placed by a syndicate offering a new security in the open market when the price of that security begins to drop too quickly after trading in the security commences. Under acceptable regulations, any stabilizing bid must be at or slightly below the initial offering price to prevent the syndicate from over stimulating demand by artificially bidding up the price of the stock in the open market. Each of the bids listed, except for $30.25, is at or below the initial offering price of $30. The correct answer is, therefore, choice A.

17. C: The problem involves three steps: the purchase of a put option, the purchase of the underlying stock, and the subsequent sale of that stock. When the client sells the put for 5, he receives $500- this is the premium received when the option is sold or written. When the option is exercised, the client must purchase the stock for $4000; this makes the client's cost-basis on the stock $3500 ($4000 - $500). When the client later sells the stock, now trading at $44, the client receives $4400 in proceeds from the sale of the stock in the open market. The client, therefore, realizes a profit of $900: $4400 - $3500 or $500 of premium plus $400 profit on the sale ($4400 - $4000).

18. B: Under normal circumstances, account statements must be sent out to customers on at least a quarterly basis (every three months). However, if the account is active (meaning that any trades were performed within the course of the month), then account statements must be sent out at least monthly. In other words, a statement must be sent for any month in which a trade took place on an account. As John is an active trader, the rep should assume that his trading activity will require monthly statements to be sent. Mutual fund statements are the exception to the general rule and may be sent as infrequently as every six months, but that exception not apply in this instance.

19. B: A limited trading authorization gives the registered representative the authority to buy and sell investment securities for the customer's account. A limited trading authorization does not give the registered representative the authority to contribute or withdraw funds from the account, neither in the form of cash nor securities. A limited trading authorization also provides for the necessity of paying a third party or for paying the registered representative for his or her services in the form of a regular monthly fees. A customer is the sole person who may add or subtract capital to and from the account.

20 B: The key to this question is to read the question carefully and notice that it asks for how many *additional* shares the investor will own after the stock split. This is an easy question and one you will get wrong if you overlook the important detail of what the question is actually asking. To determine the correct answer, multiply the original 600 share holding by (3/2) which equals 900 shares. Since the investor initially owned 600 shares and now owns 900, the correct answer to the question is 300 shares (900 shares – 600 shares = 300 shares).

21. D: In a short margin account, equity (EQ) is determined using the relationship SMV + EQ = CR. For Sally, that means that she has $3000 of EQ (the equation $5000 + EQ = $8000 solves to $3000). Remember that the question asks for the level of excess equity (SMA); when Reg T is applied to the SMV, it is determined that the required equity in the account is $2500 (Reg T * SMV = required equity, 50% * $5000 = $2500). Therefore, Sally has $500 of SMA in her account ($3000 - $2500 = $500). It is important not to confuse this with buying power, which is twice the SMA, or $1000 in this example.

22. D: The central difference between an IRA and a Roth IRA is when, in the tax stream, the contributions may be made. An IRA allows for contributions to be made from pre-tax dollars, allowing the investment of a greater number of dollars individually. When the money is withdrawn from an IRA, the withdrawals will be subject to applicable income taxes. This allows the money to grow "tax-deferred." In a Roth IRA, post-tax dollars are contributed, but any subsequent growth is not subject to additional tax; these assets are allowed to grow tax-free because taxes were paid on the initial dollars before they were invested. Each type of account has advantages and the specifics will differ according to the tax liability needs of the individual investor.

23. A: While prevailing interest rates do affect the likelihood of a company to call a bond, the recent action by the Federal Reserve is irrelevant to determining which of the listed bonds is MOST likely to be called. All other things being equal, an issuer is most likely to call a bond with the highest coupon interest rate in order to issue new debt at a lower rate. Of the two 7% bonds, the issuer is more likely to call the bond with the longer maturity; the longer maturity is more expensive to the issuer over the remaining life of the bond as the higher rate must be paid for a longer period of time. Therefore, the issuer will select the highest coupon, longest maturity bond to call – answer A.

24. C: Since one must assume that this is a normal, on-shore account that is subject to Reg T, an increase in SMA is one half as big as the increase in equity (since Reg T requires that stocks be 50% paid for by equity). You know that the account had some positive SMA before the move in the market, because the question tells you that the account is unrestricted. Therefore, a $12,000 increase in SMA implies that the long market value of the account must have increased by twice as much, or $24,000 (2 * $12,000 = $24,000).

25. C: A double-barreled municipal bond is essentially the combination of a revenue bond, backed by the municipal revenues received through a specific investment in a project, and a general obligation (GO) bond, which is backed by the full taxing authority of the issuing municipality. With a double-barreled bond, if the revenue from the revenue-producing project or facility is insufficient to service the payments due on the bond, the municipality uses its taxing power to make up any short-fall. This is considered an advantage to the bondholder, so double-barreled bonds tend to trade at a discount to straight revenue bonds.

26. C: Statement I is correct, since a reduced maximum sales charge is allowed and possible when a company is buying shares for its own pension plan. Statements II and III are both correct also- the sales charge can be reduced when an investor is either purchasing a significant dollar value of stock or when he or she agrees to have income and dividends automatically reinvested. The discount is provided as an inducement for the large purchase or for the indication that an investor wishes to hold the position for an extended period. Statement IV is incorrect. A unit investment trust may receive a reduction in the maximum sales charge only when the shares are the SOLE investment underlying a contractual plan. The answer which combines the three correct statements is C.

27. D: The United States Congress is responsible for setting fiscal policy for the U.S. Government, and by extension, the country. Fiscal policy refers to government spending which is controlled by the Congress. In some instances, these policies are implemented by the Treasury Department. The Federal Reserve Board (the Fed) is responsible for setting monetary policy for the country, which it executes by setting key interest rates and through the Federal Open Market Committee (FOMC), which buys and sells government securities in order to affect the money supply in a way that is believed desirable for the national economy.

28. B: The key to this question is to recognize that the test writers often like to provide you with an excess of information in an effort to confuse you or trick you into believing that the question is more complicated than it actually needs to be. The selling group receives the concession on the shares that it actually sells. In this case, the selling group was allotted 1,000,000 shares and earned $0.30 for each share because it sold all the shares it was allotted (1,000,000 * $0.30 = $300,000).

29. D: There are two types of annuities: immediate payment and deferred payment. With an immediate payment annuity, the customer pays a lump sum and begins receiving payments immediately. With a deferred payment annuity, the customer pays a lump sum and begins receiving payments at some point in the future; in this case, the customer may be able to opt for making periodic payments. Under no circumstances will the issuing insurance company allow the customer to begin receiving immediate payments without fully paying the lump sum prior to the commencement of payments.

30. D: A long straddle means buying a call and a put on the same underlying security where the call and the put each have the same expiration month and the same strike price. Answer B is a long combination (long meaning buys and no sells), defined as having two buys ("long" means purchase in the context of options) where the expiration month, the strike price, or both are different. A straddle is used when the investor expects a significant move in the underlying security, but is uncertain as to the direction.

31. B: This questions states that each of the options given will cover the put writer's position, except for one; in essence, the question is asking which of the listed actions WILL NOT cover the put writer's position. Answer A is not a good choice because it will not really neutralize the put writer's position (she will still have market exposure), but it will cover the dollar exposure. Answers C and D will fully neutralize the position, cover the put writer's dollar and market exposure. Answer B will not cover the put writer's position at all; if the put is exercised, the put writer will still be responsible for buying the underlying stock at the strike price; a long position in the stock provides no protection, and thus, does not cover the put writer.

32. B: Under the wash sale rule, when a customer sells a security at a loss, the customer cannot buy the same security or anything equivalent or convertible into the same security within 30 days before or after the sale and still claim the loss for tax purposes. The object of the rule is to prevent an investor from "locking in a loss" for tax purposes, while essentially maintaining the same position after the sale. (II) is a violation of the rule because the customer is buying options that are equivalent (and also "convertible" upon exercise) into Xenon common. (IV) is also a violation because a convertible bond is also convertible into shares of Xenon common. Buying put options (I) is acceptable because they are not an equivalent position. (III) is acceptable because it takes place after the required 30-day waiting period.

33. C: The NASD 5% rule is somewhat of a misnomer – it is more of a guideline than a rule which can be legally enforced. The NASD 5% rule states that a brokerage firm should not charge more than 5% for commissions, markups, or markdowns when collecting fees from customers. It was enacted to help ensure that customers were not excessively charged in the over-the-counter (OTC) market. It covers OTC trades by customers who trade in outstanding, non-exempt securities. Each of the listed answers, except answer C, is an exception to the NASD 5% rule and describes the situations where a higher fee may be charged because of the difficulty in executing the specific trade. A broker may not attempt to recoup losses by overcharging the customer and this not an allowable exception to the 5% rule. Therefore, Answer C is the best answer.

34. D: A principal must review any communication that is to be sent to customers of the firm, any complaints received by a customer of the firm, and any special documents (including those giving discretionary authority to a registered rep) pertaining to a customer's account. Internal memos and regular communications made between employees of the firm are not required to be reviewed by a principal. However, the principal is responsible for all official communications coming into and disseminated by the firm, and thus must review written recommendations and other solicitations sent to customers.

35. A: The minimum short equity maintenance required to be maintained under NYSE rules in a short margin account is 30%; this amount is calculated based on the short market value held in the account at a given time. In this case, the short market value of the account is $52,000 so the minimum amount based on the 30% rules ($52,000 * 30%) is $15,600. It is important to note that ABC Brokers may require a higher amount than is required by the rule – this question, however, pertains only to the NYSE rule and not to the broker's own discretionary limits

36. B: When a customer account has no activity, an account statement must be sent on at least a quarterly basis. During any month in which the account has activity, an account statement must be sent at the end of the monthly period. While this may seem obvious, the test-writers are very concerned with the registered representative's duties to his or her customers. Proper service and dissemination of customer account statements is one of the most basic requirements of customer account maintenance but it is important and should not be overlooked as it reflects upon the ethical behavior of the registered representative.

37. A: The cost basis for a call option is determined by adding the premium to the strike price (45 + 4 = 49). Despite the fact that the investor does not actually own the stock, the cost basis is the break-even point for the option in question. This call had some intrinsic value and some time value when it was purchased; it must appreciate in intrinsic value faster than the time decay occurs for the investor to make money. The cost basis is the price above which the stock needs to trade before the expiration date in order to realize a profit-- 49 in this problem.

38. A: When the municipality selects an underwriter (or a syndicate of underwriters) the issue is said to be done on a negotiated basis. In contrast, when the municipality publishes a notice of sale, it is putting various dealers on notice that it is accepting bids on a competitive basis. Answer D can be ruled out since A and C are mutually exclusive (both cannot be correct at the same time). Private placements usually refer only to the issuance of specialized investment vehicles like hedge funds or private equity investments, not the issuance of public debt.

39. D: The par value of a stock is set by the corporation as a placeholder to be listed on the balance sheet. There is no relationship, direct or inverse, between the par value and the market value – the par value is fixed and does not fluctuate unless the company is attempting to achieve an accounting change unrelated to market conditions. Answer C refers to the liquidation value, which is closer to the stock's book value. The balance sheet will often list the stock's par value plus the additional capital that was raised by the initial public offering (IPO) – classified as "paid-in capital."

40. C: The first step in determining the correct answer is to determine at what price Peter will acquire shares – his price is lower than the POP because he is making a sizeable investment and will receive a breakpoint discount. Keep in mind that the entire transaction takes place at this sales charge percentage. To determine the price Peter will be charged, divide the NAV by 100 percent less the sales charge: Price = NAV / (100% - 6.5%) = $9 / (1.00 – 0.065) = $9.63. Now you can determine how many shares Peter can afford to purchase at this price, determined by dividing $25,000 by the $9.63 sale price.

41. B: The "money market" refers to the market for financial instruments with maturities of one year or less. CDs, repos, and t-bills are money market instruments because they are used by investors to manage short-term cash (money) positions. CDSs are credit default swaps and are a derivative instrument that have varying maturities, but are not a part of the more liquid money market. CDSs have received a great deal of press coverage of late because of their role in =f the recent financial crisis. Money market instruments tend to be lower-yielding, but are highly liquid instruments and easily converted into cash.

42. C: Under the Securities Investor Protection Corporation (SIPC), an individual investor is covered up to $500,000 in the event of a broker's bankruptcy, with a maximum of $250,000 coverage for cash positions. Fran was holding $150,000 in cash, so all of it is covered; the entirety of her securities positions, which are in aggregate below the maximum coverage level, are also covered under SIPC. She is, therefore, covered by SIPC for $450,000.

43. D: A sinking fund is a special account into which bond issuers make regular deposits in order to pay off bond principal at maturity. The key to this question is in understanding that it asks which types of debt issue must have a sinking fund. While balloon bonds often use a sinking fund because of the large payment that is made when the balloon is due, a term bond makes a single payment to cover all of the principal and, for this reason, a sinking fund is a required provision as a protection for bondholders.

44. C: Joan's net position is a debit spread because she paid more for the option she purchased than she received for the option she sold; her net debit is $5.50. In order for Joan to profit, the difference between the two options must widen as they move towards expiration. As the options theta kicks in (time decay), if ABC stock trades below $54.50, the intrinsic value of her long put will be greater than her debit and both options could be covered for a profit. At this point ($54.50), or any point below this, at least one of the options will be in-the-money and Joan will realize a profit. In this case, one or both of the options may be exercised, but this is not necessary for Joan's trade to be profitable.

45. A: When including previous successful recommendations in an advertisement that will be seen by customers, trading regulations require that any and all similar trades suggested by the firm for the previous year be included in the advertisement. The fact that Peter is only interested in sharing *his* own recommendations for the past six months does not exempt him from including all options trades suggested by the firm during, the previous twelve months. The rule states that all similar trades must be included, so the rule means that only options trades must be disclosed.

46. D: When a customer purchases a new issue of bonds (even dubious automotive ones), the confirmation that must be sent to the customer must include: the customer's name, the settlement date, the maturity date, and the coupon rate (nominal yield on the bond). The current yield at the time of the sale is not required information on the confirmation. Of the choices listed, only answer D includes all information that is required and none that isn't. It is important to identify which statements contain faulty information and eliminate those because this will provide the most comprehensive answer choice and lead to the correct answer.

47. C: The Federal Reserve Board (also known as the FRB or simply the Fed) is responsible for setting reserve requirements for banks. When the Fed raises the reserve requirements, the money supply contracts, as banks have less capital to lend. The Fed also controls the discount rate; this is the rate at which banks may borrow from the Fed in the overnight market to meet reserve requirements. When the discount rate rises, the money supply also contracts because all interest rates increases tend to making borrow less attractive. The prime rate is the rate banks charge their most-preferred borrowers and is not controlled by the Fed The Federal Open Market Committee (or FOMC) is also controlled by the Fed When it wishes to increase the money supply, the FOMC buys securities in the open market, pushing dollars into the system; when they sell those securities, the money supply contracts.

48. B: The key to this question is that shareholders are voting using cumulative voting rights, meaning that Bill has a total of 3000 votes (1000 shares * 3 open slots = 3000 votes) to cast in any way he sees fit. Cumulative voting rights are a way for a small investor to gain greater influence by allowing him to combine his votes and get at least one favored individual onto the Board of Directors. Each of the answer choices is possible except for choice B, because that choice would imply that Bill has a total of 9000 votes rather than 3000. Choice C is acceptable because Bill is not required to use all of the votes that accrue to him.

49. D: This question is best answered through the process of elimination. In order to have a spread, the investor must have purchased one option and sold another – this eliminates answers B and C because this investor has sold two options. To determine whether the investor is holding a straddle or a combination, consider the strikes prices and months of expiration for the two options in question. If the strike and expiration months are both the same, then the investor is holding a straddle. If either is different, as is the case here, the investor is holding a combination.

50. C: The U.S. balance of payments is a measurement of all capital flowing into the U.S. as compared to the capital flowing out; this measurement includes both capital flows resulting from the export / import of goods as well as those resulting from investment. To answer this question, simply consider the effect of each choice and which direction that choice will cause money to flow. The purchase of ADRs will cause money to flow out of the U.S. and into the countries of the companies that issued the ADRs. An increase in the discount rate and the tightening of the U.S. dollar would each cause money to flow out of the U.S. in search of cheaper foreign goods. Only answer C leads to money flowing into the U.S.

51. C: The SEC is responsible for the regulation of corporations and the issuance of stock. The Chicago Board Options Exchange (CBOE) is one the exchanges upon which options are traded. The Options Clearing Corporation (OCC) is the issuer and guarantor of all listed options in the United States. The OCC determines which securities are may be sold as options, and guarantees that the holder of any options contract will have the right and ability to exercise that option according to the terms under which it was issued.

52. D: According to Rule 405 (the "know your customer" rule), Michael is required to obtain Sally's full name, address, date of birth and Social Security number. It is also advisable, though not strictly required, that he consider her risk tolerance and investment objectives in discussions with her. However, this information may be obtained from other sources. Since the question asks what information Michael should obtain, the "best" answer is all of it. Had the question asked which information Michael was required to obtain from her, only the first two statements would be accurate.

53. A: The Federal Reserve Board (the Fed) determines which securities may be purchased on margin. While both the SEC and the NASD propagate rules, which affect the ability of investors to purchase on margin and to short securities and on what terms, the various exchanges have their own rules about what securities may be listed on each respective exchange. Ultimately, the Fed determines if a given security may be sold short or purchased on margin. An easy way to remember this is to keep in mind that purchasing on margin is a form of borrowing – typically a bank lends, so borrowing and banks is regulated by the Fed as opposed to other securities regulators.

54. B: Intrastate offerings (those offered only within the borders of a single state) are exempt from SEC registration, but must be registered on the state level. Interstate offerings (those offered across state lines in several states) and variable annuities are required to be registered with the SEC. Under Regulation D, private placements are exempt from SEC registration and are not required to be registered in the individual states in which they are offered. Private placements include such investments as hedge funds and private equity funds and are often subject to other restrictions. Additional restrictions may be placed upon the investors and upon the methods by which they may be marketed (think accredited investor rules).

55. D: All bondholders (including both the holders of zero-coupon bonds and the holders of convertible debentures) are debt holders or creditors of the corporation and do not have an ownership interest. The purchase of bond debt gives investors a higher claim to the company's assets in bankruptcy, but does not give them any of the rights of ownership. Options give the holder the right to buy stock at a given price, but the holder of an option does not become an owner until the options have been exercised. Only stock holders (of both common and preferred) are actual owners of the company.

56. A: The key to this question is to recognize that the test writers often like to provide you with an excess of information in an effort to confuse you or trick you into believing that the question is more complicated than it actually needs to be. This question asks for the current yield (current yield = annual interest / market price = $80 / $1100 = 7.3%). The bond's duration, its conversion price (or even the issue of its convertibility), or the fact that it is one of Sara's major holdings is completely irrelevant to coming up with the correct answer. In questions that provide a laundry list of details, look for the few that are needed to solve the question being asked.

57. C: One of the keys to answering this question correctly is being able to distinguish between a seller, a writer, a buyer and a holder of various options contracts. A seller and a writer are equivalent, and both are short the option in question. A buyer and a holder are equivalent, and both are long the option in question. Of the choices listed, only the buyer (or holder) of a call option would end up owning the stock if the options were exercised (an investor short a put would also end up owning the stock, but this is not one of the listed choices). In order to receive the dividend payment, the investor must own the stock as of the ex-dividend date. Only answer C would result in the investor owning the stock.

58. A: Under OTC equity security trading rules, a single share that trades above $175 is considered a round lot. In this case then, with ABC shares trading at $256, each single share will be considered a round lot, so 65 round lots have traded. For lower priced securities, round lots are considered share blocks of 100 shares. If ABC were trading below $175, this would then be considered a trade of 65 odd lots. Investors should pay attention to this when trading stocks that are very near $175.

59. C: Dollar cost averaging refers to the practice of buying a set dollar amount of certain investment vehicles at regular intervals with the goal of achieving a lower average cost per share. The dollar cost averaging method of buying equities relieves the investor of market-timing uncertainties. As the stock's market price fluctuates, the investor continues to purchase shares regardless of the stock price fluctuations. Dollar cost averaging is a long-term strategy which is founded on the premise that equity market prices always climb over long periods of time. Over time, if the investment ultimately appreciates, the investor's average price per share will be lower compared to the future market price of the investment. Unless an investor is extremely lucky, the alternative method of buying a block of shares at a single price point may not achieve this goal and expose the investor to significant market fluctuation risk

60. A: Variable annuities are retirement plans issued by insurance companies whose payouts are dependent on the performance of a group of securities held in a separate account held by the insurance company. Straight life annuities, as opposed to life with period certain annuities, have the highest payouts because all payments stop after the death of the account holder. Answer C refers to the tax treatment of IRAs, not variable annuities. Finally, the assumed interest rate (AIR) of an annuity contract is unrelated to the performance of any of the U.S. equity market indexes.

61. B: The key to this question is to recognize that the test writers often like to provide you with an excess of information in an effort to confuse you or trick you into believing that the question is more complicated than it actually needs to be. The recent upgrade received by Billings by one, but not both, of the major rating agencies, has absolutely no bearing on the correct answer. The fact that the bond carries a call premium (or even the fact that the bond is callable at all) is also irrelevant. The fact that the coupon and the basis are equal means that Sam paid par, or $1000, for the bond. No calculation is required once this is recognized.

62. A: Specialists are not allowed to compete with orders from the public market. In order to determine the range of the public market, find the highest bid and the lowest offer (ignoring stop orders which are triggered only if the market trades at or through that price). Any quote entered by the specialist must be between these two prices. In this case, the highest bid is 35.20 and the lowest offer is 35.60. Since the specialist's quote must fall in between these two prices, answer A is the only one that fits this criterion, and thus, is the correct answer.

63. C: When trying to determine the inside market by looking at the specialist's book, find the highest bid and the lowest offer (ignoring stop orders which are triggered only if the market trades at or through that price). This defines the inside market. In this case, the highest bid is at Morgan for 35.20 and the lowest offer is at Merrill for 35.60. The range created by these two extremes is the inside market. These are the prices most commonly quoted as the bid/ask spread to retail clients.

64. D: Open-end investment companies trade in mutual funds and have characteristics that differ from closed-end investment companies. An open-end investment company continuously creates and issues new shares to investors, selling them at the public offering price (POP), not the NAV plus a commission. Investors must redeem the shares directly with the issuer, which may only issue common shares. Closed-end funds may issue common shares, preferred shares, and bonds, and their shares may be traded on the open market between two investors not associated with the company. Closed-end funds do not offer redeemable shares.

65. A: An in-the-money option is trading such that there is already some intrinsic value contained in the price of the option. With regard to calls, this means that the underlying is trading above the strike price and, with regard to puts, this means that the underlying stock is trading below the strike price. An at-the-money option occurs when the underlying stock is trading at the strike price of the option. An out-of-the-money option is trading such that there is no intrinsic value contained in the price of the option: for calls this means that the underlying is trading below the strike price and for puts this means that the underlying is trading above the strike price. Only answer A is an in-the-money option.

66. A: This question is one that involves selecting the "best" answer. The company will be paid in Euros, so its risk is that the euro declines relative to the U.S. dollar between the time it bills its Italian customer and that customer pays. While selling calls will provide the company with some protection against a decline in the euro, that protection is limited and could cost the company significantly should the euro rise sharply. Buying puts is the best hedge against a decline in the euro – buying options will always be the right answer to these types of questions.

67. D: The cooling off period is a part of the registration process for a new security, and is a required waiting period prior to the offering going on sale to investors. During this period, due diligence must be exercised, blue-sky laws are observed, and a preliminary prospectus, often called a red herring, is issued. A stabilizing bid is placed by the underwriting brokers if the price of the issue drops too quickly after the security IPOs – this is a part of the sales process and only takes place when the security begins to trade. This happens after the cooling off period is finished, and thus, is not a part of the process itself.

68. C: Investors in GNMAs must pay both state and federal income tax on the interest they receive. Puerto Rican Commonwealth bonds are known as triple-tax-free as they are exempt from income tax on the state, federal and local levels. Treasury bonds are also tax free in all states under federal law. Municipal revenue bonds are tax free to investors who reside in the same state as the municipality issuing the bonds, but residents of other states must pay state income tax on the interest they receive from these bonds.

69. C: An investment in a private equity fund is an example of a non-conventional investment (NCI). Other examples include hedge funds, high yield bonds (including both distressed and low-grade debt instruments), equity-linked notes, and shares in real estate or natural resource limited partnerships. When a registered rep purchases these instruments for a customer's account, FINRA rules require the rep to have prior written consent from the customer. This is relatively new material, so it is very likely that it will appear on the test – this rule is a reaction to the financial turbulence of 2008.

70. A: The last time that an investor can trade a listed option is at 4:00 p.m. on the third Friday of the expiration month (answer B). Options may be exercised until 5:30 p.m. on the third Friday of the expiration month (answer A). Options officially expire at 11:59 p.m. on the Saturday after the third Friday of the expiration month (answer D). It is important to remember that some test questions may use CST instead of EST because many options are traded primarily in Chicago at the CBOE.

71. B: Barry's tax liability is determined by calculating the annual interest he receives plus the annual accretion. The interest is calculated by multiplying the annual coupon by the par value of the bond (8% * $1000 = $80). Accretion is determined by dividing the discount received in the purchase price (par value minus market price) by the number of years to maturity ($1000 - $800 / 10 = $20). Therefore, Barry's annual tax liability is $80 of interest added to the $20 of accretion, or $100.

72. C: This is another question is which you must determine which is the "best answer." A head and shoulders topping formation is a bearish indicator, but more accurately it signals that a bullish trend is reversing. Therefore, while answer B is technically also correct, the "best" answer is C because it is more complete and more accurate. The type of formation can apply to an individual stock or the market as a whole, and it gets its name from the "picture" of a head and two shoulders "appearing" on the chart of the security being investigated.

73. B: The NASD 5% rule is somewhat of a misnomer – it is more of a guideline than a regulatory rule. It states that a brokerage firm should not charge more than 5% for commissions, markups, or markdowns when collecting fees from customers. It was enacted to help ensure that customers were not charged excessively in the over-the-counter (OTC) market. It covers OTC trades with public customers in dealing with outstanding, non-exempt securities. The policy is not intended to cover new securities – like those offered through a prospectus. Each of the other statements is false.

74. D: The first step to solving this problem is to properly accrete the bond. Accretion is determined by dividing the discount received in the purchase price (par value minus market price) by the number of years to maturity ($1000 - $800 / 10 = $20). This amount must be added to the purchase price to determine the investor's ultimate cost basis ($800 + $100 = $900). If the investor sells the bond for 89, he or she receives $890 (89% * $1000 par value = $890). The difference realized by the investor is, therefore, a loss of $10 ($890 - $900 = -$10). Remembering to add the accretion is the critical step in this problem.

75. B: When evaluating any question on the exam, pay careful attention to words that are emphasized (MUST in this case). Any of the combinations of public offering price (POP) and net asset value (NAV) could indicate a closed-end fund but, under the maximum 8.5% sales charge rule, answer B must be a closed-end fund because its sales charge exceeds 8.5%. The sales charge implied in the combinations given can be calculated as: sales charge = (POP – NAV) / POP. Each of the answer choices results in a sales charge below 8.5%, except for B, which must, therefore, be a closed-end fund.

76. D: An American Depository Receipt (ADR) represents the shares of a foreign security trading in the U.S. The very definition eliminates answer C. An investor IS able to receive dividends in cash and the certificates are held in a custodial bank; NOT delivered to the investor. Answers A and B can also be eliminated, leaving only answer D as the one TRUE statement of the four answer choices given in the question. ADR questions tend to be very straightforward and should be an easy place to gain points if you are familiar with the basics.

77. B: The key to this question is to recognize that the test writers often like to provide you with an excess of information in an effort to confuse you or trick you into believing that the question is more complicated than it actually needs to be. The fact that the bond carries a call premium after 5 years is completely irrelevant to determining the correct answer. If the basis and the coupon are equal, the investor paid par for the bond. This means that the investor paid $1000 for the bond – what has happened since is not relevant to determining the purchase price.

78. A: A Collateralized Mortgage Obligation (CMO) normally has a Standard & Poor's credit rating of AAA because they are comprised of GNMAs (directly backed by the U.S. Government), FNMAs and FHLMCs (these are agencies implicitly backed by the U.S. Government as we saw during the recent housing crisis). All of these securities are considered exceptionally safe and receive S&P's highest rating unless they are accompanied by a statement to the contrary. Whether this will remain the case remains to be seen, but for the time being, and for the current test, it is accurate.

79. C: Despite the brokerage firm's wish to sell shares using its own cost basis (the price at which the firm acquired the shares and took them into their inventory), the current market price is the only price at which the shares may be sold (plus the commission charged by the firm). Since the question asks what price the brokerage sells the shares for, the current ask or offer price ($34.15) should be used – the customer is buying at the offer. The brokerage could buy the shares from a customer at the bid, less any commission.

80. A: This is a relatively straightforward question that tests your overall knowledge of how the combination of information flow, control, and decision-making works within various organizations. Non-clearing brokers cannot extend credit to customers. They are required to pass the request through to the firm's clearing agent, who ultimately presents the request to the clearing agent's designated examining authority (DEA) for approval. This applies to both cash and margin accounts. The self-regulatory organization (SRO) may set these rules, but is not directly involved in the process on a regular basis.

81. A: This question has multiple parts, but the first consideration is to recognize that an easing of interest rates means that the discount rate will fall. The next thing to determine is the overall effect of the Fed's move – namely, that all interest rates will generally fall, leading to an increase in the price of bonds overall. If interest rates fall, the U.S. money supply will loosen, making the dollar weaker. If the U.S. dollar is weaker, U.S. goods will be cheaper, and thus, more competitive.

82. D: The "loan amount" is the amount of capital advanced or loaned to Sam by his brokerage. Since the question states that this is an initial transaction, we know that we are trying to determine the initial allowable dollar figure as opposed to the maintenance margin required. Initial margin may not exceed 50%, so if the transaction value is $30,000 ($30 * 1000 shares = $30,000), and the transaction is at the maximum allowed by Reg T, then the loan must be for $15,000 ($30,000 * 50% = $15,000).

83. C: Again, the key to this question is to recognize that the test writers often like to provide you with an excess of information in an effort to confuse you or trick you into believing that the question is more complicated than it actually needs to be. The only information required to answer this question is the market price and the coupon rate ($972 and $60 respectively). The fact that the bond is a callable muni or that it is triple tax free to Jon has no bearing on determining the correct answer. Simply use the following equation: current yield = annual interest / market price = $60 / $972 = 6.17%.

84. B: A leading indicator is believed to provide a sense of how the economy will perform in the near term. The money supply, the rise and fall of interest rates, and housing starts give forecasters an idea of what to expect over the next several months. The Institute of Supply Management's industrial production number is considered a coincident indicator – it gives an idea of how the economy is currently performing. The third type of indicator, a lagging indicator, is used to give confirmation that the leading and coincidental were correct after the fact; lagging indicators change after the economy has already changed course. The unemployment rate is the most often cited example of a lagging indicator.

85. A: The Trust Indenture Act of 1939 was passed to regulate the issuance of debt by corporations, and only covers corporate bonds. Debentures are a type of corporate bond, and thus, are covered by the Act. Treasuries, agencies, and GO bonds (municipal bonds) are backed by government (or quasi-government) entities and are exempt from the Act. Debentures, which are backed by the issuing corporation, are specifically covered by the Act. While agencies are only implicitly backed by the U.S. Government, they are also exempt from the Act.

86. C: When a company raises cash through either a debt or equity offering, including both the issuance of common and preferred shares, the company's cash position increases, but its liabilities do not (the equity section of its balance sheet is the offset for the higher asset level). Since assets have increased with the debt or equity issue, and liabilities have not, net worth increases. The cash raised qualifies as both a current and quick asset (can be liquidated in less than 6 months). Knowing that total liabilities remain unchanged immediately eliminates answers B and D – even if this is all you know; your chances have improved dramatically. Knowing the definition of a quick asset should point you to answer C.

87. D: A covered call writing program involves systematically selling call options on an underlying long position (hence the options are covered). If the options are exercised, the long underlying position is called away. An investor would pursue this type of program to enhance the yield on an underlying security, to hedge a long position by collecting premiums (this essentially lowers the cost basis), or to slowly reduce the size of a concentrated long position. If an investor believes a security will depreciate significantly, selling the security or purchasing put options would be the appropriate action, not covered call writing.

88. C: Municipal Securities Rulemaking Board (MSRB) rule G-39 addresses standards for cold-calling new potential customers (it does not address communications with existing customers). The rule states that the caller must disclose his or her name and the name, address, and phone number of the firm. Picking between statements I and II, is a matter of common sense. The local time of the person receiving the call governs the acceptable times to call as described in the rule. This rule is important in preventing global call centers from completely circumventing the rule and initiating contact with new customers at the call center local time.

89. B: The order must be split into two separate orders – an order to buy if the stock trades at or above 25 and an order to buy for a price of $25 or better. Therefore, looking at the ticker, when the stock trades at $25, the order is triggered. You must then look for the next print at or below $25 – the "SLD" print tells us that the trade was reported out of order, so the registered rep must look for the next trade at or below $25. The next trade is at $24.98, so this is the price at which the order was filled (executed).

90. A: The first step here is to recognize that the question is asking about a municipal revenue bond – the bond is backed by the revenues produced by a revenue producing facility. In a net revenue pledge, the municipality pays for operating expenses (cost of operations plus maintenance) first, and then pledges the remainder to the bond holders. Therefore, to obtain the net revenue pledge, start with the gross revenue of the facility, subtract the operating costs, and divide the remaining revenues by the debt service requirements.

213

91. B: A registered representative may remain unaffiliated with a broker-dealer for no more than 2 years without having to retake each of the licensing exams required to work as a stockbroker. A registered representative will also be required to complete continuing education requirements on an annual basis, often by the firm with which he or she is employed, in order to remain current on changes that have occurred. The registered representative is responsible for remaining current on changes as they occur and for incorporating them into their individual business practices.

92. D: The first step is to determine the conversion ratio.   The conversion ratio is obtained by dividing the par value by the conversion price ($1000 / $25 = 40 shares). Once this is accomplished, you can determine that Joe sold 40 shares for $23 (40 shares * $23 = $920). Once you have determined the dollars realized from the sale, subtract the cost basis ($850). The trade resulted in a gain of $70 for Joe. The question does not ask whether the trade is advisable as this is impossible to determine without knowing where the bond was trading at the time it was converted – selling the bond might have resulted in lower transaction costs.

93. C: Repos (repurchase agreements) are usually overnight loans between two counter-parties; in this type of financing, U.S. government securities are used as collateral. Repos cannot be transferred. Fed funds are loans made by the Fed to individual banks to meet overnight reserve requirements – these may not be transferred either. Likewise, private placements (investments like hedge funds and private equity funds) may not be transferred amongst investors because they have certain investor requirements (such as the accredited investor rules). Of the listed answer options, only ADRs trade in the secondary market.

94. C: Of the possible answers listed, only answer C does not change the number of outstanding shares of the stock, which can have a significant impact on the price of the stock. A stock split or a stock dividend will alter the number of shares outstanding and affect the price of the stock significantly. A cash dividend, while having an indirect impact on the price of the stock, is perceived as being "priced-into" the stock and the price of the options as well. The declaration or payment of a cash dividend does NOT alter the strike price of any of the listed options on the underlying stock.

95. B: For tax purposes, a limited partnership (such as hedge funds, private equity funds, or natural resource funds) may make standard deductions, including depreciation, depletion, and interest expenses. Principal expenses, such as redemptions (the return of principal invested in the fund to some of the limited partners by the general partner after the liquidation of certain assets), may not be deducted for tax purposes. The fund may treat them differently when calculating performance based on the cost of liquidating the specific assets in question, and based largely on the disclosed policies of the partnership at the time the initial investments were received.

96. B: In determining the margin position of an account, the portfolio margining method considers the net risk of the entire portfolio, rather than on assessing margin limit requirements on the basis of each individual position. It is only available when certain criteria are met and there is no minimum number of requirements that must be held in the account. As a tip, remember that when two answer choices are opposites of each other (answer B and answer C in this question), one must be the correct answer, since one must be true and the other false.

97. D: After a 2-for-1 stock split, there are twice as many shares of XYZ outstanding. The earnings of the company must now be shared by twice as many shares, and thus the earnings per share (EPS) must be cut in half ($2). Since there are twice as many shares, and the market capitalization of XYZ should not have changed, each share must also be worth half as much ($32). Each shareholder will still receive a proportional share of the earnings of the company because they will own twice as many shares (worth 50% as much) and receive the $2 EPS twice as many times (assuming no shares are sold). There are many reasons a company may do a stock split, discussed in various areas of the test material. A very common reason for a stock split is to lower the price of shares, making them more attractive to investors. The corporation may raise additional capital in this way.

98. B: The key to this question is to recognize that the test writers often like to provide you with an excess of information in an effort to confuse you or trick you into believing that the question is more complicated than it actually needs to be. To calculate the tax equivalent yield (TEY), the only information that is needed is the bond's yield to maturity (7% in this question) and the investor's effective tax rate (Sara is in the 28% tax bracket). To calculate the TEY, divide the YTM by 100% less the tax rate (TEY = 7% / (100% - 28%) = 9.7%). The additional information provided in the question can be ignored and the answer determined with a single calculation.

99. C: After the investor fills out an account transfer form with the new broker, the new broker must send a copy of the form to the old broker. Upon receipt, the original broker must cancel any and all outstanding orders for the account and place it into frozen account status. The old broker then has three business days to validate the account transfer form received from the new broker and then there is an additional four days allowed to complete the transfer. The old broker does NOT have ten days to effectuate the entire transfer.

100. C: The advantages of using an option instead of going short a stock include the downside protection, the ability to maintain the same level of exposure while risking less capital, and the fact that no dividend payments will be made if the position is held over an ex-dividend date. The downside is that the option WILL lose time value as it moves toward expiration. It is the advantages described in statements I, II, and IV that an investor must weigh against the cost described in statement III when deciding whether to buy a put option or sell the stock short.

101. A: If the Federal Reserve increases the reserve requirement, banks will have to hold a greater percentage of deposits in their vaults and will have less money available for lending. Increasing reserve requirements will lead to a DECREASE in the money supply. When the money supply tightens, interest rates tend to rise and bond prices, which are inversely related to interest rates, tend to fall. Furthermore, when money is tight, the Fed is likely to experience a greater demand volume at the Fed window, until the change is assimilated and the demand for Fed funds levels off.

102. D: When a company performs a rights offering, it hires a rights agent, which is responsible for maintaining records of the names of the rights certificate holders. In addition to rights agents, companies also hire transfer agents who are responsible for maintaining lists of shareholders, retiring old stock certificates, and issuing new certificates when required. In certain instances, the transfer agent may act as a rights agent also; were this the only given answer choice, it would be one of the "best" answers test-writers enjoy so much.

103. A: Treasury STRIPS (T-STRIPS) are purchased at a discount and mature at par value, building the return on the investment into a single lump sum payment. This type of security behaves similarly to a corporate zero-coupon bond. Despite the fact that the investor only receives a single payment, he or she must pay taxes on the accretion each year. Remember that the question asked which two statements are false. This is a question on which it is easy to get confused and, even after careful analysis, one may still get the wrong answer.

104. B: The debit balance (DR) is the amount the investor borrowed from the broker-dealer when purchasing the securities on margin. The debit balance changes only when the broker-dealer charges interest on the money borrowed, when more securities are purchased or sold, or when more money comes into the account by way of dividend or payment by the customer. A change in the market value of the securities does not change the debit balance. The investor will be responsible for paying interest on the debit balance held in the account and she may use the securities as collateral with which to borrow more funds to purchase additional securities (within the limits of Reg T). The securities will be held in street name.

105. C: The general partner signs the subscription agreement when he or she officially accepts a new limited partner (a new investor); the subscription agreement is usually accompanied by payment and wiring instructions to fund the new account. The certificate of limited partnership must be filed with the Securities and Exchange Commission (the SEC) prior to a public offering; the agreement of limited partnership describes the roles and responsibilities of limited and general partners; and a new account form is filled out when a registered rep takes on a new customer. While other documents may be involved, it is the subscription agreement that OFFICIALLY triggers the acceptance of the new limited partner.

106. A: Corporations may issue income bonds and mortgage bonds. Income (adjustment) bonds are issued by corporations that are in the process of reorganization (usually to avoid bankruptcy); income bonds do not receive interest or principal until the corporation can afford it. Mortgage bonds are issued by corporations and are secured by a pledge of property. Statements III and IV are municipal bonds: A double-barreled municipal bond is essentially the combination of a revenue bond, backed by the municipal revenues received through a specific investment in a project, and a general obligation (GO) bond, which is backed by the full taxing authority of the issuing municipality. With a double-barreled bond, if the revenue from the revenue-producing project is insufficient, the municipality uses its taxing power to cover any short-fall. Moral obligation bonds are municipal bonds that are backed by the state in the event of default.

107. A: A lagging economic indicator may conform to the same pattern as a leading indicator but reaches its peaks and troughs at a later date. It is used to give confirmation that the leading and coincidental indicators were correct after the fact; lagging indicators change after the economy has already changed course. The fed funds rate is a leading indicator and gives forecasters an idea of what to expect over the next several months. Weekly hours worked in manufacturing is also a leading indicator. The Institute of Supply Management's industrial production number is considered a coincidental indicator – it gives an idea of how the economy is currently performing. The unemployment rate is a lagging indicator.

108. B: Municipalities issue IDRs (industrial development revenue bonds) to fund the construction of a facility for the benefit of a private user (usually a corporation). In spite of the fact that the IDR is a municipal bond, it is backed by lease payments made by the corporation, and it is therefore considered the riskiest municipal bond. Special tax bonds are backed by the taxing power of the municipality (though they are often dependent on a specific segment of that taxing authority), which is NOT true of IDR bonds.

109. A: The official notice of sale, which is found in The Bond Buyer, contains bidding details for municipal bonds, including the information included in statement III - the method of interest-cost calculation used to determine the winner (net interest cost or true interest cost). The priority of execution of orders and the allotment details are present in the syndicate agreement. The reoffering yields are determined by the market and are generally not published anywhere, certainly not in the official notice of sale for a competitive offering.

110. B: A zero-plus tick occurs when the trading price of a security goes up and stays up at the same price for the next trade. Several of the answer choices have zero-minus ticks (when the price goes down and stays down at the same price for the next trade). Only in the prints listed in answer choice B does the price go up (from 8.55 to 8.60) and is then followed by another print at the same price (another trade at 8.60). This is called a zero-plus tick because it starts with a zero tick (the same price as the last trade) during an upward tick (most recent trade was up). Only answer B has this characteristic.

111. B: Betty has indicated that she wants Jon to have trading authority, not that he should be a joint owner of the account. Having trading authority means that while Jon can trade, he cannot make withdrawals or issue additional instructions (as a joint owner he would have full authority to do so). The account, therefore, requires a limited power of attorney to give Jon trading authority, but not a joint account agreement. All new accounts require a new account form, so that form is required as well. The question indicated that this is to be a cash account, not a margin account, so a hypothecation form is not required either. Despite the addition of Jon to the joint account agreement, only two of the four forms listed as answer options are needed to open the account.

112. C: In order to diminish the possibility that the certificates will be lost in transit, the broker should retain both certificates and send a stock power to the customer with instructions and a return envelope. A stock power has the same impact as signing the back of the certificate itself. Both of the certificates need to be signed in order for the brokerage to be able to successfully transfer them when the customer decides to do so. Proactively getting the appropriate documentation is the correct course of action asked for by the question.

113. D: Sellers of options, whether put options, straddles, or any other combination, make money when the options owner does not exercise the option contract because the seller then retains the premium amount. This is the objective of most options selling programs. Since the strike price and the market price of the underlying stock remained the same, neither the buyer of a put, nor the buyer of a straddle is likely to exercise the options, and thus, the seller benefits because the premium received is retained and adds to profit.

114. C: Depression and recession each have formal definitions based upon the number of consecutive quarters that the economy must experience a contraction for the respective condition to exist (6 for a depression and 2 for a recession). Fluctuation is clearly not the correct choice, as it could refer to prices trending in either direction or going from one to the other. The only remaining choice is answer C. Deflation refers to a decline in the general price level of goods, usually as measured by the consumer price index (CPI) or the producer price index (PPI).

115. D: This is a simple memorization question, but one that is likely to be found on the test. The test writers particularly like to test material that covers the ethical behavior of a registered representative. The National Association of Securities Dealers (NASD) limit of the size of a gift that may be given by a registered representative to a customer or related person within the securities business is $100 total per year. Learn this rule, as it will likely show up on the test in one form or another.

116. B: A sell stop-limit order would be the best choice because it specifies a price, but will not become a market order. This order will only get executed at the price specified or a more favorable one. Pure stop orders, although quicker in execution, become market orders when the stop price is reached and the customer will not be guaranteed a specific price. Stop-limit orders are somewhat risky, in that the order may or may not get executed. If the price of the stock continues to fall, the order will not get executed and the customer's position will continue to depreciate.

117. A: Treasury bills (more commonly known as T-bills) are issued in 1 month, 3 month, and 6 month maturities. Treasury notes have maturities ranging from 1 year up to 10 years. Treasury bonds are government-backed debt securities with maturities over 10 years. Treasury strips are longer term as well, and are derived from a combination of treasury notes and bonds. Treasury STRIPS (T-STRIPS) are purchased at a discount and mature at par value, building the return on the investment into a single lump sum payment. This type of security behaves similarly to a corporate zero-coupon bond.

118. B: According to rule 144, an individual who has held shares of restricted stock for a minimum of a one year holding period is the greater of 1% of the total number of outstanding shares or the average weekly trading volume as determined by the previous four weeks of trading activity. In this case, with 5 million outstanding shares, 1% of the total outstanding shares is 50,000. However, when the average weekly volume over the most recent four weeks is considered (240,000 / 4 = 60,000 shares), this is the larger of the two numbers and the correct answer to the question. Answer choice D is tempting because it stands out, but this is a common test-writers trick and should be ignored.

119. B: Bonds purchased at a premium will have a lower yield to maturity than the coupon rate. The coupon rate is based on and paid against the par value of the bond. The premium (price above par) will be lost over the life of the bond, as the face value of the bond moves to par at maturity. While this premium is lost, that loss is what is figured into the lower yield to maturity and is the reason why it is lower than the coupon. This phenomenon occurs when rates in the general market fall. Investors bid up the price of the bond "chasing" the higher rate until the premium brings the bond's yield to maturity (all other factors being equal) into equilibrium with the prevailing rates available in the market.

120. D: An order where a customer wants an immediate execution and wishes to cancel any portion that is not executed immediately is termed an immediate or cancel order (IOC). A fill or kill (FOK) order is one where the broker is to take the order to market and if it cannot be filled at the specified price, the order is to be cancelled. An all or none order (AON) is one in which the investor specifies that he or she wants the entire order filled as a block or not at all; AON strategies are far less common with equity orders and tend to be used when trading futures or options contracts.

121. D: Shareholder approval is required for stock splits, including reverse stock splits. Decisions about dividends, whether cash or stock dividends, is the sole purview of the Board of Directors (BOD). The shareholders elect the BOD and they are expected to make the bulk of decisions affecting the day-to-day operations of the corporation. Dividends (if the company is performing) are a part of the "regular" operations of the company. Stock splits are far less common, and thus require special approval from the shareholders – the true owners of the corporation.

122. D: Because the assistant is not a Series 7 Registered Representative, he or she may not accept such an order under any circumstances. The alternative answer choices in questions such as these are designed by the test-writers to provide plausible sounding exceptions to the rules – such as the notion that it's acceptable if a principal signs off after the fact. Most of the ethical and procedural rules are hard and fast. Advisory decisions are more subjective occasionally, but if you are working a question wherein the prohibitions and limitations are very explicit, do not assume there is an exception.

123. D: It is impossible to tell because the question does not indicate that the options are now worthless or that they have expired. It is possible that the assumption will be made and that only numbers will be given as possible answers. If this is the case, assume that the options have expired. In this case, look at the two purchase prices ($45 and $3.50). This forms the cost basis for the problem. Since the option value has been lost, the stock must be trading at this price in order for the investor to break even.

124. A: When opening a corporate margin account, a registered representative is required to obtain the corporate resolution and the corporate charter. An income statement is not required to demonstrate the corporation's ability to take on risk, nor is required to provide a list of outstanding securities issued by the company. Statement I is included in every answer choice, so you know that it must be included. Picking up on the subtle nuances in the way the question is posed will not only help you to answer questions, it will help to save time. If a given statement is obviously correct on the face of it, it is not necessary to spend much time evaluating it.

125. B: Accrued interest is the interest due to the seller of a bond as calculated from the last day that interest was paid until the end of the current interest period (the seller is paid for the interest he or she has earned, but not yet received). Corporate bonds pay on a 30-day basis month and a 360 day basis year. They also settle on the 3rd business day following the trade date (T+3). The trade settles on October 7tH. The last pay date was July 1st. The customer is owed 30 days for July, 30 days for August, 30 days for September and 6 days for October. You do not include the interest due for the settlement day of the 7tH.

126. A: A customer should buy long term bonds when she feels interest rates are going to decline after the purchase of the bond.   The long-term bond purchase locks in the higher rate for a longer period of time and provides her with the opportunity to realize a capital gain as the price of the bonds rise. This is due to the fact that when interest rates decline, bond prices go up. The short-term rates have less of an impact on overall rates, and will not necessarily affect the price of long-term bonds.

127. C: While each of the answer choices listed is important, Sam's investment objectives are the starting point and most important factor when considering how to invest and which mutual funds are appropriate. Answer A pertains to front and back loaded funds – meaning that brokerage fees are collected at time of purchase or when sold later.   It is important to include the front- or back-loaded fees as a percentage of the initial investment or the funds that are returned. No load funds may be a more desirable purchase decision. The sales charge is the amount of commission charged by Mighty Sure and must be disclosed, as must the ongoing management fee that will be charged by the fund manager.   All fee and charge information must be contained in the prospectus. Each is important, but the overall investment objectives are critical and of top concern to Sam. It is the overall investment objective which must be discussed and determined with the assistance of Might Sure.

128. A: Level I on NASDAQ is the inside market and is defined by the highest bid and the lowest offer – a process ultimately creating the tightest bid / ask spread. Nasdaq is called the inside market because, when all the bids and offers are listed in ascending order, the bid and the offer that are closest together or inside all of the others represents the inside market. NASDAQ displays these inside bids and ask prices as level I quotes. The NASDAQ exchange provides level II and other level data to offer market depth analysis to investors who believe this data benefits their positions.

129. B: A growth stock is one issued by an emerging company which is thought to have great potential for upside price increases. Normally, such companies are not in an income position to offer much in dividends, as they are still investing their profit into the company. In addition, these companies tend to be more affected by the direction of the general market and by news events. Investors buy growth stocks for the chance at capital appreciation, rather than income (no dividends means no income). This greater sensitivity to moves in the general market (a higher level of volatility) translates into higher beta – the measure of how much a given stock moves relative to the broad market.

130. C: The key to this question is to recognize that the test writers often like to provide you with an excess of information in an effort to confuse you or trick you into believing that the question is more complicated than it actually needs to be. The only relevant information is that the investor owns 10 6% bonds, and that the question asks for the semi-annual payment amount, not the annual amount. If par is $1000, then 6% * $1000 = $60; and $60 * 10 = $600 (annual amount received). Therefore, $600 / 2 = $300. The correct answer is $300 is received by the investor on a semi-annual basis.

131. A: The portfolio margining method considers the net risk of the entire portfolio, rather than on a position by position basis, to determine the margin position of an account. It is only available when certain criteria are met and there is no minimum number of requirements that must be held in the account. As a tip, remember that when two answer choices are opposites of each other (answer A and answer B in this question), only one can be the correct answer.

132. C: To determine the status of Diane's account, the first step is to calculate the account's equity and compare that to the SMA as allowed by Reg T. LMV – DR = EQ, so $35,000 - $18,000 = $17,000. Reg T required equity = 50% * $35,000 = $17,500. This tells you that the account is restricted by $500 and that there is currently no SMA in the account. There is no margin call at this point, however, because the maintenance level has not been reached. To calculate the maintenance call level use (4/3) * DR; in this case (4/3) * $18,000 = $24,000. A maintenance call will occur if the current market value of the securities held falls to $24,000.

133. A: Of the choices listed, selling options is the only way to create income. The customer should sell calls, which are covered by the underlying stock. If the calls were exercised, the stock would be delivered to meet the obligation, protecting the customer from any sharp moves in the stock. In another sense, the income generated through the sale of the options lowers the investors cost basis on the stock, or increasing the profit received at any given price in the open market. This is known as a call writing program – it is usually reserved for instances when the customer's positions will not seriously deteriorate by losing ownership of the underlying shares.

134. D: Potential money laundering activities include excessive wiring of money between accounts. Since the September 11, 2001 terror attacks, the SEC and FNRA have taken an increasing interest in monitoring and preventing illegal activities involving securities accounts. Frequent deposits and withdrawals in large sums, excessive money wiring activities, and transfer to or from countries "of interest" could trigger investigations with which the registered representative must cooperate. Overall, these occurrences are rare, but this additional oversight by government regulations makes this prime test material for the test-writers.

135. D: The maximum gain for the investor in the purchase of a call option is unlimited. The appreciation of the underlying stock can go up without limits, giving the holder of a call option the right to call (or purchase) the stock at the strike price and sell it at the limitlessly high market value. The maximum loss that the investor can incur by the purchase of the call option is the premium paid of $300. For this reason, buying call options is considered the safest form of options investing and is most readily granted by brokers to retail clients. Selling naked options is the riskiest, and is usually more tightly regulated and limited to certain investors.

136. B: Rule 144 applies to restricted stock only; control stock and registered shares are not covered by the rule. Under Rule 144, restricted stock must be held by both affiliated and nonaffiliated persons for a minimum of six months. Of the three different nonaffiliated persons given in the answer choices, the only one who has held the restricted stock less than the required 6 months is the one in answer choice B. This person will be required to hold the shares for an additional 3 months before the shares can be sold.

137. C: A workable indication is the price at which one municipal securities dealer is willing to purchase securities from another municipal securities dealer. Therefore, a workable indication is a likely bid price. One of the key features which distinguishes the bond market from the stock market is the lack of a central clearinghouse. Bonds trade amongst dealers, so when an investor wishes to sell a bond, his or her broker calls other dealers to establish the price at which the bond can be sold. It is in this context that a workable indication would be encountered.

138. A: In spite of the fact that the shares may not fit into the investor's investment objectives, the registered rep can still accept the order. However, as a precaution, the order should be marked as unsolicited in case the shares lose money. If an order ticket is marked unsolicited, it serves as some protection against the investor later claiming that he was manipulated into purchasing the security. A registered rep is prohibited from accepting unsolicited orders on options and DPPs (limited partnerships), unless the rep previously received an ODD and the options account was reviewed and approved.

139. B: In order to be exempted from the discretionary order account rules, a customer must specify the security, indicate whether the order is a buy or a sell, and also specify the number of shares or dollar-value of a trade he/she will accept when the trade is executed. If these characteristics are not specifically described in the customer order, the trade will be a discretionary trade and the registered rep will be required to obtain a limited power of attorney from the customer before executing the order. Market orders by definition are executed at the best available market price and thus are not subject to the registered representative's discretion. Limit orders set a particular price range at which to purchase or sell an investment and therefore involve discretion.

140. B: A trade in the first-market involves a listed security trading on an exchange (such as the NYSE or AMEX). A trade in the second-market is an over-the-counter (OTC) security trading over-the-counter. A trade in the third-market is a listed security trading over-the-counter. A trade in the fourth-market is any type institutional trading that does not use the services of a broker-dealer, such as when two institutional trading desks trade directly with each other (usually with large blocks of securities). This is a straight memorization question, but can provide easy points if you know the answer.

141. B: Under the wash sale rule, when a customer sells a security at a loss, the customer cannot buy the same security or anything equivalent or convertible into the same security within 30 days before or after the sale and still claim the loss for tax purposes. The object of the rule is to prevent an investor from "locking in a loss" for tax purposes, while essentially maintaining the same position after the sale. This investor bought a call option, which gives him or her the right to buy XYZ stock at a fixed price, thereby violating the wash sale rule. Therefore, the loss is disallowed for tax purposes and the cost basis would have to be adjusted for the purchase.

142. D: Starting with expansion, the normal economic cycle is expansion, peak, contraction, trough. This is another very straightforward question that is regularly on the test because it forms the basis of understanding much of the other material. In a sense, it is the opposite of those questions where the test-writers purposefully try to confuse you by giving you far too much information. In this type of question, there is no fluff – either you know the answer or you do not. Don't waste precious time trying to reason through this type of question; simply mark your best answer and move on.

143. A: The customer sold short at $43 per share and bought a call with a strike price of 45; the call gives the customer the right to buy back the stock at $45. If the stock rises, the call can be used to limit the loss to 2 points. The customer can lose $200 on the stock. The customer also paid a $300 premium. Therefore, the maximum loss on the combined position is $200 + $300 = $500. The maximum gain is $40 * 100 = $4000 (this would occur only if the stock went all the way to zero).

144. C: A Regulation D offering is also called a private placement. Regulation D offerings are exempt from SEC registration as long as the securities are sold to no more than 35 unaccredited (small) investors per year. A Rule 147 offering is an intrastate offering that is exempt from SEC registration, provided the issuer conducts business only in one state and sells securities only to residents of that same state. This provision also encompasses the 80 percent rule, which states that at least 80 percent of the issuer's assets should be located within the state and at least 80 percent of the offering proceeds should be used within the same state. Regulation A offerings are exempt from full registration requirements, provided the issuer doesn't sell more than $5,000,000 worth of securities in a 12-month period.

145. A: The allocation of orders, which details the priority by which customer orders will be filled, is found in the syndicate agreement. The official notice of sale is an invitation to underwriters from municipalities announcing that they're accepting bids on a new issue. The indenture is a contract between a bond issuer and bondholders that states certain contract terms, such as whether the bond is callable, when the bond matures, and the coupon rate. The official statement is a document prepared for municipal offerings that contains similar information as to offerings as a prospectus.

146. C: The question states that the stock's market value increases, but makes no mention of any additional action taken by the investor. The investor does not have a capital gain or loss until he or she sells the security. Passive income is income received from limited partnerships, and ordinary income is interest received from bonds or dividends received from stock. Passive income also includes income earned through wages or salary, and may include rents received. The increase in stock value by itself, if no other subsequent action is taken, is in the category of *appreciation*.

147. B: When a company issues cumulative preferred stock, this means that it may make the required payments as the Board of Directors best decides. However, before the company pays a dividend to common stockholders, it must first make up any delinquent payments to the cumulative preferred shareholders. The preferred carries an annual dividend of $6. Since the company fell short by $2 in the second year, it must make up this shortfall, as well as making the third year's payment (preferred stockholders receive dividends before any common dividend is paid). The $2 short plus the additional $6 means the company must pay $8 before issuing a common dividend.

148. C: A bond indenture includes important information such as the nominal yield (coupon rate), the collateral backing the bond (if any), and the maturity date. The rating is not on the indenture, however, because it is not static and may change as the issuer's financial condition changes. Companies such as Moody's and Standard & Poor's place ratings on the bonds based on their analysis of the financial condition of the issuer. Bond rating companies may also issue warnings about impending changes in status to signal the market before a significant change has occurred. Over the past year or so, these ratings have been called into question as several companies, which issued bonds receiving high ratings, were not as sound as those bond ratings might indicate.

149. A: Matty, with a defensive investment strategy, is attempting to safeguard principal, generate current investment income, and maintain a reasonable degree of liquidity for unexpected events. High yield bond funds and exotic options strategies are considered speculative (risky investments) and would likely not have a significant (if any at all) place in his portfolio. Municipals and global bonds would be appropriate because they are generally considered safe investments, particularly when diversified through a vehicle like a fund. It would be useful to know Matty's tax status, because only certain investors benefit from municipals. Since statement III alone was not an option, answer A is the best choice.

150. A: Because this account is set up as JTWROS (joint tenants with rights of survivorship), the deceased investor's portion of the account is transferred to the remaining survivor(s) named on the account. This is another very straightforward question that is regularly on the test because it forms the basis of understanding much of the other material. In a sense, it is the opposite of those questions where the test-writers purposefully try to confuse you by giving you far too much information. In this type of question, there is no fluff – either you know the answer or you do not. Don't waste time trying to reason through this type of question; simply mark your best answer and move on.

151. B: The debt-to-equity ratio measures the capitalization of a company. The higher the debt-to-equity ratio, the more leveraged the company is (the more money it owes). A high debt-to-equity ratio often indicates that the company has financed its growth by borrowing large quantities of capital. The earnings for companies with high debt-to-equity ratios tend to be more volatile, so they'd be considered somewhat riskier investments. Examining a company's debt-to-equity ratio relative to its peers is important, as some industries are more prone to high debt levels than others.

152. B: A Rule 147 offering is an intrastate offering that is exempt from SEC registration, provided the issuer conducts business only in one state and sells securities only to residents of the same state. This provision also includes the 80 percent rule, which states that at least 80 percent of the issuer's assets should be located within the state and at least 80 percent of the offering proceeds should be used within the state. A Regulation D offering is also called a private placement. Regulation D offerings are exempt from SEC registration as long as the securities are sold to no more than 35 unaccredited (small) investors per year. Regulation A offerings are exempt from full registration requirements, provided the issuer doesn't sell more than $5,000,000 worth of securities in a 12-month period.

153. C: The question asks you to identify the false answer in the group of answer choices. Buying a put option protects a long position, not a short position. To protect a short position (when selling short), the investor can buy a call option. The maximum loss when purchasing an option is the premium paid, the maximum gain on a put is equal to the strike price minus the premium paid, and the OCC does guarantee that the holder of the option can exercise the option and receive delivery of the underlying shares.

154. A: A numbered (street-named) account is a common occurrence in brokerage firms; a customer who wishes to remain anonymous in the market can have the account set up as a numbered account. All order tickets contain a number or code; however, the brokerage firm needs to have a customer-signed document on file stating who owns the account. There is no requirement that the customer be accredited (have a net worth over $1,000,000 and/or have had an annual income of $200,000 or more for each of the preceding two years) in order to be able to open up a numbered account.

155 C: Debt securities are senior securities, meaning that in the event of issuer bankruptcy, holders of debt securities will receive payment before preferred stockholders and common stockholders. This has been the case excepting recent bankruptcy activity in the automotive industry, in which case it may be difficult to determine. Debt securities (bonds) are loans to the issuer, as compared to stocks, which represent ownership of the issuing corporation. Issuers issue bonds to raise working capital (the amount of money a corporation has available), so statement III is true as well.

156. C: Minimum maintenance equity on a short margin account is 30% of the short market value held in the account. The NYSE rule states that, after meeting the initial Reg T requirements, an investor's account may not fall below 30% equity based on the current short market value. In this case, the short market value of $40,000 must be multiplied by 30% (30% * $40,000 = $12,000). If the account falls below this value, the investor will receive a margin call and be required to deposit more money into the account in order to avoid having his or her positions liquidated.

157. A: When a variable annuity is annuitized during the payout phase, the investor receives a fixed number of annuity units based on the value of the accumulation units. This is another very straightforward question that is regularly on the test because it forms the basis of understanding much of the other material. In a sense, it is the opposite of those questions where the test-writers purposefully try to confuse you by giving you far too much information. The only trick in this question is to read carefully and be sure that you pay attention to wording – the distinction between number and value is key in this question.

158. A: There is an inverse relationship between interest rates and bond prices – they move in opposite directions. If interest rates rise, outstanding bond prices fall; if interest rates fall, outstanding bond prices rise. The distinction to be made in this question is that, if the bond carries a variable rate, the coupon rate adjusts proportionally to interest rate changes. This leads to far greater stability in the price of the bond, which, under certain circumstances, is an advantage to an investor and a reason to select a variable rate bond over one with a fixed rate.

159. B: Liquidity is essentially the ease with which an investor may move into and out of a given investment. Limited partnerships are generally considered illiquid as they require extensive documentation, approval of the general partner, approval of the registered representative, and often contain a lock-up period (a set amount of time during which the investment may not be sold). In addition, there is generally not a secondary market for these types of investments, so relative to all of the other listed choices, B is the best answer.

160. A: The easiest way to answer the question is to break the question into 2 parts and calculate the gain or loss on each side. The customer bought the shares for $65 and sells them for $70, resulting in a profit of $5 per share (100 shares * ($70 - $65) = $500). On the option side, remember that the customer sold the option and has to buy it back to close the position (100 * ($2 - $4) = -$200). When the two sides of the transaction are combined, the result of the overall trade is a gain of $300 ($500 + (-$200) = $300.

161. C: The key to this question is to remember that index options are always settled for cash – this should make sense since an index option has an index representing its underlying value and so it may not be deliverable in pure form (instruments that track an index may have slight performance deviations from the index they follow). Investors who exercise their options are required to pay the buyer cash equal to the intrinsic value (the in-the-money amount) multiplied by 100 shares. Index options are settled at the end of the business day.

162. A: Term bonds, also called dollar bonds, are quoted as a percentage of the dollar value of their price. For example, a term bond trading for $1,050 would be quoted as 105 (105% * $1,000 par = $1050). This is another very straightforward question which appears regularly on the test because it forms the basis of understanding much of the other material. In a sense, it is the opposite of those questions where the test-writers purposefully try to confuse you by giving you far too much information.

163. C: The de minimus filing threshold feature of Rule 144 provides that no filing is required when the total sale within the defined period is less than $50,000 and the number of shares is less than 5000. This applies to affiliates selling restricted shares in keeping with Rule 144. This is a straight memorization question, but can provide easy points. Rule 144 is a favorite test topic because it covers both ethical and insider behavior in different contexts – the major tenets of the rule should be learned for the test.

164. C: A defined contribution plan is distinguished from a defined benefit plan in that the amount an employer will contribute to the plan is defined, as opposed to the amount that will be paid as a benefit upon retirement. The shift toward defined contribution plans is the result of employees switching jobs more and more frequently. In these types of plan, the contribution generally remains fixed, although both the employee and the employers may make adjustments to the amount contributed (by the employee) and the % match provided (by the employer). An employer may not discount its contribution based on the company's performance, but there is no requirement that an employer pay into the plan at all.

165. C: While there are no NASD rules specifying the percentages that brokerage firms are required to charge customers, charges must be fair and reasonable and must not discriminate between customers. The test writers particularly like to test material that covers the ethical behavior of a registered representative or of the brokerage firm; non-discriminatory practices by each of these entities is of particular interest, so if such discrimination or ethics violations stands out among the answer choices, there is a fair possibility that this answer will be the correct answer.

166. D: Stopping stock is a method a specialist uses to guarantee that a customer's order will be executed at a specific price. Stopping stock may be done only for public orders and cannot be executed for the specialist's own book. Since the specialist has his or her own inventory, a specialist does not need permission to stop stock, but is limited to performing this service on public orders only. The NYSE uses specialists, which is one of the things which distinguish it from the over-the-counter (OTC) market.

167. D: In order to protect both investors and brokers from having orders executed that were not intended to be filled, and were simply forgotten, any good-til-cancelled (GTC) order that remains unexecuted at the end of either April or October will automatically be cancelled. A registered representative should contact his or her customer to determine if the customer wishes to re-activate these orders. If so, the orders can then be re-entered. Un-executive GTC orders will not carry over beyond the automatic expiration months, so the registered rep should be sure to communicate this information to the customer when the orders are first placed.

168. C: A put option gives the holder (buyer), the right, but not the obligation, to sell shares of an underlying security at a specific price until the expiration of the contract. The best way for an investor to protect against a sharp decline in the underlying security is to buy a put. Selling options will help the investor to generate additional income, but the seller is basically transferring the right to exercise the options to others. Buying a call option will benefit the investor if the underlying security rises, but will not protect against a decline in the stock price upon which the option is based.

169. D: A government regulatory agency that oversees the municipal securities, bonds and notes issued by cities, counties and states. It sets standards for municipal securities dealers. It was established by the U.S. Congress in 1975.

170. A: Each of the answer choices provided details the result of the Fed raising rates except answer A. A higher discount rate leads to a higher prime rate. When the discount rate rises, interest rates rise in general, lifting bond yields. As lending rates rise and the cost of borrowing goes up, fewer loans will be taken out. A rise in inflation is often one of the reasons the Fed chooses to raise rates. Thus, it follows logically that an increase in the discount rate can be expected to curb inflation, not increase it.

171. D: The key to answering this question correctly is to remember that a dividend will never increase or decrease the total value of the investment. Therefore, if the investor started with 1000 shares at $45 ($45,000), then the investor must still own a $45,000 investment even though the share amount has changed. To recalculate the share price, first determine the new number of shares, then divide the total dollar investment by the new share amount (1.05 * 1000 shares = 1050 shares, $45,000 / 1050 = $42.86 per share).

172. A: Firstly, when a firm sells securities out of its own inventory, the firm charges a markup, not a commission. Secondly, the sale is not subject to the NASD 5% policy because municipal bonds are exempt securities. Thirdly, a bond's rating is never reported on the confirmation because ratings are subject to change over time. The firm does consider the overall size of a sale when deciding on the size of the markup that will be charged to a customer – this amount is agreed to in advance of the sale and disclosed on the confirmation sent to the customer.

173. A: The short-sale rule applies to NNM (NASDAQ National Market) securities, and prohibits entering a short sale (selling borrowed securities) at or below the current inside bid price whenever the current bid price is below the previous inside bid price. The idea behind this rule is to keep short sellers from continually driving down the price of a security. This is slightly different from the old uptick rule, and both rules are currently under review as a result of the 2008 financial crisis. The ramifications of enforcement or non-enforcement of both these rules are considered partly to blame for the demise of several Wall Street firms.

174. B: When a syndicate sells a new issue, the spread is broken down into the manager's fee and the takedown. The takedown is the amount that syndicate members earn when selling shares or bonds. If the syndicate hires selling groups to help sell the shares, these groups receive the concession, which is a percentage of the takedown and also paid out of the takedown. Firms outside of the syndicate (also called selling groups) receive the reallowance – this amount tends to be smaller than the concession and is also paid out of the takedown. The manager's fee is the lowest, but the syndicate manager receives a fee on every share (or bond) sold by any of the selling entities.

175. B: The premium of an option is made up of intrinsic value and time value: intrinsic value is by what amount the option is in-the-money (what it could be converted for immediately); and time value is the amount the buyer pays for the time to allow the option to appreciate in value. The question tells you that the premium is 7. For a call option, the intrinsic value is calculated as the market price minus the strike price ($62.50 - $60 = $2.50). Since the total premium is equal to the intrinsic value plus the time value, time value can be calculated by subtracting the intrinsic value from the premium ($7 - $2.50 = $4.50).

176. B: Fiduciary accounts such as UGMA (Uniform Gift to Minors Act) accounts are required to follow the prudent man rule or legal list of the state in which the account is set up. The prudent man rule or legal list establishes a guideline of appropriate investments for accounts that involve trusts. UGMA accounts are created to allow the custodian to allocate money to a minor in a tax-advantaged way, but limit the custodian's ability to withdraw the money once it has been "gifted" to the minor.

177. B: The key to this question is to remember that index options are always settled for cash – this should make sense since an index option, by definition, has an index representing its underlying value and as such may not be deliverable in pure form (instruments that track an index may have slight performance deviations from the index they follow). As a tip, remember that when two answer choices are opposites of each other (answer A and answer B in this question), one must be the correct answer, since one must be true and the other false.

178. A: The two keys to this question are: 1) recognizing that the S&P 500 and housing starts are leading indicators, and 2) to recognize that 3 of the answer choices are cyclical and 1 is counter-cyclical. When leading indicators are rising, cyclical market segments are likely to be rising; when leading economic indicators are rising, counter-cyclical market segments are likely to be falling. Gold tends to be counter-cyclical, so it is likely to be falling when the leading economic indicators and the cyclical security listed are all rising.

179. D: Stop orders, not limit orders, are used to protect a stock position (limit orders are used to protect the investor entering a position). Sell stop orders are placed below the market price, but close enough to limit losses; if the market price of the security drops to or below the stated price, the order is triggered and sold on the next trade. Placing a stop too far beneath the current price does not provide sufficient loss protection, but if it is too near the current price point, it will be too easily triggered since a certain amount of price fluctuation is normal. A registered representative should discuss this with the investor in order to determine how much of the profit the investor is willing to risk in order to gain additional upside potential.

180. A: Regulation A offerings are exempt from full registration requirements, provided the issuer doesn't sell more than $5,000,000 worth of securities in a 12-month period. A Rule 147 offering is an intrastate offering that is exempt from SEC registration, provided the issuer conducts business only in one state and sells securities only to residents of the same state. This provision also encompasses the 80 percent rule, which states that at least 80 percent of the issuer's assets should be located within the state and at least 80 percent of the offering proceeds should be used within the state. A Regulation D offering is also called a private placement. Regulation D offerings are exempt from SEC registration as long as the securities are sold to no more than 35 unaccredited (small) investors per year.

181. C: The Sarbanes-Oxley Act of 2002 established more stringent standards for all U.S. publicly traded companies, their boards of directors, and the public accounting firms they hired. It was a response to several accounting scandals, and in addition to addressing accounting and reporting standards, it required self-regulatory organizations (SROs) to establish research analyst conflict of interest rules. It also created the PCAOB (Public Company Accounting Oversight Board) to specifically oversee public accounting firms and to establish and enforce disciplinary standards for all the groups discussed in the Act.

182. A: Most securities settle on the third business day after the trade date (T + 3), but U.S. government instruments generally settle (known as regular way settlement) one business day after the trade date. This is another very straightforward question that is regularly on the test because it forms the basis of understanding for much of the other material. In a sense, it is the opposite of those questions where the test-writers purposefully try to confuse you by giving you far too much information. Know regular way settlement for the most common instruments.

183. B: A tight money yield curve is one indication that interest rates have recently increased and that short maturity bonds are yielding more than long maturity bonds. This is the opposite of what is generally considered "normal" because, when this occurs, the yield curve is said to be inverted. Normally bond holders are compensated for buying longer maturity bonds by receiving higher rates and charting would show an upward sloping yield curve. When money is tight, often due to an increase in rates, short-term bonds are in greater demand and the yield curve may be temporarily distorted.

184. A: John's intention to take an additional paid position would mean that he wants to moonlight. The NASD moonlighting rules require John to inform and receive permission from his employer, the broker-dealer. The regulations do not require him to seek additional permission or to report this to any of the regulatory agencies or exchanges, such as the NASD and the NYSE. There is no special trick to getting this question correct; it is a single fact question requiring a familiarity with the various rules governing the conduct of a registered representative.

185. D: When a municipal bond is issued, it is accompanied by a legal opinion. A legal opinion is a statement prepared by a bond attorney which states that the interest received from the bond being issued meets the requirements for exemption from federal taxation. All municipal bonds must be accompanied by such an opinion prepared by the issuer's bond counsel, or the bond must be marked as ex-legal (this makes the bond less attractive as the purchaser will need to obtain his or her own legal opinion or risk violating federal tax law).

186. B: The fed funds rate is the rate that banks charge other banks for overnight loans; this is distinguished from the discount rate, which is the rate charged by the Fed to member banks for similar overnight loans. When the Fed raises the discount rate, the money supply tightens; if it lowers the discount rate, the money supply is eased. Reserve requirements set by the Fed determine the percentage of deposits banks must hold each night. The Fed can also control the money supply through open market activities (buying and selling U.S. government securities).

187. B: This is a straightforward question that is asking you to calculate the tax-equivalent yield (TEY) for the investor in question. The only information needed to do this calculation is the effective tax rate and the yield to maturity; any additional information provided in these types of questions is put there to create confusion. The relationship needed is TEY = YTM / (100% - tax rate). In this case then, TEY = 7% / (100% - 28%) = 9.7%. A prepared test-taker will be readily able to recognize basic municipal bond calculation and make them quickly.

188. A: Government National Mortgage Association (GNMA) securities are directly backed by the full faith and credit of the U.S. government. The other listed securities (FNMA's, Farm Credits, and Freddie Mac's) are sponsored by various government agencies, but are, in fact, issued by independent corporations that list and back these securities. During the recent financial crisis, the extent to which the government "stood behind" agency securities was tested, and was shown to be weaker than these securities had historically been treated (often trading at near zero spreads to treasuries).

189. B: Each of the answers given, except accrued interest, affects the quality of the bond. Accrued interest is the amount of interest a buyer has to pay a seller when purchasing a bond in between coupon dates. The investor earns the same amount of interest each day, regardless of the specifics of a given bond (all other factors being held equal), so an investor is indifferent to the amount of accrued interest. Therefore, the accrued interest does not impact the marketability of the municipal bond being considered.

190. B: Simplified arbitration is used to settle disputes between members and customers when the amount in dispute is not more than $25,000. The customer (the non-member in the dispute) is allowed to decide whether the dispute should go to arbitration or through the NASD's formal procedure for handling complaints. Decisions made in the arbitration process, which is less formal than the NASD code of procedures process, are binding and not subject to appeal. The arbitration procedure also tends to be quicker and generally results in faster resolution of disputes.

191. D: Preferred stocks have characteristics similar to those of fixed income instruments – priority over common to assets in the case of bankruptcy, priority over common to dividends, and a fixed rate of return. One of the distinguishing features is that preferred stock, unlike fixed income securities, does not have a specified maturity date. This means that answer D is the single answer among all the answer options that combines all of the characteristic features of preferred stock. In addition to the features in the question, holders of fixed income securities take priority to assets over the holders of preferred shares.

192. D: The first step in resolving this question is to determine the conversion ratio – this is done by dividing the par value by the conversion price ($1000 / $25 = 40 shares). This calculation tells you that Frank will receive 40 shares of stock when he converts the bond into shares of common stock. If he sells those shares for $23, the sale results in proceeds of $920 (40 shares * $23 = $920). Frank bought the bond for $850 (($85 / $100) * $1000 = $850), so Frank is into the trade for $850. If he closes the trade for $920, then he realizes a $70 profit ($920 - $850 = $70).

193. C: IRAs (individual retirement accounts) and municipal bonds provide tax advantages to investors. Capital invested in a traditional IRA can be written off from the individual's income taxes and not paid until the money is withdrawn. IRAs are not entirely exempt from taxation; payment of taxes on IRA gains is merely deferred. The interest payments received from municipal bonds are tax-free at the federal level (some are tax-free at the state level as well) Investors in higher tax brackets benefit most significantly from this advantage of municipal bonds. Despite being issued by a private corporation which has the implicit backing of the federal government, FNMAs are still taxed in the regular way for all investors.

194. C: When issuing a limited tax bond, the municipality is issuing a general obligation municipal bond that has the maximum tax rate increase permissible to service the debt defined in the bond indenture. With the majority of GO bonds, the interest payments are backed by the full taxing authority of the municipality, meaning that it can levy whatever taxes are necessary to service the debt obligation created by the bond. Limited tax bonds fall between GO bonds and revenue bonds in perceived safety from any given municipality.

195. A: In order to offset passive income, Tracy needs to find an investment that provides passive losses, as only passive losses may be used to offset passive gains. Passive income and losses are derived from rental properties and limited partnerships. Oil and gas exploration typically provide large write-offs initially for purchasing land, equipment, and other required costs to get the project started, without yielding any cash flow until oil is found and being pumped out of the ground, a process which could take several years. By employing this strategy, Tracy will be able to offset her current passive gains, in hopes of realizing future gains when the oil project begins to produce.

196. D: The order department receives an order from the registered rep, transmits the order to the appropriate market for execution, and then returns a completed trade ticket to the registered rep who initiated the order. The cashiering department handles incoming and outgoing checks from and to customers; the margin department handles credit issues resulting from credit the broker-dealer has extended to its customers; and the purchase and sales department sends trade confirmations to customers and addresses any trading errors. Each of these is generally known as a "back-office" department within the broker-dealer business, as distinguished from the "front-office" where the registered rep interacts directly with customers.

197. B: After a customer fails to pay for a trade and the broker-dealer freezes his or her account, any subsequent trades must be paid for ahead of the execution of any new buy orders. Likewise, before the customer will be allowed to execute any sell orders, the securities that are the subject of the planned trade must first be delivered to the broker-dealer. This type of customer activity is tracked, which prevents the customer from simply opening another securities account with another broker-dealer and repeating (potentially) the same mistake which is in violation of regulations.

198. D: The easiest and fastest way to answer this question is to identify the fact that the current yield will be higher than the coupon since the bond is trading at a discount to par. The only answer that fits this criterion is answer D. To calculate the correct answer, simply divide the annual interest payment by the current market price ($78 / $983 = 7.93%). This question is full of extra information that is meant to serve as distraction in an otherwise simple, straightforward question.

199. C: Closed-end funds issue a set number of shares and then the holders of those shares must trade them with other investors in order to close their respective positions. Mutual funds, UITs, and face amount certificates all have provisions by which the investor holding the respective instrument may redeem the shares when he or she no longer wishes to hold the investment. Mutual funds (open-end funds) create and destroy shares in accordance with investor demand, unlike closed-end funds that only issue a specified number of shares.

200. D: This is somewhat self-explanatory as a combination program offers diversification across the other three types of programs listed in the answer choices. Similarly, each type of program is what it sounds like: an exploratory program attempts to find and recover previously undiscovered oil; a development program drills near already existing oil wells; and income programs invest in currently producing wells to earn a return. Combination programs diversify across all three of the above types in varying degrees, depending on the specific mandate of the given program.

201. C: Hypothecation is the pledging of the securities bought on margin as collateral for the loan that finances the same purchase; it is not prohibited by regulation and is a common practice. Commingling refers to combining customer securities and firm securities in the same account (or a customer's fully paid securities with those bought on margin). Interpositioning refers to standing between a buyer and a seller to illegally act as a middle-man. Backing away refers to a market maker failing to honor a firm quote and refusing to complete the transaction at the quoted price.

202. A: During the registration process, a broker-dealer may contact its existing clients to gauge the level of interest those clients will have in purchasing shares of the new issue when it becomes available. The customer may indicate his or her level of interest in the hypothetical purchase of shares, but is not obligated to complete the transaction when the shares are actually available for sale. In spite of a customer's enthusiasm for a new offering, a customer may change his or her mind at any time. Likewise, the broker-dealer is not obliged to have as many shares available for sale as the brokerage initially indicates because the assignment of shares has not yet taken place.

203. B: Each of the answers given would change the amount of cash held in the account, except for answer B. Cash deposits affect the cash balance in the account, and thus will offset any debit balance held. Cash dividends all lead to a higher level of cash being held in the account, thereby driving down the debit balance. The sale of securities will also raise cash in the account and affect the debit balance. The receipt of additional shares from a stock dividend is the only answer choice which will have no impact on the amount of cash held in the account, or on the debit balance held by the customer.

204. D: Each of the items listed is considered promotional material and must be approved by a principal prior to being disseminated to customers. A form letter is a generic letter sent to several customers or potential customers. A market letter is a newsletter that a brokerage firm uses to promote its services. A research report usually states the firm's opinion on a specific security. An abstract is an excerpt or synopsis of the official statement and requires approval as it may adjust the original language but not the overall message of the official statement.

205. A: Initial margins may not exceed 50%, so if the transaction value is $22,500 ($45 * 500 shares = $22,500), and the transaction is done at the maximum allowed by Reg T, then the customer must make a deposit for $11,250 ($22,500 * 50% = $11,250). The remainder of the purchase may be financed on margin, assuming that the broker-dealer is willing to advance this quantity to the customer. In some cases, broker-dealers may place additional constraints on customer accounts, including higher margin requirements or simple caps on the dollar value that the firm is willing to advance to a given client.

206. D: The investor is concerned about an increase in the price of the underlying security, so the strategy used must be targeted at profiting when the stock rises, and fixing the price at which the trade can be closed. The investor could either use a buy-stop order, which is not offered as an answer choice, or buy calls. The owner of a call is entitled to buy shares at a fixed price. If the stock rises (moves against the investor's short position), the owner of a call can buy back the shares required by the short position and close out the position at a set price.

207. B: The "takedown" refers to the amount divided between the various syndicate members when selling new securities to the public. Questions about the various fees involved in bringing new securities to market, the parties involved, and who is to receive what fees for what services will certainly appear on the test in one capacity or another. Memorizing these relationships is an easy way to accumulate needed points on test day. These questions may be complex, or simple (like this one), but they will show up in some form or another.

208. D: This is somewhat of a trick question because there are occasions when warrants may be perpetual. Warrants give the holder the right to buy stock at a fixed price. Warrants are long-term investments and may have an expiration date or they may be perpetual. The question asks for which answer choice is not true. Since answer choice D states that warrants are perpetual (I.E. under all circumstances), this is the correct answer because some warrants have an expiration date, making that answer option (D) false.

209. B: The majority of instruments that trade in the money market, including banker's acceptance, T-bills, corporate paper, and repos all sell at a discount to face value and mature at their full value, thus helping the holder to realize the expected profit. Jumbo CDs, however, are an exception as they pay regular periodic interest. They can also be distinguished by the fact that they do not, in most cases, trade in the secondary market. Issued by banks, jumbo CDs usually must be held to maturity to avoid a penalty.

210. B: This question tests a single fact that needs to be memorized for the test: if the coupon and the basis are equal, the bond was purchased at par. Any additional information is provided only to confuse or distract you. The reason this information is so important for the test is that it may help you to eliminate wrong choices on questions where you're not sure how to perform the needed calculation. If the basis is higher (on a percentage basis), the bond traded at a discount and vice

versa if the basis is lower. Knowing this will help to narrow your focus in on correct answers when you're not sure how else to proceed.

211. A: To determine the advance-decline ratio, you need to divide the number of advancing stocks by the number of declining stocks (in this case 2100 / 1250 = 1.68). The advance-decline ratio gives an investor a strong indication of the true market movement because it considers breadth. If more stocks are advancing than declining (the ratio is greater than one), this is considered a bullish sign. If more stocks are declining than advancing (the ratio's less than one), this is considered a bearish sign. In addition, when there is a disparity between the direction of the major indexes and the advance-decline ratio, traders may look for a reversal in price levels.

212. B: A company tends to use a reverse-split when its stock price falls too low – as has been the case with many financial stocks in the recent banking crisis. The market price increases due to the split, but the total value of all shares remains unchanged; therefore, the number of outstanding shares decreases. Sue will end up owning 1 share of stock for every 4 shares that she owned prior to the effective date of the split (12,000 / 4 = 3,000). Her total investment in ABC will not change.

213. D: A U.S. citizen who owns stock or bonds issued in another country is responsible for federal and state taxes on any interest and dividends received on his or her U.S. tax return. However, if there has been withholding made by the country of origin, the investor may claim a tax credit against the amount of such withholding. If the withholding is greater than the amount of U.S. taxes that would be owed, the investor will not need to make additional payments to the U.S. Government.

214. C: Treasury receipts or treasury STRIPS (T-STRIPS) are purchased at a discount and mature at par value, building the return on the investment into a single lump sum payment. In this way, they behave just as any type of zero-coupon bond. Treasury notes and treasury bonds make regular interest payments at regular intervals until maturity. Treasury bonds and treasury notes are distinguished from T-bills (which also behave like zero-coupon bonds) in that they have maturities over ten and one year respectively; T-bills have maturities under a year.

215. B: After an existing customer goes through the approval process and is given permission by the firm to trade option contracts, he or she must return a signed written options agreement to the firm within 15 days of receiving the approval. If the signed written options agreement is not tendered, the customer's trading privileges for options will be permanently suspended until the agreement has been received and the suspension is lifted by one of the broker-dealer's principals. The broker-dealer is required to keep these agreements on file in case a dispute arises in the future.

216. C: Most large municipal issuances require a legal opinion to be attached to the bond indenture. A legal opinion is a statement prepared by a bond attorney which states that the interest received from the bond being issued meets the requirements of exemption from federal taxation. When no legal opinion is obtained, the bond trades ex legal. Many small issuances trade ex-legal because the issuance is too small to justify the expense of obtaining a formal legal opinion. In this case, the investor must rely on his or her own resources when preparing annual tax returns.

217. D: To begin with, it is important to know that there are options on the U.S. dollar that trade in the U.S. Consequently, any U.S. dollar-based answers will be wrong – the answer will always be in terms of the foreign currency (in this case, the Japanese yen). Since the customer is concerned that the Japanese yen will weaken against the U.S. dollar while he or she is waiting to receive payment, the best answer is one which will protect the customer against depreciation in the currency. Puts offer downside protection against the value of the Japanese yen relative to the U.S. dollar.

218. C: The first step to solving this problem is to properly accrete the bond. Accretion is determined by dividing the discount received in the purchase price (par value minus market price) by the number of years to maturity (($1000 - $850)/15 = $10). This amount must be multiplied by the number of years the bond has matured, then added to the purchase price to determine the investor's ultimate cost basis ($850 + $50 = $900). If the investor sells the bond for 92, he or she receives $920 (92% * $1000 par value = $920). The difference realized by the investor is, therefore, a gain of $20 ($920 - $900 = $20). Remembering to add the accretion is the critical step in this problem.

219. A: Treasury stock is defined as stock that has been issued and then repurchased by the issuing company. The stock is not considered part of the outstanding shares for the company because it is not outstanding in the market. The company neither pays itself dividends on the shares, nor does it acquire voting rights (which would presumably be "against" the public shareholders) when it repurchases the shares. Answers B, C, and D are all true statements about treasury stock, so answer A is the correct or UNTRUE answer. It is important to read the question carefully – you are looking for the false ("NOT TRUE") answer in this question.

220. C: The best answer is a AA rated bond. Although convertible preferred stock pays a consistent dividend, it's not considered as safe as AA rated bonds. AA rated bonds will provide current income and carry only moderate risk relative to the other answer choices. Hedge funds are generally considered risky investments as an asset class, despite the fact that many hedge funds provide less risk than other, traditional investments. The shares on a growth stock are unlikely to provide current income (through a dividend), and might also be considered speculative.

221. C: Buy limit orders and sell stop orders change on ex-dividend date, while sell limit and buy stop do not. This makes sense if you consider that the first types of orders generally apply to entering and exiting a long stock position, while the second two generally deal with entering and exiting short stock positions. An investor would likely change his trading decisions around the lower ex-dividend price because he or she may receive the dividend. On the short side, the investor does not receive the dividend (he or she must actually pay it), so he or she is less likely to change trading decisions based on the dividend.

222. D: A trade that takes place directly between two institutional parties and without the use of the services of a broker-dealer are considered to have taken place on the fourth market. A trade of exchange-listed securities trading on an exchange takes place on the first market; a trade of over-the-counter securities trading over-the-counter takes place on the second market; and a trade of exchange-listed securities trading over-the-counter takes place on the third market. First and second market trades are the most common and encompass the bulk on U.S. trading on any given day.

223. D: All the choices listed may change an investor's investment objectives. A customer may, and often will, change his or her investment objectives for the reasons listed or for no reason at all. The best answer choice is one that represents a significant life change which will require the registered rep to review a customer's investment objective to assure that they are still appropriate. Even in the absence of such apparent changes in life status, the registered rep should still review these investment objectives with a customer on a regular basis.

224. A: When an investor holds a bond to maturity, the investor receives par value from the issuer on the maturity date. After a bond matures (whether corporate, U.S. government, or municipal), an investor stops earning interest. As the bond gets closer and closer to maturity, its market value is likely to move towards par since that is what will be received at maturity. This is similar to an option contract moving toward its intrinsic value as it gets closer and closer to the expiration date.

225. B: The settlement date is defined as the day on which ownership officially changes from the buyer to the seller, and the issuer updates its records to reflect the new ownership. Current ownership will determine who has a claim to the next interest payment when it becomes due. Municipal securities settle regular way in three business days after the trade date, which is the same as common stock transactions. "Regular way" is often referred to as "T plus 3." Transactions for cash settle the same business day.

226. A: The Securities Act of 1933 is the federal law that defines the rules issuers must follow when selling new securities. The Glass-Steagall Act prohibited commercial banks from underwriting securities; the repeal of this law led to banks expanding into multiple areas and has been offered as one of the roots of the financial crisis of 2008. The Securities Exchange Act of 1934 is the federal law that defines the rules governing the treatment of outstanding securities. The Securities Exchange Act of 1934 created the SEC, which regulates the various exchanges and the over-the-counter market. Regulation T regulates the maximum amount of credit that can be extended to customers for cash and margin accounts.

227. C: As the name suggests, a collateral trust bond is collaterized by securities owned by the issuer and held by the trustee. The collateral pool stands in reserve until the issuer misses an interest payment, at which time the trustee sells some of the securities to satisfy the debt service payment. Debentures are backed by the faith and credit of the issuer. Guaranteed bonds are backed by another entity, such as a parent company, which is obligated to make any missed payments on behalf of the issuer. Equipment trust certificates are secured directly by equipment owned by the issuer.

228. C: When purchasing a period-certain annuity, the annuity is guaranteed to make payments for at least as long as the period-certain states. If the purchaser of a period-certain annuity dies prior to the lapse of the specified period, payments are made for the duration of the specified period to the purchaser's designated beneficiary. However, if the purchaser lives beyond the period specified by contract in the period-certain annuity, the annuity will continue to make payments for as long as the purchaser is alive, with payments stopping immediately upon the death of the purchaser.

229. C: There are two steps to answering this question. The first is to know that rights are issued on a 1-to-1 basis for shares held – a customer will receive one right for every share of stock that he or she owns. The next step in the question is to know that a rights offering will be anti-dilutive, meaning that if the company is issuing 5% more stock (200,000 / 4,000,000 = 5%), then every current share holder will be granted a proportional increase in the number of shares they can purchase (20,000 shares * 5% = 1,000 shares). When these two steps are combined, the right number of rights and shares gives you answer C.

230. B: If the stock market is consolidating, it is trading in a very narrow range and the trendline will be sideways. The term *consolidating* comes from the idea that there are roughly an equal number of buyers and sellers who are "consolidating" their positions by bouncing the traded shares back and forth. Consolidation periods are often followed by *breakouts*, a period during which the narrow range that has persisted over an extended period of time is replaced by a wider range in which the indexes make large moves up or down. Technical analysts tend to believe that the longer the consolidation period, the more severe the breakout is likely to be when it occurs.

231. D: This is another very straightforward question that is regularly on the test because it forms the basis of understanding much of the other material. In a sense, it is the opposite of those questions where the test-writers purposefully try to confuse you by giving you far too much information. A shelf-registration gives the issuer the ability to delay the sale of all or a portion of the securities for up to two full years. A shelf-registration gives the issuer the ability to be nimble in planning the precise timing of the offering, without the delay of the registration process.

232. A: As soon as the trade is executed, the customer is obligated by contract to complete the transaction, regardless of any subsequent moves in the price of the stock, positive or negative. Neither the broker-dealer nor the registered rep is permitted to repurchase the shares (there is the implication that the repurchase would take place at the original purchase price), because this would essentially allow brokers and registered reps to guarantee or backstop customer stock trades. The rep may not assure the customer that the stock will recover because this is guaranteeing performance that may or may not be true.

233. D: An IDR (industrial development revenue bond) is issued to build a facility for a private user or corporation, but they do not need specific voter approval. Because the facility, owned by a third-party, is responsible for earning the revenue needed to make principal and interest payments, the municipality is not directly responsible for the payments. Furthermore, IDRs are, in fact, subject to the substantial user rule, which prohibits substantial participants in the project from buying their own bonds and receiving tax-free payments from the project.

234. A: There are a few keys to getting the correct answer to this question. Firstly, you have to know that the assessed value, rather than the current market value, is used when calculating taxes. Secondly, it is important to know that a mill is equal to 0.001 or one-thousandth when performing the calculation. These two facts are the key, and if you know them, the question is easy. Therefore, in the instance of this question, the taxes are calculated by multiplying the assessed value of the property ($550,000) by 16 by a mill ($550,000 * 16 * 0.001 = $8,800).

235. D: The MSRB (Municipal Securities Rulemaking Board) rules are enforced by each of the following entities in varying capacities and with varying responsibilities: the SEC, the NASD, the FDIC, the Federal Reserve Board (FRB), and the Comptroller of the Currency. The **FGIC** is not a regulatory body, but rather is an insurer that underwrites various municipal securities. On the test, the details that you will be expected to know about the MSRB is relatively limited and will generally be limited to straightforward, single fact type questions.

236. D: To be considered good delivery, the certificates should be in multiples of 100 shares (100, 200, or 300), divisors of 100 shares (1, 2, 4, 5, 10, 20, 25, 50), or amounts that add up to 100 shares (80 + 20, 70 + 30, 60 + 30 + 10). These rules do not apply to any odd lot portions of the delivery, and only apply to the round lot portion of the trade. The 30 shares portion of answer D is not good delivery because 30 is not a divisor of 100.

237. B: As the Federal Reserve Board increases the reserve requirements, the multiplier effect decreases. Under the multiplier effect, a bank will lend any money it is not required to hold as reserves. This money will end up in another bank and a portion of it will be again loaned to customers. This process repeats until all of the money is held as reserves in various banks. As the reserve requirements rise, the number of times the money can be loaned out again falls quickly. This results in a decrease in the money supply, which in turn, leads to a rise in interest rates.

238. B: Call protection refers to the number of years an issuer would have to wait before calling its callable bonds. When interest rates fall, an issuer will prefer to call its bonds and reissue new bonds at lower rates. Keep in mind, however, that the question is focused on the value of call protection. As rates fall, then, investors will prefer to hold their higher rate bonds, making call protection increasingly more valuable as rates fall. Beware of misdirection in test questions and don't confuse the perspective and interests of the issuer with those of the bond holder.

239. B: In order to open a cash account with a broker-dealer, a corporation must provide a copy of its corporate resolutions. Among its resolutions, the document will specify the individuals who have trading authority. If the corporation wanted to open a margin account, it would also need to provide a copy of its bylaws and a signed margin agreement. The bylaws are required because they will warrant (or might not) that the corporation is allowed to purchase securities on margin and assume debts in its own name for this purpose.

240. A: A syndicate member is guilty of the illegal practice of withholding when it does not sell available shares of a hot issue to interested investors, and rather holds the shares in hopes of selling them at an even higher price at a later date. Freeriding is when a customer purchases a security and never sends in payment but sells the security to pay for the trade. Marking to the market is adjusting the market value of the securities in a margin account to determine the equity available within the account; this is a legal practice, although marking to market has come under much discussion in terms of banks and their balance sheets. Commingling is the prohibited practice of holding customer funds and firm funds in the same account.

241. B: A trade confirmation must be sent on or before the date that the transaction is completed (the settlement date). This is another very straightforward question that is regularly on the test because it forms the basis of understanding much of the other material. In a sense, it is the opposite of those questions where the test-writers purposefully try to confuse you by giving you far too much information. These are single fact based questions which, if studied and acquired through rote memorization, can accumulate valuable test scoring points.

242. B: A registered rep may open a joint account with a customer after obtaining approval from a principal of the firm. In addition, the registered rep and the customer are required to sign a proportionate sharing agreement, which states that they will share gains and losses proportionately based on the amount of money invested in the account. Generally speaking, sharing an account with a customer is not an advisable practice as it invites scrutiny and offers little in the way of advantage for either the customer or the registered rep.

243. C: Under the 1940 Act, if an individual is receiving a fee for the advice they are giving to clients, as opposed to receiving a commission for executing trades, they must be registered. Individuals who give advice for free, or who provide general information in the form of mass marketing publications are not required to register. The important distinction regarding registration is whether the financial advisor solicits a fee for the advice dispensed. These guidelines do not apply to hedge fund managers, who are subject to a different set of criteria to which they must adhere under the accredited investor rules.

244. C: The question asks you to follow the transaction from the purchase of the option, to the purchase of the underlying stock, to the sale of the stock. In the example provided, the customer sells the put option and receives $600 in premium. However, due to the price action of the stock, the customer is obligated to produce the shares and must buy 100 shares of the stock at its strike price of $65. This phase of the transaction sequence results in a total debit of $5900 ($600 - $6500 = $5900). The customer then sells the stock for proceeds of $6900 for a total of a $1000 profit ($6900 - $5900).

245. C: The official statement is often left in an intermediate stage without a final version being prepared, even though certain changes have been made. For a revenue bond, the official statement will not include information about the tax base of the municipality because the bond will be backed by revenues from the project rather than by the taxing authority of the municipality. The official statement does not need to be filed with the SEC, but it does need to be sent to all prospective purchasers, regardless of whether they end up purchasing shares or not.

246. D: The question is asking you to distinguish between bearish and bullish strategies and match up the two types of options that have the same directional bias. In general, buying one type of option will produce the same directional bias as selling the opposite type of options. Buying calls and selling puts are both bullish strategies, while buying puts and selling calls are both bearish strategies. Answer D identifies each of these combinations as having the same directional bias; the other choices reflect a combination of bullish and bearish strategies.

247 D: In a firm commitment underwriting, the broker-dealer serving as the underwriter keeps whatever shares it was not able to sell. Both mini-max and all or none underwritings are examples of best efforts offerings. In a mini-max underwriting, the broker-dealer must sell a minimum number of shares of the offering or the entire underwriting is cancelled. In an all or none underwriting, just as it sounds, unless all of the shares of the underwriting are sold, the entire underwriting will be cancelled. In each case, the broker-dealer agrees to use its best efforts to meet the minimums.

248. A: The resistance level of a stock is the upper bounds of its recent trading range. When a stock hits a resistance level, the stock has difficulty continuing to appreciate above that price. When a stock is at or near the top of its trading range, this often signifies that the stock is overbought. Many prospective buyers are exhausted and have reached their purchase limits, and the stock encounters resistance to further appreciation. If the stock breaks through a resistance level, a technical analyst would expect the stock to then experience a significant period of appreciation as a new upper ceiling or resistance point is established.

249. A: The question asks you to calculate the current yield (current yield = annual interest / market price = $75 / $1050 = 7.3%). This is a straightforward, single fact question that will be determined by your ability to memorize the preceding formula. The test writers use this type of simple memorization question in cases where the knowledge being tested forms the basis of a great deal of other information. The bond section on the test is important as it covers a sizable percentage of the test.

250. A: Civil penalties for insider trading may be imposed on anyone violating insider trading rules, whether they are a registered representative or not. Insider trading results when a party uses non-public material information to make trades within a given security. The penalties levied may be as high as three times the gain or the loss that resulted from the illegal transaction. Insider trading violations are extremely serious for a registered rep and may lead to a loss of license as well. These rule infractions are often referred to as 10b violations.

How to Overcome Test Anxiety

Just the thought of taking a test is enough to make most people a little nervous. A test is an important event that can have a long-term impact on your future, so it's important to take it seriously and it's natural to feel anxious about performing well. But just because anxiety is normal, that doesn't mean that it's helpful in test taking, or that you should simply accept it as part of your life. Anxiety can have a variety of effects. These effects can be mild, like making you feel slightly nervous, or severe, like blocking your ability to focus or remember even a simple detail.

If you experience test anxiety—whether severe or mild—it's important to know how to beat it. To discover this, first you need to understand what causes test anxiety.

Causes of Test Anxiety

While we often think of anxiety as an uncontrollable emotional state, it can actually be caused by simple, practical things. One of the most common causes of test anxiety is that a person does not feel adequately prepared for their test. This feeling can be the result of many different issues such as poor study habits or lack of organization, but the most common culprit is time management. Starting to study too late, failing to organize your study time to cover all of the material, or being distracted while you study will mean that you're not well prepared for the test. This may lead to cramming the night before, which will cause you to be physically and mentally exhausted for the test. Poor time management also contributes to feelings of stress, fear, and hopelessness as you realize you are not well prepared but don't know what to do about it.

Other times, test anxiety is not related to your preparation for the test but comes from unresolved fear. This may be a past failure on a test, or poor performance on tests in general. It may come from comparing yourself to others who seem to be performing better or from the stress of living up to expectations. Anxiety may be driven by fears of the future—how failure on this test would affect your educational and career goals. These fears are often completely irrational, but they can still negatively impact your test performance.

> **Review Video: 3 Reasons You Have Test Anxiety**
> Visit mometrix.com/academy and enter code: 428468

238

Elements of Test Anxiety

As mentioned earlier, test anxiety is considered to be an emotional state, but it has physical and mental components as well. Sometimes you may not even realize that you are suffering from test anxiety until you notice the physical symptoms. These can include trembling hands, rapid heartbeat, sweating, nausea, and tense muscles. Extreme anxiety may lead to fainting or vomiting. Obviously, any of these symptoms can have a negative impact on testing. It is important to recognize them as soon as they begin to occur so that you can address the problem before it damages your performance.

Review Video: 3 Ways to Tell You Have Test Anxiety
Visit mometrix.com/academy and enter code: 927847

The mental components of test anxiety include trouble focusing and inability to remember learned information. During a test, your mind is on high alert, which can help you recall information and stay focused for an extended period of time. However, anxiety interferes with your mind's natural processes, causing you to blank out, even on the questions you know well. The strain of testing during anxiety makes it difficult to stay focused, especially on a test that may take several hours. Extreme anxiety can take a huge mental toll, making it difficult not only to recall test information but even to understand the test questions or pull your thoughts together.

Review Video: How Test Anxiety Affects Memory
Visit mometrix.com/academy and enter code: 609003

Effects of Test Anxiety

Test anxiety is like a disease—if left untreated, it will get progressively worse. Anxiety leads to poor performance, and this reinforces the feelings of fear and failure, which in turn lead to poor performances on subsequent tests. It can grow from a mild nervousness to a crippling condition. If allowed to progress, test anxiety can have a big impact on your schooling, and consequently on your future.

Test anxiety can spread to other parts of your life. Anxiety on tests can become anxiety in any stressful situation, and blanking on a test can turn into panicking in a job situation. But fortunately, you don't have to let anxiety rule your testing and determine your grades. There are a number of relatively simple steps you can take to move past anxiety and function normally on a test and in the rest of life.

Review Video: How Test Anxiety Impacts Your Grades
Visit mometrix.com/academy and enter code: 939819

Physical Steps for Beating Test Anxiety

While test anxiety is a serious problem, the good news is that it can be overcome. It doesn't have to control your ability to think and remember information. While it may take time, you can begin taking steps today to beat anxiety.

Just as your first hint that you may be struggling with anxiety comes from the physical symptoms, the first step to treating it is also physical. Rest is crucial for having a clear, strong mind. If you are tired, it is much easier to give in to anxiety. But if you establish good sleep habits, your body and mind will be ready to perform optimally, without the strain of exhaustion. Additionally, sleeping well helps you to retain information better, so you're more likely to recall the answers when you see the test questions.

Getting good sleep means more than going to bed on time. It's important to allow your brain time to relax. Take study breaks from time to time so it doesn't get overworked, and don't study right before bed. Take time to rest your mind before trying to rest your body, or you may find it difficult to fall asleep.

> **Review Video: The Importance of Sleep for Your Brain**
> Visit mometrix.com/academy and enter code: 319338

Along with sleep, other aspects of physical health are important in preparing for a test. Good nutrition is vital for good brain function. Sugary foods and drinks may give a burst of energy but this burst is followed by a crash, both physically and emotionally. Instead, fuel your body with protein and vitamin-rich foods.

Also, drink plenty of water. Dehydration can lead to headaches and exhaustion, especially if your brain is already under stress from the rigors of the test. Particularly if your test is a long one, drink water during the breaks. And if possible, take an energy-boosting snack to eat between sections.

> **Review Video: How Diet Can Affect your Mood**
> Visit mometrix.com/academy and enter code: 624317

Along with sleep and diet, a third important part of physical health is exercise. Maintaining a steady workout schedule is helpful, but even taking 5-minute study breaks to walk can help get your blood pumping faster and clear your head. Exercise also releases endorphins, which contribute to a positive feeling and can help combat test anxiety.

When you nurture your physical health, you are also contributing to your mental health. If your body is healthy, your mind is much more likely to be healthy as well. So take time to rest, nourish your body with healthy food and water, and get moving as much as possible. Taking these physical steps will make you stronger and more able to take the mental steps necessary to overcome test anxiety.

> **Review Video: How to Stay Healthy and Prevent Test Anxiety**
> Visit mometrix.com/academy and enter code: 877894

Mental Steps for Beating Test Anxiety

Working on the mental side of test anxiety can be more challenging, but as with the physical side, there are clear steps you can take to overcome it. As mentioned earlier, test anxiety often stems from lack of preparation, so the obvious solution is to prepare for the test. Effective studying may be the most important weapon you have for beating test anxiety, but you can and should employ several other mental tools to combat fear.

First, boost your confidence by reminding yourself of past success—tests or projects that you aced. If you're putting as much effort into preparing for this test as you did for those, there's no reason you should expect to fail here. Work hard to prepare; then trust your preparation.

Second, surround yourself with encouraging people. It can be helpful to find a study group, but be sure that the people you're around will encourage a positive attitude. If you spend time with others who are anxious or cynical, this will only contribute to your own anxiety. Look for others who are motivated to study hard from a desire to succeed, not from a fear of failure.

Third, reward yourself. A test is physically and mentally tiring, even without anxiety, and it can be helpful to have something to look forward to. Plan an activity following the test, regardless of the outcome, such as going to a movie or getting ice cream.

When you are taking the test, if you find yourself beginning to feel anxious, remind yourself that you know the material. Visualize successfully completing the test. Then take a few deep, relaxing breaths and return to it. Work through the questions carefully but with confidence, knowing that you are capable of succeeding.

Developing a healthy mental approach to test taking will also aid in other areas of life. Test anxiety affects more than just the actual test—it can be damaging to your mental health and even contribute to depression. It's important to beat test anxiety before it becomes a problem for more than testing.

> **Review Video: <u>Test Anxiety and Depression</u>**
> Visit mometrix.com/academy and enter code: 904704

Study Strategy

Being prepared for the test is necessary to combat anxiety, but what does being prepared look like? You may study for hours on end and still not feel prepared. What you need is a strategy for test prep. The next few pages outline our recommended steps to help you plan out and conquer the challenge of preparation.

STEP 1: SCOPE OUT THE TEST

Learn everything you can about the format (multiple choice, essay, etc.) and what will be on the test. Gather any study materials, course outlines, or sample exams that may be available. Not only will this help you to prepare, but knowing what to expect can help to alleviate test anxiety.

STEP 2: MAP OUT THE MATERIAL

Look through the textbook or study guide and make note of how many chapters or sections it has. Then divide these over the time you have. For example, if a book has 15 chapters and you have five days to study, you need to cover three chapters each day. Even better, if you have the time, leave an extra day at the end for overall review after you have gone through the material in depth.

If time is limited, you may need to prioritize the material. Look through it and make note of which sections you think you already have a good grasp on, and which need review. While you are studying, skim quickly through the familiar sections and take more time on the challenging parts. Write out your plan so you don't get lost as you go. Having a written plan also helps you feel more in control of the study, so anxiety is less likely to arise from feeling overwhelmed at the amount to cover.

STEP 3: GATHER YOUR TOOLS

Decide what study method works best for you. Do you prefer to highlight in the book as you study and then go back over the highlighted portions? Or do you type out notes of the important information? Or is it helpful to make flashcards that you can carry with you? Assemble the pens, index cards, highlighters, post-it notes, and any other materials you may need so you won't be distracted by getting up to find things while you study.

If you're having a hard time retaining the information or organizing your notes, experiment with different methods. For example, try color-coding by subject with colored pens, highlighters, or post-it notes. If you learn better by hearing, try recording yourself reading your notes so you can listen while in the car, working out, or simply sitting at your desk. Ask a friend to quiz you from your flashcards, or try teaching someone the material to solidify it in your mind.

STEP 4: CREATE YOUR ENVIRONMENT

It's important to avoid distractions while you study. This includes both the obvious distractions like visitors and the subtle distractions like an uncomfortable chair (or a too-comfortable couch that makes you want to fall asleep). Set up the best study environment possible: good lighting and a comfortable work area. If background music helps you focus, you may want to turn it on, but otherwise keep the room quiet. If you are using a computer to take notes, be sure you don't have any other windows open, especially applications like social media, games, or anything else that could distract you. Silence your phone and turn off notifications. Be sure to keep water close by so you stay hydrated while you study (but avoid unhealthy drinks and snacks).

Also, take into account the best time of day to study. Are you freshest first thing in the morning? Try to set aside some time then to work through the material. Is your mind clearer in the afternoon or evening? Schedule your study session then. Another method is to study at the same time of day that you will take the test, so that your brain gets used to working on the material at that time and will be ready to focus at test time.

STEP 5: STUDY!

Once you have done all the study preparation, it's time to settle into the actual studying. Sit down, take a few moments to settle your mind so you can focus, and begin to follow your study plan. Don't give in to distractions or let yourself procrastinate. This is your time to prepare so you'll be ready to fearlessly approach the test. Make the most of the time and stay focused.

Of course, you don't want to burn out. If you study too long you may find that you're not retaining the information very well. Take regular study breaks. For example, taking five minutes out of every hour to walk briskly, breathing deeply and swinging your arms, can help your mind stay fresh.

As you get to the end of each chapter or section, it's a good idea to do a quick review. Remind yourself of what you learned and work on any difficult parts. When you feel that you've mastered the material, move on to the next part. At the end of your study session, briefly skim through your notes again.

But while review is helpful, cramming last minute is NOT. If at all possible, work ahead so that you won't need to fit all your study into the last day. Cramming overloads your brain with more information than it can process and retain, and your tired mind may struggle to recall even previously learned information when it is overwhelmed with last-minute study. Also, the urgent nature of cramming and the stress placed on your brain contribute to anxiety. You'll be more likely to go to the test feeling unprepared and having trouble thinking clearly.

So don't cram, and don't stay up late before the test, even just to review your notes at a leisurely pace. Your brain needs rest more than it needs to go over the information again. In fact, plan to finish your studies by noon or early afternoon the day before the test. Give your brain the rest of the day to relax or focus on other things, and get a good night's sleep. Then you will be fresh for the test and better able to recall what you've studied.

STEP 6: TAKE A PRACTICE TEST

Many courses offer sample tests, either online or in the study materials. This is an excellent resource to check whether you have mastered the material, as well as to prepare for the test format and environment.

Check the test format ahead of time: the number of questions, the type (multiple choice, free response, etc.), and the time limit. Then create a plan for working through them. For example, if you have 30 minutes to take a 60-question test, your limit is 30 seconds per question. Spend less time on the questions you know well so that you can take more time on the difficult ones.

If you have time to take several practice tests, take the first one open book, with no time limit. Work through the questions at your own pace and make sure you fully understand them. Gradually work up to taking a test under test conditions: sit at a desk with all study materials put away and set a timer. Pace yourself to make sure you finish the test with time to spare and go back to check your answers if you have time.

After each test, check your answers. On the questions you missed, be sure you understand why you missed them. Did you misread the question (tests can use tricky wording)? Did you forget the information? Or was it something you hadn't learned? Go back and study any shaky areas that the practice tests reveal.

Taking these tests not only helps with your grade, but also aids in combating test anxiety. If you're already used to the test conditions, you're less likely to worry about it, and working through tests until you're scoring well gives you a confidence boost. Go through the practice tests until you feel comfortable, and then you can go into the test knowing that you're ready for it.

Test Tips

On test day, you should be confident, knowing that you've prepared well and are ready to answer the questions. But aside from preparation, there are several test day strategies you can employ to maximize your performance.

First, as stated before, get a good night's sleep the night before the test (and for several nights before that, if possible). Go into the test with a fresh, alert mind rather than staying up late to study.

Try not to change too much about your normal routine on the day of the test. It's important to eat a nutritious breakfast, but if you normally don't eat breakfast at all, consider eating just a protein bar. If you're a coffee drinker, go ahead and have your normal coffee. Just make sure you time it so that the caffeine doesn't wear off right in the middle of your test. Avoid sugary beverages, and drink enough water to stay hydrated but not so much that you need a restroom break 10 minutes into the test. If your test isn't first thing in the morning, consider going for a walk or doing a light workout before the test to get your blood flowing.

Allow yourself enough time to get ready, and leave for the test with plenty of time to spare so you won't have the anxiety of scrambling to arrive in time. Another reason to be early is to select a good seat. It's helpful to sit away from doors and windows, which can be distracting. Find a good seat, get out your supplies, and settle your mind before the test begins.

When the test begins, start by going over the instructions carefully, even if you already know what to expect. Make sure you avoid any careless mistakes by following the directions.

Then begin working through the questions, pacing yourself as you've practiced. If you're not sure on an answer, don't spend too much time on it, and don't let it shake your confidence. Either skip it and come back later, or eliminate as many wrong answers as possible and guess among the remaining ones. Don't dwell on these questions as you continue—put them out of your mind and focus on what lies ahead.

Be sure to read all of the answer choices, even if you're sure the first one is the right answer. Sometimes you'll find a better one if you keep reading. But don't second-guess yourself if you do immediately know the answer. Your gut instinct is usually right. Don't let test anxiety rob you of the information you know.

If you have time at the end of the test (and if the test format allows), go back and review your answers. Be cautious about changing any, since your first instinct tends to be correct, but make sure you didn't misread any of the questions or accidentally mark the wrong answer choice. Look over any you skipped and make an educated guess.

At the end, leave the test feeling confident. You've done your best, so don't waste time worrying about your performance or wishing you could change anything. Instead, celebrate the successful completion of this test. And finally, use this test to learn how to deal with anxiety even better next time.

> **Review Video: 5 Tips to Beat Test Anxiety**
> Visit mometrix.com/academy and enter code: 570656

Important Qualification

Not all anxiety is created equal. If your test anxiety is causing major issues in your life beyond the classroom or testing center, or if you are experiencing troubling physical symptoms related to your anxiety, it may be a sign of a serious physiological or psychological condition. If this sounds like your situation, we strongly encourage you to seek professional help.

Thank You

We at Mometrix would like to extend our heartfelt thanks to you, our friend and patron, for allowing us to play a part in your journey. It is a privilege to serve people from all walks of life who are unified in their commitment to building the best future they can for themselves.

The preparation you devote to these important testing milestones may be the most valuable educational opportunity you have for making a real difference in your life. We encourage you to put your heart into it—that feeling of succeeding, overcoming, and yes, conquering will be well worth the hours you've invested.

We want to hear your story, your struggles and your successes, and if you see any opportunities for us to improve our materials so we can help others even more effectively in the future, please share that with us as well. **The team at Mometrix would be absolutely thrilled to hear from you!** So please, send us an email (support@mometrix.com) and let's stay in touch.

> **If you'd like some additional help, check out these other resources we offer for your exam:**
> **http://MometrixFlashcards.com/Series**

Additional Bonus Material

Due to our efforts to try to keep this book to a manageable length, we've created a link that will give you access to all of your additional bonus material.

Please visit https://www.mometrix.com/bonus948/series7 to access the information.